Wired for Wealth

Wired for Wealth
Unlocking Your Brain for Financial Success

Dr. Alok Trivedi

Published by Game Changer Publishing

Paperback ISBN: 979-8-9880752-6-4
Hardcover ISBN: 979-8-9880752-7-1
Digital: ISBN: 979-8-9880752-8-8

www.GameChangerPublishing.com

ACCESS YOUR FREE GIFTS

Read This First

Just to say thanks for buying and reading my book, I would like to give you a few free bonus gifts, no strings attached!

To Download Your Free Gifts Now, Scan the QR Code Below:

Wired for Wealth

Unlocking Your Brain for Financial Success

Dr. Alok Trivedi

www.GameChangerPublishing.com

Foreword

Welcome to "Wired for Wealth-Unlocking Your Brain For Financial Success" – a book that will take you on a journey of self-discovery and help you harness the power of your mind to achieve financial abundance. In today's fast-paced world, financial stability and success are crucial for a fulfilling life. However, many of us struggle to attain it due to limiting beliefs and negative thought patterns that hold us back.

This book will show you how to reprogram your mind for success, using scientifically-proven techniques and practical strategies that will help you unlock your full potential. You will learn how to identify and overcome limiting beliefs, develop a positive money mindset, and leverage the power of visualization to manifest abundance in your life.

At the heart of this book is Dr. Trivedi, a renowned expert in the field of brain rewiring and personal development. With over 20 years of experience, Dr. Trivedi has helped countless individuals achieve financial success and maximize their health and wellness. His unique approach combines cutting-edge neuroscience with ancient wisdom, creating a powerful and effective system for transforming your life.

In these pages, Dr. Trivedi will guide you step-by-step through his proven process for rewiring your brain for financial abundance. You will learn how to cultivate a growth mindset, overcome self-doubt, and tap into the power of your subconscious mind to achieve your goals. Dr. Trivedi's expertise and guidance will empower you to take control of your financial future and live the life of your dreams.

"Wired For Wealth-Unlocking Your Brain For Financial Success" is a must-read for anyone who wants to achieve financial success and abundance. Whether you are just starting out on your journey or looking to take your finances to the next level, this book will provide you with the tools, insights, and inspiration you need to create lasting change in your life.

Randy Garn, New York Times Best Selling Author

Table of Contents

Introduction

Money is such a sensitive subject for so many people. Most of us have been blinded by it for years and we do not understand where it comes from. A very small group of people do understand it and, when they get it, there comes a tremendous power that they are able to access. And this is one of these things that you can achieve, if you master the art of money through true mastery. But if you do not achieve this mastery, you will end up spending your entire life working in misery for it, and so, it is a challenge for many people to know how to do this. Most people will not be able to master this.

When it comes to money—as I go into the content of these lessons, and we are going to get into lots of content—you are going to learn how to transform yourself from someone who is at the effect of money into a master over it. I really put an effort into this book toward your transformation. My work is not, "Oh, I hope you just take in the information and it magically and methodically gets into your head and you are now going to be masters of money." It does not work that way. This is going to take work on your part. I want to be very real with you. I am a straight shooter. If anything I say offends you, I do not know what to tell you. I am still going to do it, so I hope that is okay with you. Being friends is not my aim here; my objective is to help you transform.

The reason I sometimes offend people is because I get very inspired about this topic. I would rather be real and authentic with you than feed you a bunch of crap. And there is a lot of crap out there. Wouldn't you agree that there is a lot of crap out in the market space? Yeah, there is. And I want to thank you for trusting me enough for me to teach you some of the truths behind this.

I am going to do everything in my power to make sure that this lives up to your expectations, or exceeds them. I have been on the other side—the side where I bought thousands and thousands of dollars' worth of garbage and I did not get any of the results I expected. It did not get me what I wanted— did not give me the answers. At first, I could not figure it out and I put my hopes and dreams—like many of you probably have—in other people's hands and realized that they were only in it for themselves. And I thought, "That's not teaching."

I am an entrepreneur businessperson, as well, but I want to make these lessons as effective as possible for people to win in the game of life, and I say this humbly and honestly.

Maybe you saw your parents struggle with this thing called money and you have been trying to figure it out for yourself. But somehow it just does not make sense. You do not understand it and how to move forward with it. Perhaps, you are looking at your life—I don't know, maybe you are 20, 30, 40, 50, 60 years old—looking back and saying, "What happened? How did I get here? How is it that I am here and I am looking at my bank account, my assets and my money and I don't have what I thought I was going to have?" And that is a tough place, right? You look at your entire life—you look back at it—and you have nothing left.

I remember I had a patient one time, in practice, and this was in 2008. Very clearly do I remember this. His name was Jerry, and he was about to retire. This guy had worked as a corporate executive at an insurance company. He had worked there for almost 45 years of his life. Everyone knows what happened in 2008, right? The stock market crashed, and this guy had all his money in his 401K. The stock market crashed, and he was ready to retire on December 31, 2008.

His portfolio was cut by 65-70 %. His entire retirement was just shot down a month and a half before he was about to retire, and I remember him sitting on the table and just crying to me, saying, "Dr. Trivedi, my money is gone. My entire life savings is gone. Everything I worked for is now history. In one day!"

And he is not alone.

I thought about it. Man, that sucks. That really sucks—to work all your life and to look back and say, "There's nothing left for me. What was the purpose of it all? Where's my retirement? Where is this all coming from?"

I never forgot Jerry for it. And I remember what he said: "Doc, whatever you do"—and I was a young kid at the time—he said, "Diversify! Just diversify, diversify, diversify." I never forgot that, but the bigger thing that he taught me was that it is wise to spread your money and to understand the concepts of money. So, I did.

By no means am I going to sit here and preach from an Ivory Tower. I am not that guy. I have made millions of dollars. I am not going to lie. I have lost millions of dollars, too.

I have been to the point where I have had millions of dollars in my bank account, and I have had lots of money in my wallet, and then I have also been to the point where I have had one lemon to eat for four days.

I have been rich and I have been broke. So, what is my authority to speak on this? It is that I have been on both sides and I understand both sides of this money "coin." That is why I am going to teach you the truth around money because there are a lot of people out there who are teaching bullshit about money—that you magically sit under a tree and meditate, and money just shows up.

I asked a fellow doctor if they had ever tried such a thing—meditating and having new patients walk in the door—just magically show up. No advertising, no screenings—nothing. They just show up at their office, like, "Oh, here I am." And naturally, he had never experienced such a thing.

Life does not work that way. There are components of that worldview which might help. Does it help your own mindset? Of course it does. I am not taking away from any of that. But there are strategies around this thing called the Law of Attraction. A few things work, but a great many approaches do not.

Understand this: If you can attract something, then something can also be repelled. The law of physics says that if something can be attracted—if something is a magnet—then you can reverse the polarity and push something away.

To think that there is only one side—where there is only attraction without repulsion—is just not true. It does not work that way. You cannot have a north magnetic pole without a south pole. You cannot have electrons without protons. In this action-reaction universe, you cannot have attraction without repulsion. Most people in our lives, however, are repelling money and not attracting money.

And though there is some truth to these ideas, we will not be going into them in greater depth. The curriculum I have laid out puts your focus on the things you need for your own transformation. If you do the work that is in front of you, your financial world will change. Your consciousness around money will change.

I cannot promise you how much you are going to make on the other side of this work. I cannot say, "Doctor Mike, you're going to have 100 new patients walking through the door every week. Or Tim, you got an extra $70,000 coming through the door every day." I cannot tell you any of that. But what I can tell you is this: Your consciousness around money is going to shift. How far you take it will depend on your own diligence and hard work.

When you do this work, money starts to show up. Opportunities show up.

Full disclosure right off the top—I am not here to be your friend. We can get together and have a beer, later on. But now, I am here to make a transformation. I am committed to that and I hope you are committed to that, too because we can be friends, but later. I am here to help you get through your consciousness, which, until now, has been stuck here. When you transform your consciousness, you can get to the other side. Sometimes,

I am going to be tough. Sometimes, I am going to be intense. Your work ahead is not going to be easy. So, you need me to be intense.

And I hope that is okay with you. I want you to know that my intensity and toughness are not out of malicious intent. It is not just to be an asshole. That is not it. It is to get you to the other side. And those who get to the other side—I promise you—every single person who stays with me and goes to the other side always says, "Thank you."

Between you and the other side is where that "block" sits. And if I do not take you over that, by pushing—by getting intense, sometimes swearing, whatever I have to do—you are less likely to get there. Whatever it takes to get you through to the other side is what I am willing to do because if you do, then your world will be entirely different.

I can tell you story after story of people who have made an additional 40, 50, 60, 70 thousand dollars a month in their income when they get through these blocks that we will be talking about. But, please—in all honesty—please give me permission to do that—to push you out of your "comfort zone." Would that be okay?

I am here to get results, and I am a straight shooter. So, I am going to be honest with you.

I have spent thousands of dollars on people trying to help me, but in the end, I taught myself. I made discoveries which gave me real traction.

And now, I have to teach you about this thing called money. I am committed to your transformation. Every exercise I give you is neurologically based. It is going to challenge you. It is not one of those things where it is meant for you to say, "It's okay. It's supposed to be easy." It's not. This is about transformations. It is not supposed to be easy. But when you do it, step-by-step, you will get through it.

Summing it Up and Looking Ahead

Most people repel money instead of attracting money. And here, you are going to learn why you repel money before you learn how to attract it. In other words, you need to learn how you self-sabotage before we make you stronger on the things that matter.

I want you to grow and to transform.

Some people may be burdened by credit card debt. Others may have suffered through bankruptcy and divorce. But even a seeming tragedy like divorce can be a beautiful process for teaching you about money.

Some people feel as though they are being blocked by an invisible wall. Here, you will find out exactly what that wall is and how to overcome it.

I am not comparing myself to Einstein, but I think there is some truth to what he said. His contempt for authority is one thing that helped make him into an authority.

My contempt for the existing personal development field is what led me to neuroscience and interpersonal neurobiology in order to become an authority on thinking, psychology, the mind and how it works, plus the brain and the behavior of it. So, every exercise I give you has a neurobiological basis. Through this process, I will be helping you to remyelinate your brain.

One of my students is also a doctor, but suffered a brain injury which left her life in a shambles. Because of it, she went through five years of rehab. She was not able to think straight. Her memory was affected. She was able to hold only three numbers in her short-term memory. Normally, a person is able to hold ten.

After working with me, she was able to get that up to 15 numbers. The neurologist working with her rehabilitation was floored at the results. She now has more brain power than she ever had before.

This is the type of work we will be doing here—changing your neurobiology.

When I talk about consciousness, this deals with the way you think and the way you process information. And I am not talking about consciousness from a Deepak Chopra standpoint—you know, "infinite consciousness"—but this is consciousness from what you create based on how you think about things. It also involves you doing things.

Part of what you will be doing involves certain concepts and attitudes about money—certain emotions, certain beliefs—that have to happen for you to achieve the desired transformation.

First thing, I have to have you understand your own beliefs about money—the context of money. As with any journey, you need to know your starting point.

Second, we will explore the fact that money is more about avoidance of pain than it is about an abundance of pleasure. But there is a lot of bullshit out there that teaches you that it is actually all about an abundance of pleasure—having more of it right now. Abundance. Knowing what truly drives your mind on money will make all the difference. This is what makes transformation possible.

Third, we are going to talk about emotions and money. One point I have made in many of my videos is that your resentment toward money prevents you from attracting money. Your guilt and shame around money gives it away. So, if at any point in your life you have had resentment, guilt, or shame around money, you give it away, or you do not bring it into your life, and I will talk about that heavily. And most people are not aware that they do this.

Most people have been taught the idea that money is either fear or abundance, and that we live in a land where it is all fear and abundance. That is just not true. It is not just about fear or abundance. There are stages within each of these. There are stages of consciousness that exist in between these that nobody wants to talk about because it is easier to sell a fantasy life. That is a wonderful paradigm to tell people, but it doesn't create transformation in people. It does not create results for people, so we are going to talk about that, as well.

Fifth is about relationships and money. People get a bit crazy when they mix the two, like, "Oh, my God!" So, in section five we are going to talk about balancing relationships and money, and how to make that happen in the most effective way for yourself.

Section six is going to be about spirit and matter. Because, for many people, there is a lot of guilt and shame around having money, and having possessions. Because we have been taught this construct that it is better to give than to receive. Have you ever heard that before? It is a bunch of nonsense, but we have been taught that. I am going to show you why it is nonsense in section six. Many of my students, when I tell them this, they look at me as if to say, "I don't know if I like this—if he's really going to break the myths."

Stay with me. We are going to crack through all of the myths and barriers. And there are a lot of myths and bullshit to break through, so stay with me.

Assignments

Throughout the book, you will be given assignments to go with the breakthroughs I present. The ideas in these lessons prepare you for your transformation. And, like any instruction, they give you direction and enough understanding to implement those instructions. But the assignments are what activate the transformation. Therefore, it is vital that you do the assignments in a timely fashion and with a sober commitment to do your best possible work.

If any of this feels uncomfortable to you, know this: You are not alone; the discomfort you feel is part of your transformation. And this transformation is your reason for being attracted to this book in the first place. This is you doing the vital work. And trust me—the work will not get done without your commitment and follow-through.

Also, please note that the work you will be doing builds on past assignments. So, please keep what you write down for future reference.

How To Write Benefits/Drawbacks

Everything in life has benefits and drawbacks. There are no "perfect" solutions. No perceived benefit is free of negative connotations; otherwise life would be simple. But more than that, your perception of a concept, idea or solution can have multiple layers. Becoming aware of those various qualities and attitudes helps with your mastery.

For example, ask yourself, "What is a drawback to having money?" One of my students told me that "management" was a drawback.

And here is where it starts to get really interesting. Drill more deeply into the subject by asking, "What is a drawback of managing money?" The same student told me, "Organization." Being organized, of course, could be a benefit, but many people view the chore of getting organized to be a drudgery. These are very personal attitudes.

But we take this even deeper. When asked, "What is a drawback of organization?" the same student replied, "Time." In other words, it takes time out of an individual's already busy schedule. Getting organized about money is "time consuming."

Digging into a fourth layer of drawbacks, we ask, "What's the drawback of being time consuming?" The student replied, "You feel frustrated because you're not doing it—because it is time consuming."

Do you see? Here we have multiple layers of drawbacks, one built upon another—primary, secondary, tertiary and quaternary layers.

Once you are done drilling down four layers with one set of drawbacks, you have to start fresh again. Simply ask the same starting question: "What's a drawback to having money?"

Consider the answer: "People will come to borrow it." That's your primary. Now, what is the drawback of people borrowing money? An obvious answer might be, "They won't pay it back."

Drilling down into your tertiary layer, you might find that a drawback of people not paying back what they borrow is that it "ruins relationships."

And then you ask, "What is a drawback of ruining relationships?"

For an exercise such as this, the objective is that you keep going until you have done 50 based on this four-layered approach. For some other exercises you might do 100 repetitions.

When you do these exercises, again and again, you are literally creating new neurons—new neural pathways. It is a process called "myelination" which you are doing inside of your own brain. By following these steps, I will be helping you rewire your brain around the subject of money.

But why 50? Or why 100? Is it because this is my book and I decide? Of course not. Based on my experience, this is what works for most people. In the realm of experience alone, I feel that these *could* be enough, but I do not know in your specific case. It could take someone even more. Every individual has their own unique differences, and it might take twice as many for this to be very real with you.

What will work with you? I do not know. I do not have an exact formula. Every person is going to be distinctly different, but it has to be to the point where you see behavior changes in yourself. And when you see that—then it starts to become very exciting.

Early on, doing these things, sometimes I would not see any of my behaviors changing. I am like, "Man, I'm going to do this! I know this should work." And I would have to go through and write another 200 to see my behaviors change. But if the neurology is set up the right way, the behavior will follow. The neurology leads the behavior to change. This is the law of neurology.

I may assign a specific number—like 50 repetitions—but you have to be honest with yourself. Did you achieve a transformation? If not, keep going. A lot of masters have to do 200.

Statement of Presence

At the end of the evening, just lay in bed and say to yourself,

- I am grateful for the opportunities that today had to show.
- I love myself for whatever I did and didn't do, and I am present with my heart.
- I love who I am—not what others want me to be.
- Where I am in my life is perfection for me.

Keep doing this every evening before you sleep. Gradually, you will become more and more aware of your own mind and attitudes and more relaxed about living in the moment.

CHAPTER 1

Old Belief System

Throughout modern times, people have held a great many different beliefs about success and prosperity. The old model basically said that your beliefs led to your behaviors which led to your habits.

For example, you will get pissed off at your habits and this creates anger toward who you are. You will judge yourself because of your habits.

"I spent too much money, damn it! I did it again." Or, "I spent it and I lost all my money." These are all habits. We tend to judge the habits without looking at the beliefs. But you have to ask, "What are my beliefs?"

I used to ask this question when I was going through a rough time in my life. Backstage with all the personal development gurus, I used to ask them this question and never seemed to get a satisfactory answer.

In my business, I thought I was making all the required phone calls, doing everything I was supposed to do, but I did not seem to be making the kind of progress I desired.

I made money. I have made millions of dollars. But I asked myself, "Why don't I have more money in my hands? Where's all the money?"

I was trying to make new money—attract new wealth into my life. I was putting in long hours—sometimes 250 to 300 calls a day. Voicemail after voicemail. You know, "Smile and dial." I should have been the Wolf of Wall Street, with the relentless work I put in. Call, call, call, call, call and I was not attracting any wealth. I wasn't attracting any type of sales.

Slowly, it dawned on me, "I must be pushing this thing away." After all, that is the result I had been achieving. Trust the evidence.

I kept on meditating and this term "belief" kept on coming up in my head.

And so I started asking a lot of these gurus, "What is this 'belief' thing? How do we change our beliefs?"

They would say, "Well, you just change your beliefs."

"Wait a minute! What do you mean? You just change your beliefs?"

I wanted to know, "How do you change them?" And the answer was always the same: "Well, you just change them." And that seemed horribly glib.

That's like saying, "Guys, I want you to focus differently," to which we could ask, "Well, how do you do that?" Instead of a usable answer—one which gives us meaningful traction, I would always hear a shallow response: "Well, you just focus differently. Just focus, don't screw around. Just focus."

"Well, how do I focus?"

"Focus! That's it."

See? Frustrating!

But I will not do that to you. I want you to understand sufficiently what is required of you so that you can take the necessary steps to make the desired transformation. With the "focus differently" example, you need to know what "focus" means and what are some meaningful ways, first, to become aware of your focus, and then how to change that focus.

So it was with beliefs. "Change your beliefs!" Instead of insisting that we merely change them, I wanted to understand beliefs well enough so that I could accomplish exactly that. I started digging into this subject—into the anatomy of belief.

And then, I realized the cause of everything on this topic—truly the new model. It starts with the perception, plus the values, plus the emotions, plus your beliefs, plus your behaviors, plus your habits—these are what create the output that you want from all your activities.

The input starts back at the beginning of this sequence—at the perception. The output shows up at the habit and behavior. It started back here—perception.

But no one had talked about these things.

I realized that in order to change something—in this case, beliefs—I should first try to know more about the thing I am attempting to change. This is me thinking like a doctor—attempting to diagnose what the patient is trying to tell me.

I am thinking objectively. If I want to lose 30 pounds, I have to know my starting point. Am I starting at 180 to get to 150? Or am I starting at 80 and attempting to get down to 50? That would be very unhealthy.

In other words, there has to be an understanding of your starting point.

If I am in a race, with the goal of crossing the finish line first, and I am not at the starting block, then I have a problem. If I am still in the locker room, I cannot very well start running from there when I hear the sound of the starting gun. I might trip over a bench or slip on some water on the floor. And really, I am at a disadvantage. But I am in an even worse position if I happen to be viewing the race from up in a tree. Starting to run from there could end up breaking my neck, falling off the branch in which I am perched. So you see, knowing your starting point is critical.

I have been told that you merely look at the results which you have been getting and that this will tell you what your beliefs are. For me, that was the stupidest thing I had ever heard.

And they were like, "No, that's how it is. That's how we've taught it for 40 and 50 years. That is the law of success."

Then I said, "The law needs to be changed because that makes no bloody sense whatsoever."

From a general standpoint, not having money can tell you that your beliefs are somehow negative, but that's like looking through a microscope with lots of mud plastered over the lens. You know there is some light on the other side, but you have no details. You really have no idea what is on the slide under the microscope.

Let me give you an example from my own medical practice. As a doctor, I used to look at spines and backs all day long. If someone were to come in with lower back pain, I would need more specific information before attempting to help. Their problem could be the result of a sprain, a subluxation, a herniated disc, a prolapsed disc, a spinal fracture, cancer of the spine or a vertebra which had become collapsed. Each one of these would require a different treatment. Each one of these is a different starting point. And the result of each—the pain in the lower back—definitely does not tell me the details of the cause.

The gurus were using "malpractice logic," for if I had attempted to use their logic in diagnosing my patients' ailments, I could, very quickly, have become neck deep in malpractice lawsuits.

There must be a better way—a better approach to understanding these things. In the health industry, we know that it is far better to treat the root cause, rather than merely the symptoms. My symptom was that I lacked money. And this is why I started asking deeper questions about these things.

The symptom, for most people, is that they do not have money. They are resisting money. I knew that I had to get to the isolation point to figure out what the belief is around all this. No one had created a process to accomplish this. I looked high and low and no one had figured out how to decipher what it was behind the symptoms.

How do I know what my current state of beliefs are? Only then would I know how to change those beliefs because if I don't objectively know where I currently am with regard to money, then I will never know how to shift toward more money. Does that make sense so far?

I like to ask my students for their own thoughts as we go through these materials. One student told me, "It's always about change, change, change, but you don't know what to change. Don't you know? It's always, 'make lots of phone calls and work your butt off.' But if you don't know what your belief is behind it—you're not making the money—then it's just like a perpetual cycle and you're wondering why you're not getting anywhere. What the heck is wrong with me?"

But you have to know this: There is nothing wrong with you. Think about this concept. What if there's nothing wrong with you? You are perfect as a human being and you can love yourself for who you are. What do you think that is going to do to your psyche and to your life?

If you think this might "blow your mind," then welcome to my world where this happens every single day.

You no longer need to feel as though you are on a roller coaster—going up and down—with regard to money. You have to figure out what these beliefs are. Then, if you understand what these beliefs are, you will understand what the construct is around all this. And only then can you truly understand what money really is.

The steps you will be taking, I have been through them. I went through this process. But when I first did it, I had to figure out whether any of this would work because my life depended on it.

When I did this process—what I call a Belief Inventory—it changed my life. Finally, I was able to move past the "invisible wall" most people feel, but toward which most people feel utterly helpless. That helplessness ends now. You are on the road to financial mastery.

Now, I understood that I had created this belief. I realized that this is why I was repelling money, repelling sales and repelling work from my life.

A majority of people seem to want you to believe that you need to grind it up—work your ass off and then work even harder!

But is life really about grinding? To be perfectly honest, I am not into a life of grinding; I am into a life of living.

I created this Belief Inventory process and started making new and surprising discoveries. I realized that, as I got more specific with the details, there are many other components all around those details.

Sample Exercise

Up ahead, there are a number of timed assignments on this Belief Inventory process. But here, I want to give you a taste of what to expect. Those will have a duration of 90 seconds each, but here we will use only 10 seconds. You will need some kind of timer to let you know when to stop. This can be on your watch, a cell phone app or software on your computer.

At the start of each timed assignment, you will be given a word, but you are not to think of the word. Instead, with pen and paper, or a text file on your computer, you need to write down every thought which comes into your mind. Do not think about what you are to write; simply write it down. As fast as you can, write, write, write, write, write—whatever comes to your stream of consciousness. Do not try to filter it; do not try to make it right; do not try to make it wrong. It is what it is.

Are you ready?

For this brief exercise, give yourself 10 seconds.

Consider the word "Porsche" and go!

Once you are done, read over what you wrote, and next to each item label it either positive or negative based on your perception of what you wrote.

For instance, one of my students wrote down: "fast, rich, classy and mid-life crisis." And then, she classified "fast" and "rich" as positive.

When I asked her about "rich," she seemed hesitant, but said "positive" using a questioning tone.

Sometimes, your physiology will tell you what you really think, even though intellectually you may think a different way. This will affect your tone of voice—the firmness of the way you say things. So, I called her on it. I pointed out the change in her vocal tone and she admitted that it was probably more on the negative side.

For her, "classy" was positive, but she was "on the fence" with "mid-life crisis."

Digging more deeply, I asked, "Why is 'fast' a positive statement?"

And she replied, "Because I like driving cars fast."

She had been more hesitant on "rich"—leaning toward classifying it as "negative"—because she did not perceive herself to be "rich."

Details like these become a self-reflection of who you are on the inside.

One of my male students wrote, "horsepower, car, wealth, red, fast." For him, all of these, without hesitation, were positive, so he is more likely to move toward a Porsche if given the opportunity, whereas the female student was going to move away from it.

Another female student wrote, "wealthy, executive, professional, black, fast, classy and rich." All of these she labeled as "positive."

And another male student had all negative items: "big money, luxury cars, too expensive."

I told him that if I had started the short exercise with something like "Honda Accord," he likely would have viewed it as a positive thing because it is so affordable.

He sheepishly admitted that he owns a Honda Civic. So, there you go.

When you do your Belief Inventory, later in chapter 2, you will have a full 90 seconds for each concept in the field of finance—11 topics in all. Remember to save the positive-negative assessments for after you are done with the eleven, 90-second exercises.

One objective is to find out if you have any conflicting ideas around money. The fact that you are reading this book likely means you have plenty of those. Superficially, many people will say, "Oh, I like money. I want money." But once they do their own Belief Inventory, they discover that it is not so simple. There are other aspects of money, like credit, debt and liability.

Of course, people are going to say positive things about money, assets and building wealth. And, naturally, they will say negative things about bills and expenses. But if they do not value bills and expenses, how are they going to bring in more money in order to pay those bills and expenses?

The answer is, they are not going to bring in more money. Instead, they will continue to resist money because they do not value some aspects of money.

Once you have completed your Belief Inventory on money, you can look at life and see exactly why you have this conflict with finances. Many people look at assets as a positive, but if you remember the gentleman who, in 2008, lost most of his savings, you can see a negative possibility with assets.

One of my students brought up a great question that gets at the heart of this difficulty. She asked, "In your Porsche example, I had a Porsche as an 'expensive car,' but I don't have a problem with it being expensive. I like expensive stuff, so that's what I'm trying to understand. Is this supposed to be a negative thing for me? I don't think it's a negative thing."

She said she likes "expensive stuff," but the word "expensive" has a special meaning to those who cannot afford such things. The word "expensive" usually means "difficult to purchase." For the person who has more than enough money, they would not use the word "expensive." They may not even look at the price tag. The thing does not change when we use the word "expensive," but our perception of it does.

Another student was a stay-at-home Mom homeschooling her children. She considered her work with her kids to be her "job," but she asked me, "So, even though I'm not bringing in income it's still my main responsibility?"

I told her, "Yes, and we're going to change you not bringing in income because you are bringing in income. You're just not aware of where you're bringing it in."

When you do the upcoming assignments—especially on the Belief Inventory—you may look at the first couple of answers and think they look pretty simple. The real answers are going to come fourth, fifth, sixth, seventh and down the line.

Let me give you an example. Some time ago, I was working with a sales team and we were doing "rejection" as a Belief Inventory. After going through the exercise, one guy said, "Doc, I don't know why, but I got 'insulin' as one of my items." The word "insulin" was number nine on his list. "Yeah, Doc, what does that mean?"

At first, I was just as puzzled as he was. So, we talked and I started digging—asking probing questions to get more understanding. Then, I found out that every time he goes through a sale and gets rejected, he has sugar. Rejection? He reaches for candy. That is the neurology that was built inside of his brain. His physical body was evidence of this behavior. And it was obvious that he got rejected a lot.

So, you are going to see what your beliefs are around your assets, around liabilities, around debt, around cash, around investing, around bills. And you are going to have a new awareness of what your deepest beliefs are. If you have any conflicting beliefs in certain areas, you are going to see why you have problems with money.

What you have got to do over the remaining pages of this book is to see objectively. You will discover your starting point, and at the end of all this, you will change everything you have regarding money. You will end up with a positive direction and relationship with regard to money.

One remarkable discovery in all this involves the real pay dirt in the exercise. The true value will almost never be found in the first few answers you write down. You have to dig into your latent awareness to find the real gold. If the first few, superficial answers were all you needed, then you would never have needed any help. Through the upcoming exercises, you will be getting into the deep subconscious—the latent awareness in your amygdala (the fight or flight center of the brain)—and from there you will extract the information you require. That is where your real beliefs are regarding money.

Until we are masters of our own finances, we will have some real wounds to heal on the subject of money. One of my students was a single mother and had grown up seeing her Mom give money away—an act which had made their situation even more difficult. Because that wound had remained a part of her life, she had kept attracting more of the same. During the course, she revealed her own story and we got her to change her story.

And now, it is time to change your story, beginning with your first assignments.

Assignments: Current Beliefs Around Money

On a piece of paper, or in a computer file, write down your answers to the following questions.

1. What are your current beliefs around money? (Both positive and negative.)

2. What general beliefs did you learn from your parents growing up? (As many as you can think of)

3. What money beliefs did you learn from your parents growing up? (As many as you can think of)

CHAPTER 2

Beliefs Around Money

Beliefs Around Money, Part 1

One nice thing about becoming a financial master, besides making millions of dollars, is the ability to look back at the tough times and to be grateful for those difficulties and those hidden, self-defeating beliefs. I remember a time, looking at the topic of money and saying to myself, "I don't have anything to show for myself. I don't have any money. I don't have anything to show for who I am, or what I am."

And it was probably the greatest time in my life because it let me reinvent myself.

So, wherever you are, as your starting point, feel good about it. You are on your way and you now have a proven direction ahead of you. Are you starting with a blank slate? That is perfectly okay. If you are starting with some money, but merely want to make more, that is great, as well.

The more deeply you understand your starting point, the more intimately you will know how to move forward.

First of all, we have been taught a great many things about money—from our parents, relatives and friends, and from our interactions with others. It should be no surprise that most of us have widely divergent ideas about money and how it is defined.

One of my students defined money as "a reward for a service or transaction or product." And that is a pretty fair explanation.

Another student merely said, "I've always been taught that you have to work hard for money. It is a reward system. I've always made six figures ever since I've been in business for myself. And teaching other people about making money—that's where my challenge is."

After hearing both of these definitions, I offered my own feedback: I told them that, as soon as you say, "It's a reward system," and you are not making any money, you have to be aware of the obvious problem. How do you feel about yourself in such a situation? Obviously, the feeling is one of being unrewarded. This automatically associates, for many people, a negative feeling toward money. A person starts to wonder, "Am I worth it?"

Or is it worth all of the effort I have been putting into all this? And when your own self-value goes down, if the reward is money, and you are not having the reward, then the question becomes, "Am I worth it?"

So, if your self-worth goes down because you are not being rewarded for your efforts, then the whole game of money becomes a matter of how much you value yourself and how much self-worth you create for yourself.

This is a very key distinction.

Another problem we face in doing the upcoming assignments involves clarity and accuracy. We have to become more aware of how well we comprehend what is asked and how well the answers we give match up to what is asked.

Another student replied to my earlier question, "What is money?" with, "Money gives me power and leverage over things."

See the problem? He did not answer the question. Because I care, I challenged him on this. I had not asked, "What does money give you?" I asked, "What is it?"

When you pay attention to details like this, you start to become more critically aware of your own thoughts and feelings. This type of clarity is critical for your progress.

As soon as you answer the wrong question, "What is money to me?" it becomes "my context"—subjective instead of objective. If you say generally what it is, you understand it from a consciousness perspective. I understand what it does for you once you own it. When you have it, that is great, but if you do not have it, then you have no power. That does not define money, objectively; instead, it defines you.

The more value you put into the market space, the more money you have. If you look at something from the perspective of value, and you look at the amount of value with which you are serving people, you find that this is tied to the amount someone is willing to pay for it. If they receive a greater amount of value in it, they are willing to pay more for it.

It is all about the law of supply and demand. If something is merely "rare," then that does not automatically mean that someone is going to be willing to pay more for it. An individual may perceive that an object is "rare," but that does not automatically translate into a perception of value or demand.

Let me give you a perfect example.

The Diamond Illusion

Diamonds are not particularly rare, but there is the perception of rarity. If you get a chance, check out the history of the De Beers marketing scheme. They cornered the market on diamonds, and because they owned most of the diamond mines, they could control the supply. By artificially withholding diamonds from the marketplace, they created the perception of "rarity."

Then, they worked on creating the perception of desirability—the "demand" side of the equation. Instead of selling "the hardest rock known to man," they created a mystique—a fairytale—that women will love their men even more if they get them a bigger diamond. They added catch phrases, like, "A diamond is forever." They plucked at the heartstrings, appealing to emotion. It was, and still is, a brilliant marketing scheme. By the early 20th century, De Beers owned close to 90% of the world diamond supply—a virtual monopoly. With their marketing ploy, along with artificial scarcity, they were able to make an incredible profit from their enterprise.

Quite often, it is only the perception of value—not the intrinsic value—that people see.

Your values are driven by things you perceive as voids. When something is missing, you perceive it to be more valuable. Most people perceive money to be missing, which is why this book can seem valuable. And the intrinsic value is even greater for delivering on the implied promise—teaching you how to master your finances.

Perhaps you are looking at money, saying, "I don't have enough. I want more."

Whenever you perceive something in your life as "not enough"—in our current case, money—then that state of "not enough" makes money become more important because of the law of supply and demand. Supply and demand also work in your consciousness. The voids that you perceive make something seem more valuable.

What is consciousness? It is a collection of ideas. It is information, but it is also your own perceptions and, quite often, it includes the old model of thinking.

A History of the Old Models of Thinking

If you consider the old model and what it means—the ideas on money that were around from 60 to 100 years ago—from Earl Nightingale, Napoleon Hill and the other guys from the success testament, they were rather limited. Remember, these were the guys who said, "You have to change your beliefs." "The beliefs you have will determine your life." "Your beliefs create your reality." "Change your thinking and change your life." That all sounded great. It sounded fantastic! If you were to do a rigorous study of their fans, you would likely find that for every million people who tried the old model, only a handful ever achieved significant success. The leaders of that movement were successful largely because so many people were hungry for answers. The demand was high.

But now we return to the question, "How do you change your beliefs?" Do you read lots of books? I suspect that most of my students have read *Think and Grow Rich*. And I would ask them, "So, you're all rich by now?"

After the "change your beliefs" movement proved unsatisfactory, it was replaced with a newer model called, "You've got to do a lot of affirmations." You look in the mirror and tell yourself, "I'm rich. I'm rich. I'm rich." Oddly, you are flat broke, the debt collectors are calling, but you are "rich." Sadly, it does not work that way.

The next new model we might call, "Fake it till you make it." But what does "fake it till you make it" turn you into? Quite simply, a farce.

In reality, all you have done is to buy a bunch of stuff on the outside to mask your internal perception. And all it really accomplishes is to create or worsen the debt cycle. It puts you in the rat race of finance.

That is what most people end up doing. The world is currently built on this flawed paradigm.

If you tie your identity to the idea that money is going to give you power, then you are simply saying to yourself that, if you do not have money, you have no power.

For too many people, money becomes their identity. And if you define your success by money, then you will always be a failure. You will never have enough. You will always say, "There's more, there's more, there's more." And this is why I wrote the book, *Chasing Success*. People become trapped in the never-ending cycle of "more."

Someone might say, "I made a million. What about two million? What about ten million?" What you do is end up collapsing yourself into this cascade of never having enough because fulfillment is filling and fooling the mind with what you perceive as missing.

True Fulfillment

> **The fulfillment you want does not come from the outside; it comes from the inside.**

The popular myth tells you that money is going to give you that fulfillment, but it never does. The truth is this: fulfillment happens first and *then* you get the money.

Money is attracted to you when you are in a state of self-worth and self-love.

If you are not in a state where you are attracting wealth, you are repelling wealth. This is because you do not love who you are as an individual. And if you do not know how to love who you are as an individual—through all you have been through on your journey, the good, the bad, the highs, the lows, the challenges, the drawbacks and the setbacks—you end up resenting yourself.

Think about this for a moment: Let us say you have an evil twin brother. Everything good in your life, he ruins, or steals and claims as his own. You do your homework and the next morning it goes missing. At school, your homework is turned in with his name on it. You make some money, but it ends up in his pocket or wasted on junk. Do you think you would want to give him more money? Or would you resent him for his bad behavior? And there is an old saying: If you reward bad behavior, you will get more of the same.

Now, imagine that your "evil twin brother" is really just you. And the label of "evil" is not something you specifically apply, but the feeling is there hidden deep down. You do not want to give yourself more money because you have been a disappointment, so far. Do you see how this is a self-defeating attitude?

Because of self-resentment, you are unwilling to give yourself more money. Because you do not have money, you may consider that you are a failure—not everyone does, mind you, but just as an example—and you do not want to reward such a failure by making that self a success. This kind of internal logic gets pretty dark. It is self-destructive.

How can you love yourself if you resent yourself? And have you ever been at a point in your life where you resented who you were as an individual?

There is no question about it. If that resentment does not clear up, then you will end up repelling money and you will stop it from being part of your life.

The old idea that changing the beliefs around money is somehow going to make you successful, that is just a bunch of nonsense. And now I hope you are starting to see why.

When one of my students encountered this idea, he realized something about his own behavior—specifically, his procrastination. He realized that he had not been valuing himself enough to complete the required work.

The whole game of money is about your self-value. Your outside world is a manifestation of what is going on inside you. But behind things like "beliefs" you have a fundamental decision—whether or not to love yourself. If you decide on an unconscious level to resent yourself, then things will not go smoothly for you.

The Be, Do, Have of Existence

You have the "you"—the "self." And you have the "be," the "do" and the "have." Most people are going to define their lives by what they have, and this will be their "identity." This identity will be how they present themselves to the world. It will be the cars, it will be the yachts, it will be whatever it is on the outside—including the Rolexes. That will be the identity of what is real for them. And they will show this off. They will brag about this all day long.

They will do everything in their power to try and get that because they think their identity is outside of themselves. They structure their life by sitting in this world going back and forth. They say to themselves, "I've got to do more to have more. Do more to have more. I gotta do more things to have more things because my identity is wrapped up in the idea of having more things and if I don't have more things, I'm a nobody."

Behind all of this crap, the individual is actually trying to be somebody.

But ask yourself, "What does being "me" mean?"

It means being okay with who you are as an individual—for both the positive and the negative—loving who you are, and who you are designed to be. This is who you are intended to be. And let us be clear, here: This is not a glib, "I'm okay with myself." That can be superficial or shallow. And the exercises you will be doing dig more deeply into your real feelings about yourself—not the "logical" view of self, but the visceral, core feelings which control your behavior.

Most people never ask the question, "Who am I?" They say, "What do I do and what do I have?" That becomes the source of their existence. In this case, if the identity is in what you have, it will never be enough. You will keep consuming. And this is called consumerism.

Consumerism

Consumerism is driven by shame. This is the shame that people feel about themselves because they do not feel worthy of having and being who they are. Instead of starting with high self-worth, they will go and buy more stuff to make themselves feel better. Many people call this behavior being a "shop-o-holic," but the truth is far deeper. The source is the shame that they feel on the inside. And that shame on the inside actually prevents them from being authentic with who they are.

Shame drives you to buy more stuff, which in the marketplace is called "consumerism."

So, the market wants to own you by making you feel more shame about yourself. The more shame you have, the more money you are going to spend. You need to buy more because it is the only way you can feel good. People do this with food. All these addictions come from shame because you do not feel worth it on the inside. Marketers have known this for a century or more and they have become experts at pushing the right "consumer buttons" — "buy the latest and greatest."

There is much more on this subject of shame and we will cover this more deeply in a later chapter.

But this shopping addiction, some people characterize as "shopping therapy." When you do not feel good, you need stuff from the outside to make you feel good on the inside. That becomes your identity.

Going back to what one of my students had said earlier—about money giving them power—in reality, it gives them an identity. They are attempting to treat a symptom rather than the root cause. They are trying to fix the internal feeling with an external patch. And that is "outside-in"—backwards.

People keep chasing this external "identity" to make them feel fulfilled on the inside. They think the outside is going to solve their inner discomfort.

We live in a society today where as much as 40% of the population is on psychotropic medication. More people are messed up in this world than ever before, and a big part of the problem comes back to this misguided attempt to fix what is on the inside with something from the outside. And it is because they do not value who they are.

That is what the mission is: To help people change their misguided "solution" to a far deeper problem.

Your beliefs around money have been taught to you by marketers, peers and supposed experts. They distract you with ideas about "doing" and "having," but never about "being." They imply that you are not good enough because you need to do more and have more.

So, if you are made uncomfortable or otherwise challenged by the idea of money, and your relationship with money, why would you have more of it? If you have gone through an episode where money has been a negative thing, on an instinctual level, you will try to avoid it. Some people have gone through the double-whammy of divorce and bankruptcy, creating for them a mountain of pain. Are they going to want more of that pain in their lives? Of course not! They would do everything in their power to push that money away from them. Remember, the amygdala is not the logical, thinking part of the brain; it is the fight-or-flight, feeling part of the brain. To its one-dimensional processes, money equals pain.

A lady I met at one of the money programs told me, "No, I don't have a problem with money."

I asked, "Do you have any money?"

"Well, no."

Then, I asked her, "If someone gave you $10,000 in your pocket, could you hold on to it?"

"Well, uh, no," she replied. "I couldn't do that."

She could not hold onto the money because the more she held onto it, the more horrible she would feel about herself.

The thinking part of her mind is clever; it came up with ways to make excuses and to cover up the problem she did not consciously know she had. She could not admit that she had a problem, but my simple questions were all it took to reveal the problem she could not easily face.

Most every one of my students work very hard to get the results for which they are looking. But if hard work was the answer, the factory workers would be the successful ones. Hard work is not the answer. We all work hard, so why isn't that the solution?

The Real Importance of Beliefs

Let us define what a belief is. According to my definition, a belief is a collection of ideas about which you have conviction that they are true.

And your conviction around this belief is going to drive your neurology and the frequency of your life. Your frequency is the energy in which you function as a magnet.

At some level, you are a magnet. If you have a perception, or a belief, that money is negative, are you going to keep more of it in your life, or less of it in your life? By simple logic, the answer is, "Less."

If you have a perception, or a belief, that money is positive, are you going to have more of it in your life, or less of it in your life. Again, the answer is pretty simple: "Probably more."

But what if you believe neither? What if you do not care? Are you going to have more of it, or less of it? With such indifference, you can take it, but you do not have to. You know money will show up when you need it, and it does.

Reviewing the Old Model

This is the "old model" of thinking on money: Your beliefs lead to your behaviors, and your behaviors lead to your habits. Some of the so-called experts attack the "beliefs" end of this process, while others attack the "habits" end. They will say, "You have to change your habits! That's the secret to you succeeding!" And that is just not true.

But here is something which is true: How you believe is going to lead to how you behave, and how you behave is going to lead to the habits you have with your money.

A study at Stanford University showed some interesting results on habits and the attempts to change them. And many of us do not need a university study to tell us the results. We see similar results every year with New Year's resolutions.

Only 5% of people were able to change old habits into new ones. A total of 12% were able to change their behaviors. And statistically, 27% actually changed their beliefs around something. But look at what this means: 73% of people try to change and fail to do so.

Moving Beyond the Old Model

You know that the beliefs are there, but how do they get created? That is the question which dials into the real problem.

You have a moment in your life—an experience—which you consider to be positive or negative at that specific moment. And your life is made up of an infinite collection of moments. So, you have an infinite number of decisions or judgments based on your values. Each of these leads to an emotion which is either going to attract or repel the object or situation being considered. Two non-financial examples might be a painful bruise and a delicious meal.

So many of my students complain how they work so hard, but have virtually zero results to show for their efforts. This is as a result of too many negative events about money. Inwardly, you cringe at the thought of money. Logically, you may like what you can buy with money, but smacking you in the face—keeping money beyond reach—are the buried memories of those negative events.

Consider for a moment what it might be like to grow up in a household where you had only positive events with regard to money. Those people have an advantage—not because of the money their family already has, but because of the positive events in their memory. They will automatically attract more money because of their deepest feelings about money. So, when you hear the phrase, "The rich get richer," do not be distracted by the easy conclusion that this is because they have some unfair advantage with all their family's money and connections. It goes much deeper than that. It is all about their positive moments.

And so, their apparent advantage is now yours through the exercises in this book. You can start with nothing—zero dollars—and with the mindset of only positive experiences regarding money, "luck"—whatever that is—seems to be all yours. Luck is not an accident; it is something you create—good or bad.

One of my students described her negative experiences this way: "I grew up with a single Mom. She busted her butt and never had anything to show for it. And she would say things like, 'Money doesn't grow on trees,' or 'We don't need that' or, you know, there was always something—an excuse, or something—and for some reason, we couldn't do certain things, or have certain things, that other kids had. I just see where—you know—but she spent everything she made and I do a lot of the same stuff."

Parents and Blame

What my student said is very revealing and quite common. But her assessment of her own situation is somewhat misguided. What I am talking about now involves personal responsibility. And this is an important issue.

From this moment on, you are no longer allowed to blame your parents for your life.

If ever you might want to cripple yourself so that you could not become a master of your own finances, blaming others would do it. So, it needs to stop now.

Instead of blaming them for all of the negative experiences, you should be thanking them for what you will discover are some of your greatest gifts.

Once you master your own past events—redefining them into something positive—you will gain a strength never experienced by those who had it easy.

There are many parallels to this in life. Childhood illnesses make the body's immune system stronger. Doing uncomfortable repetitions during physical exercise will make your muscles stronger. And doing crossword puzzles or some other mental challenge will help keep your mental faculties sharp.

Personal responsibility empowers you; being a victim does the opposite.

Here is what I told the student: "If we hold onto the stories of victimhood and say things like, 'Because my Mom was a single Mom,' or, 'My Dad worked in a factory,' or 'I lived on the streets,' we will never rise above our story. Our story becomes the barrier we use to trap ourselves in a box that will never let us go. It becomes the paradigm of our existence. If you could understand the greatness and the benefits of your Mom being a single Mom and the benefits of your Mom actually giving away all her money, and what it taught you, you would be able to move forward from it. You need to see how it served you and your life, rather than stopped your life. You will be able to use it as a catapult. With that source of strength, you can stand on your mother's shoulders rather than in her shadow."

As a parent, the notion that a son or daughter will play victim pisses me off. If you grow to be 60, 70 or 80 years old, and your child says, "Well, you thought this or that about money, and that is the reason why I'm now broke," you will likely feel pretty bad at the blame and their playing the victim in all this.

Is that really what you intend for your child? No, of course not. You are doing the best with what you have.

Now, your kid—who you love with all your heart—down the line, may very well blame you for their life. We need to teach the next generation responsibility because if you blame others, you are making yourself powerless; but if you take responsibility, you at least have a chance.

Emotions and Chaos

Logic and responsibility empower you; emotions and victimhood disempower you. Your emotions are the delusions that create chaos in your life. Every emotion that you perceive is an additional reason you have chaos in your life. Very few people actually control their emotions. For most people, their emotions are merely a random reaction to circumstances and sometimes from flawed perception.

Without emotions you do not have chaos, but most people have an emotional addiction, especially to money. And that addiction is what is causing so much chaos in their lives. This is why money can hold you back, if it does.

Ninety-nine percent of your actions, on a day-to-day basis, are not your conscious will, believe it or not. They are habitual actions and neurological responses from the past. You have had a memory triggered by something in your environment, and your nervous system automatically responds to that. And if you have a response to something that is negative around money, based on your perception, your sympathetic nervous system fires up, and all of the sympathetic nervous responses—your cortisol, your fight-or-flight mechanism—comes up, and you are now in a state of defense against money.

If, on the other hand, you have a parasympathetic response—sometimes referred to as "rest and digest"—money is a positive, and you like it. You wine and dine with it. You relax with it. You have a welcoming response around money.

Yin and Yang—Positive and Negative

There is a positive in everything, but there is also a negative in everything, including a negative in a positive. Every event in life is neutral until you put a perception to it—a decision about what it means. Every event is neutral until you give it a meaning, whether positive or negative. You decide, based on your value system and value structure, whether something is going to be positive or negative. How you decide on that polarity will determine your response, whether you attract or repel.

One of my students told me that she had been taught to do a lot of affirmations. But think about this. Let us say for a moment that your life is all about affirmations. Therefore, a lack of wealth is because you do not affirm wealth enough based on the definition of affirmations.

Look at the definition of the word: The suffix, "-tion," means "the condition of." "Affirm" comes from the Latin *"ad-"* + *"firmare"*—to make firm or solid, as in one's mind. That is what it really means.

Now, let me tell you what an affirmation is not. It is not taking something you perceive to be a negative and saying its opposite a sufficient number of times to turn the negative into a positive. It does not work that way. That is a delusion. When you make something firm in your mind, it is not because you keep saying it over and over. It is because you see the positives and negatives equally within what you are considering and now it is firm because the mind is balanced and because your nervous system is balanced 100% of the time.

Assignments: Beliefs Around Money, Part 1

1. How do you define money? (Your definition.)
2. What are the benefits of your definition to you? (Make a list of 25.)

Beliefs Around Money, Part 2

Risking Emotion

You have to stop being timid about your own growth.

One of my students was usually very quiet, holding everything in. During my training sessions, the students share their celebrations before we dig into the meat of the topic for the day. So, when this one student who had not yet offered any celebrations again remained quiet, I called her on it.

She replied, "I don't know if I actually have any celebrations, but I did the assignment. Well, not until this morning, unfortunately, but, you know, I am learning a little bit more about myself. On the cash part of it, my thoughts tended to be all negative." She hesitated. "I stay quiet because I feel like I'm going to get emotional and I don't want to."

Even though emotion is a source of chaos, I want you to be emotional during this transformation process. You need to let it out while you are doing this work. This is because, only through emotions are you going to crack the code inside of you. You need to risk the chaos in this more controlled environment so you can burn off that chaos to get to the real reasons for your beliefs, behaviors, habits and real-world results. If you stay quiet—holding in your emotions—you are not going to get breakthroughs.

You are going to stay where you are because, the truth is, the emotions are the things holding you back on the subject of money. The objective of all your work—the assignments—is to give you that breakthrough. If you do not risk the emotional release, you will have spent the money, done the work and stayed exactly where you were. So, if you feel a sudden urge to cry, do not suppress the emotion. Beyond that mental storm is the golden realization you seek.

Imagine that you take a course in creative writing, but you sit quietly in the corner and never share your work with your classmates. You never risk their valuable criticism. You pay the money and spend the time in class, but miss the most valuable part of the learning. You need to be fearless—laying your soul on the anvil of risk.

Like I said earlier, transformation is not going to be easy. And a big part of your work is more than merely going through the motions. You have to be deeply involved. And that is all about emotional risk.

The Power of Decision

So many of my students have told me that shortly after making the decision to take full responsibility for their own financial mastery by taking one of my courses, they found the money they needed to do just that. When you make a life-changing decision like that and actually move into it, the money will follow. I hear it all the time—people decide to come into the work, and to start doing the work with me, and all of a sudden new business opportunities and new money show up. That is the power of decision.

Money vs. Fulfillment

Once you understand money, it no longer has any power over you.

We live in a world where our identities are defined by what we have and the things with which we live. And if we exist only with the idea that money is the answer, then we will eventually lead to a condition I call, the "continuum of chaos." This dark condition never allows us to find fulfillment.

Fulfillment is the secret to the joys that you strive to achieve.

When you understand that fulfillment is a game from the inside out, money is no longer the objective. It merely becomes part of the process of giving value. And the more money you create, the more value you bring.

Money will never make you good or bad, right or wrong, happy or sad. Let us be perfectly real about this. While you likely know people who are broke who are miserable, you might also know people who are broke, but who are extremely happy. You may know people who are rich who are extremely happy, and you may also know people who are rich but who are extremely miserable.

The delusion of our modern society is that we think that money is going to solve the emptiness we feel inside. It won't.

When I went to India, I was 11 or 12 years old. I remembered that everyone traveled on trains. And I remember that where we stayed was not a slum, but it was not the wealthiest of communities, either. And I remember very clearly, people sitting on the side of the road in a squatting position. It took me a moment, but then I realized that they were defecating in public. They did not have a toilet or a place to go. But in their poverty, they were smiling. They were happy, even though, monetarily, they were the poorest of the poor.

Without anything of material worth, they had joy.

There I was, at age 11, wondering why is this happening? Why are so many people in my own, more affluent, middle-class world, feeling miserable, but these poor people are living with joy? This memory created quite an impression on me and it helped to set me on my journey of discovery.

I want you to remove the emotion of money. I do not care if you have bills. I do not care if you have mountains of debt. I do not care about any of that stuff because you can eliminate all of that stuff. All of that stuff is just in your head. Something deep in your mind is destroying your bliss—your sense of fulfillment. And it is not the lack of money.

Your solution comes from the inside out; not the other way around.

Perhaps you took on credit that you did not feel you deserved. And now, you have debt because you do not appreciate what you have.

I want you to realize that the state of joy in which you live has nothing to do with the income you make. It has nothing to do with the car you drive, the house in which you live, or the wealthy people with whom you mingle. Those things have nothing to do with your fulfillment—your joy.

Fulfillment has everything to do with the internal state in which you decide to live every single day and that state is gratitude and love. When you sit in that state of gratitude and love, just appreciating life for what it is, then money does not become the almighty entity that so many people make it out to be. If you put fulfillment first, then money becomes an entity which allows you to do more of what you want with life.

If you believe that money is a source of pride—that it will get you high and bring you happiness—that addiction to money will eventually have you crash. Eventually, you will find yourself resenting money. For some people, that is called a mid-life crisis.

If you become too haughty with what you have accomplished, other people will begin to resent you. They will do little things, or leave out critical items, just to see you brought down a notch. In Australia, they call this the Tall Poppy Syndrome. In a way, you do that to yourself, as well.

If you are chasing the wrong thing and get high, eventually you are going to crash. The higher you get, the more feedback you get to humble you. On this topic of money, I am trying to get you to midline—to be balanced all the way through.

Not long ago, the richest man in the world—Jeff Bezos, founder of Amazon—was caught having an affair. Now, he is suffering a divorce. Some people become easily tempted with pride and power. They become the almighty, richest man in the world and can do anything. He conquered the world, achieved great heights, and was then brought low.

Investors and financial advisors do not base their assessments on the highs or the lows, but on the means—the averages. In a very real sense, the "mean" equals meaning. The mean is where you are at—your stable midpoint. You are always going to come back to a midline of balance.

My fellow doctors have a word for this principle—homeostasis. At this state, you are not parasympathetic or sympathetic, but in balance between the two. And, homeostasis is the essence of health.

The meaning is the essence of your psychology. Mean is the essence of your money. So, understand that if you get addicted to the idea of money you will eventually end up crashing from it.

So, it is wise to stay in the means and to stay balanced with it. Realize that money is an exchange of value.

This state of balance is so important—between pride and discouragement. Not only is the mean a very real phenomenon in health, with homeostasis, it touches on every other aspect of your life. There is a calm power to you being in balance, like the balance of a martial artist who does not overreach or flinch.

Today's personal development gurus want you to be excited, happy, joyful, and to live in the world of a dopamine, artificial high. But such things cannot last. Eventually—and very likely far sooner than later—you return to your balanced "comfort zone," and sometimes with a little crash and burn to offset the artificial highs.

Finding the Authentic You

One of my students works in the financial services industry and had been struggling with the exercises given to her. She admitted that she had become somewhat confused. For one thing, she had given advice to her clients which was nothing like the lessons she was learning here. While doing one of the assignments, she began to wonder if she had been authentic with herself or had merely been repeating the things she had always told her own clients.

I asked her if she had done the assignment for the full 90 seconds, and she confirmed that she had. I then told her that the last five answers were her most authentic responses.

Remember, these exercises are meant to transform you. The first few answers are likely to be the glib kind of response—shallow, easy answers which give you no traction with who you really are. But as you dig more deeply into your own mind, you start to uncover the real pay dirt.

The first 30 seconds of a 90-second assignment usually produce nothing of real value. The answers consist of the same bullshit you have been programmed to say.

The second 30-second portion of the assignment usually consists of you trying to decide what is real. Sometimes, the answers might be helpful, but quite often they contain a degree of confusion. The third and last 30-second portion touches on what is really sitting in your amygdala and in your limbic system, which are where your real beliefs reside. These are the things which knock you out of balance and drive you to chase after things like money and possessions. These drive you to adopt an outside-in strategy.

Money Is Not a Tool

Whenever I ask about money, the first question is, "So, what does money mean?" and most people tell me, "It's a tool!"

Really?

That is a programmed response perpetuated by the personal development crowd. What if I called someone else a "tool?" Is that a positive or negative statement? Naturally, it is negative!

And, of course, that other person is not a "tool," but a human being with value to exchange.

Consider this question: "What kind of relationship am I building with a tool versus something that has a far deeper, intrinsic value?" Do tools have value? In a limited sense, perhaps. But money has greater value because it has behind it the intent to reward value which has been added to someone else's life.

Money is a relationship, and if you value a relationship, you are going to take care of it. You are going to nurture it. You are going to want to spend time with it. You are going to want to pay attention to it—to make sure it grows.

In a way, it is like a child. There are obvious differences, but the similarities are worth noting. With a child, you value the relationship. You nurture him or her and help them to grow. And when it is time to let go of your child, perhaps through marriage or them setting out on a career, you hope you have prepared them well.

With money, you nurture it to help it grow. And when it comes time to spend it on something, you hope you are sending that money off in the proper direction, well spent.

Money is a communication of value from someone else that you have provided them something of value. This is all about exchange of value and relationships.

If you value money, you will want to help it grow. The limbic system is what determines whether or not you value something. But your amygdala is where you will sit and create the belief constructs around it. From there, it will run your life from pain and pleasure.

Amygdala Gold and the Process

My courses, and indeed this book, provide a process to those who are interested. Some students want to know right away how their discovery of the bottom third of the lists produced in their assignment will apply to their future success. The process of transformation requires multiple steps taken in the right sequence. Like baking a cake, you do not cook the ingredients and then mix them. Some students and readers will likely start to feel an awakening as they discover the truths they have been hiding deep down inside. But be patient with the process.

This is one key reason that you keep all of your assignments. In other words, do not write an assignment down on a napkin and then throw it away. Hold on to your work because in later assignments you are going to have to go back to those. We are going to take these negative things that you perceive around money and we are going to flip the coin on it, so to speak. We are going to change those negative feelings so you no longer have those constructs to throw you off balance.

Latent memories are creating within you some conflicting ideas around money. I do not like to use the term "subconscious." My goal for you is that, through your assignments, you will be digging up these latent thoughts and changing their alignment. You need them pointing all in the same direction, removing those hidden conflicts.

Your thoughts need to be internally consistent on the subject of money so that you no longer have a negative connotation attached to money. By the time you have finished reading this book and doing all of the assignments, you will finally "get it."

One of my students who is also a doctor told me that he still had a difficult time understanding this notion of removing emotion and staying in the "mean" or "average" state. Though he enjoys his work, helping patients feel better, he feels even better when he has a very profitable day. He feels super elated to have both the joy of helping people plus the joy of "killing it" financially.

This is a bit like a professional baseball player feeling the same emotions whether they just won the World Series, or—the opposite—lost an important game. My student wanted to know how such a thing is even possible.

It is all about the state of Zen. And perhaps that word means nothing to you.

Most people react to the events in their lives—revulsion or aversion to the negative events, and bliss or elation to the positive events. That is "outside-in" thinking and behavior. Instead, we need to be "inside-out" in our approach to the events of life. Zen is like a one-sided coin or one hand clapping. Perhaps a better description would be that it is not action-reaction—what is referred to as "dichotomous," or two-sided. Zen is all about the perfect state of the positive without any corruption by the negative.

I had my student do a simple exercise. I told him, "Close your eyes for just a second. Okay? Go to a moment where you actually had a great day with your patients and your practice. You crushed it. Then, picture having gone home after work. What happened? Something happened to humble you and to bring you down."

The student replied, "Yeah, you know, well, I have two kids, so I'm dealing with kids, and dealing with a bad time. The whole parenthood and marriage thing fills me with joy, but there's shit, too, that goes along with it."

What he had experienced at work was a state of addiction to something external. And I had done the same thing with my own practice. One week, we had 1,247 patient visits—over a thousand. It felt great for a few hours. But then I started to feel let down. From then on, I could only resent my practice because I had nowhere else I wanted to go. I had reached the peak for my practice. I had maxed out.

Life tries to bring you back into balance—similar to the parasympathetic system sending you one way and the sympathetic system sending you in the opposite direction. People tend to have a dopamine—"feel good"—addiction. It is the addiction to dopamine and to the "feeling good" that makes you feel like crap. The bad feeling is you coming down from an artificial high.

So, you go home, and the universe is going to balance you out because you cannot live in a perpetually parasympathetic state. The sympathetic nervous system is going to kick in and you might have the wife beating you up for some little thing, or telling you, "Take out the trash," or, "Really? I don't give a shit what you did that was so fantastic. That was work. Here, at home, I've been dealing with the kids all day. I'm tired. I'm exhausted. Please! You deal with it."

And you are like, "But I just saw 200 people. What are you talking about? I'm the man. I'm amazing."

And she replies, "I don't care."

In other words, life is not going to let you stay in that artificial state of bliss.

The challenge is that people go home after work and do not know how to balance what they have accomplished with this side of their life. The truth is that there are downsides to seeing a lot of patients because you have staff issues and management issues. And sometimes some of the customers did not get better. If you do not open your awareness to those things, you will have the universe humble you in order to help you see it.

So, what I am trying to teach you is that it is wise to govern yourself rather than to have the universe govern you.

In chiropractic practice, we learn that about 95% of the subluxations we handle are entirely psychosomatic. In other words, it is all in the patient's head. Stress from the job, worrying about their finances—you name it. The patients end up creating their own health problems by what they allow to operate in their own minds.

And in the work you will be doing, here, it is all in the way you think. Sure, physical trauma exists, but most of the time, the real problem is up there, in the mind.

Assignments: Beliefs Around Money, Part 2—Finding Money

1. Find the monthly mean (average) of your income.
2. What is your strategy to save money?
3. What strategy do you have to grow your savings?

Beliefs Around Money, Part 3

Latent Focus and Reflection in Reality

When you do the assignments which include judging items as positive or negative, please keep in mind that your assessment is based on the context. Sometimes an item can be positive and sometimes it can be negative. So, do not let this confuse you. Pick one which seems to apply the most to your current situation.

In 60 seconds, you can empty your mind of all the superficial or shallow ideas on a topic. The last 30 seconds will contain the items which are running your life. You do not need to have experienced those things; you merely need to have a strong feeling about them.

One student told me, "Nah, I've never been in a bankruptcy." Yet, "bankruptcy" was near the end of his list.

The fear of bankruptcy can still be very real. That fear can drive you to push money away. I am not saying that bankruptcy is right or wrong. Your reaction to the subject can have a powerful impact on what you do to attract or repel money. It depends on how you view it. The problem is not bankruptcy, but the perception of bankruptcy.

Some people feel bankrupt—empty. Like they have nothing. Thus, they fear bankruptcy and this drives their behavior and their results.

Another of my students was a real estate consultant who helped families who were in financial distress. He felt gratified that he had helped so many people, but then it became less and less gratifying. He told me, "It made me think of the irony that I'm working with thousands of people going through financial distress, and helping them, but at the same time, I am in financial distress myself."

Yet, it is not really irony. It is the nature of things. Our experiences tend to reflect what is held in our latent memories—the things which come up in the last 30 seconds of your 90-second assignments.

If you are in financial distress, you are going to attract people in financial distress. So, the way out of that negative situation is to change your consciousness around money.

The student I mentioned earlier, who is a fellow doctor, is a perfect example of this. When he decided to change his own consciousness around money, the decision alone was powerful enough to change his circumstances. Suddenly, his practice was booming. He went into a state of consciousness around money, and said to himself something like, "Okay, I'm going to grow my consciousness."

Sometimes, things suddenly get better not because of anything you do, but because of a decision which gives you hope and certainty, like growing your consciousness around money. Decisions can directly affect who you are on the inside. The inner thought is what is going to be shown to you on the outside.

Most people resist what happens in their environment, not realizing that their situation is trying to teach them and to balance their minds. The mind looks for balance, just like your body's internal chemistry looks for balance. The nervous system looks for balance. Even the universe is doing this. And, relevant to this topic, your finances are looking for balance.

If we remain unaware of what is going on, internally, we seem bewildered by what our latent memories are trying to tell us. Like the one student who said, "The customers I am attracting are broke," they do not realize that their inner belief is, "I am broke."

You attract your level of customers based on you.

Money is a game of resonance. How you resonate with money will determine how much money you bring in the door, and the type of customers with whom you are working.

There is no judgment here. Working with broke customers is not bad or good. It just is what it is. And if you understand what the dynamics are, you can have control over your situation. It is the lack of awareness of the latent memories that drives people to commit self-sabotage. They consciously want to move in one direction, but get frustrated when they cannot seem to move in that desired direction.

Say you work at a financial services company. If you have a million dollars in your pocket, you are not going to be doing business with people with no cash flow; that is going to be delegated out. You are not going to be playing at that level.

It is all about your innermost thoughts being reflected back. And after doing the work ahead, you will no longer be creating the addiction to money which sours your attraction of more desirable clientele.

Consider for a moment that you have a scale that measures your various attitudes around money. If you plot your attitudes and then take the average, it will always equal zero relative to your mean, except for brief moments of imbalance. The imbalance is going to create emotional chaos to force you back into homeostasis—into balance.

Savings, Self-Worth and Net-Worth

Now, let us use a different scale—one of financial income magnitudes— $10, $100, $1,000, $10,000, $100,000, $1,000,000. Your emotional self-worth determines how much you will go through the process of saving.

If you start with low self-worth, you might save $10. And how do you get past this level? It is not through affirmations. Your self-worth, however, determines your net worth.

Now, if you keep yourself at that negative self-worth you have guilt and shame that affect you, and they ruin your life. The greater the self-worth, the greater the ability to hold on to money. You remember when I started this book, I said money is nothing but the exchange of value. If you have more value for yourself and what you do for the world, then you, in essence, live a life where you will save more money and have more money with which to do more things.

This is not about simply getting rid of low self-worth. You need to find out why you do not love yourself and remove those barriers so you can thrive.

See the difference? As you increase your value of yourself—as you are going through this work—you end up creating more wealth.

This is why my clients end up making more money. It is not because I teach them how to invest or to put their money into index funds or into real estate. I do not teach you that stuff.

Of all the people who go to real estate seminars, most are broke. Usually, only about 5–10% actually have money to invest.

The housing market crash of 2008 created in many people—even in some formerly successful investors—a lack of self-worth. This is because they were emotionally attached to the success that they had had. If we do not see things from a neutral stance, self-worth will become emotionally diluted.

Your job here is to increase your self-worth up the ladder, from wherever it is now toward higher levels. And, again, this is not chasing after money, which uses an outside-in strategy, but building from within toward the outside. And I promise you that, throughout this entire book, I am not going to teach you anything concerning where to invest.

I am going to teach you everything on how to manage your emotions around money, and how to master your consciousness around it. In addition, I will teach you how to master your consciousness around yourself—to be able to love yourself more so that you can actually bring more wealth into your life.

Guilt and Shame

Though we will cover the topic of guilt and shame regarding money in far greater depth in a later chapter, I want to touch on it here because these are such a big part of the beliefs people have around money. Clearing up guilt is thus a big part of helping you achieve financial mastery.

Not long ago, one of my students asked about guilt and shame. As a moderately successful businesswoman, she had arranged to have her young adult son attend the course with her.

I asked her, "Have you ever sworn at your son?" She admitted that she had, so I asked, "Did you feel guilty about it?"

Again, she replied, "Yes."

Finally, I asked, "Have you ever done something to punish him?" to which she admitted that she had. "And didn't you feel guilty in the process?"

Thoughtfully, she replied, "Yes."

"I remember, when I was a kid, my Mom used to punish me, and I'd be like, 'You hate me!' And she used to tell me 'It hurts me more to punish you than you even know.' Right?"

Naturally, my student understood. As a parent, she had gone through all of these things. But, when we perceive that we have caused someone more pain than pleasure, in an action that we did, that is what we call guilt. That guilt makes us think that we did something wrong—that we hurt them.

Similarly, the student I mentioned earlier who had been a real estate consultant had felt shame for failing his clients and his business partners—losing money in the real estate mess. That shame is running his life. By the end of this book, you will learn how to clear similar emotional forces from your own life. You will no longer need to hold onto that feeling, whatever it is, and you are going to learn how to let it go.

Guilt and shame become the anchors which prevent you from having money. Shame is the biggest thing that will stop you from having wealth in your life.

Wisdom and Fair Exchange

My real estate consultant student also shared his experiences with business partners, college roommates and friends. He was always helping others, but when he needed help, no one was there for him. He had loaned others money, but all too frequently the others never paid him back.

Most of us have been taught that it is good to give and good to help, but there is a right way and a wrong way to do things. Doing this the wrong way causes you to give away your soul.

If you are lending money to people without holding them accountable, then you are creating a destructive, emotional cycle. You need to stop that kind of self-destructive activity.

True wealth sits in fair exchange, where giving and receiving are in balance. In order for you to give, you must get something in return. You are getting the positive emotions of thinking that you are doing something powerful, including states of pride. We will come back to this aspect later in the book on the topic of emotion and money.

But you giving, and giving, and giving, puts you in a state of imbalance. This is the kind of giving which is not good. They keep taking from you which throws them out of balance, too.

It is wise to stay in fair exchange for what you give and for what you receive.

Take for example this book. The retailer charges a certain amount of money which helps them with payroll, utilities and everything else to keep their business running. But my intention is to provide more value than you expect for the money you spent. Does this throw me out of balance to give more than you expect? Not really. And this is the wisdom of adding value.

Now, if I gave you something "under" what you were expecting, then you might feel that you did not get what you paid for, right? You might feel disappointed or let down—perhaps even cheated.

This is also partly perception. Let us say you go to a coffee shop and they charge more for a large cup of coffee than do other coffee outlets. They serve in the same, large paper cups, but their cups are only half full. It does not matter that their coffee costs more because it is imported from Vietnam, or some such. The customer sees half as much coffee, which costs more than they are used to paying. If, on the other hand, the coffee shop provided the same amount of coffee in a smaller, but fancy, porcelain cup that was filled to the brim, then the customer might perceive greater value. Not that I am comparing life-changing wisdom to a cup of coffee, but sometimes the packaging or presentation is part of the product—the ambiance or experience. If the customer does not perceive the value, then it does not matter how hard the service or product provider works.

And so if you give, and the other person receives, you have to be in balance. Giving a little more can help with the perception of value. But there is a wildcard at work behind the scenes—in the latent memory. If your latent memories contain shame for having money, then you would give it away. And you would give it to other people because that made you feel good. It alleviated the feelings of shame for having money.

Societies and businesses grow, not by giving, and not by receiving, but by finding a balance of giving and receiving. If we step back for a moment and look at the American economy, we see that it is on the brink of collapse. I am not trying to be alarming, but look at the facts. When you have $30 trillion in debt, built on pride because that is what we are living in, it has to collapse. This is not sustainable. It may not be today or tomorrow, but it is going to be in the next five to seven years. All through history, every country that has gone into states of pride has collapsed. It has to because we are too far into the state of debt. Our pride and our shame are imbalanced, and we have to crash because of it. And the more we keep printing money and putting ourselves in debt, the more deeply in trouble we become.

There is a limit, but more debt does not make more money. More debt builds more debt. It may produce jobs in the economy, but are they adding value? Or is it, as the old saying goes, "taking in your own laundry?" If the work done is merely internal—doing your own family's laundry—you can be very busy, but not be making any income.

If you study history—societies and economies—over the last 2,000 years, including the Roman Empire and the British Empire, they had to crash because they got too far into a state of pride.

Wisdom supports the business of fair exchange. For example, if you had not paid for this book, was the retailer going to give you the book? Of course not! Why would they do that? In a very real sense, that would rob you of your own initiative.

Discounts and buy-one-get-one-free programs are good for increasing interest and exposure, but also know, whatever you do not pay for, you do not value nearly as much. Paying for something is a measure of your commitment to getting as much value out of the product or service as you possibly can. "Free" simply does not generate the same level of commitment.

And in training such as this, which demands a great deal from the reader or student, a lack of commitment means that they never realize the value that was promised.

The ones who do the required work are going to be the ones who paid for it. Their commitment ensures they get the value for which they paid.

In the health industry, a similar dynamic is at work. A large percentage of patients who are insurance-based and do not pay directly for their care, are rarely, if ever going to get better. The patients who pay cash are more likely to get better.

Removing the Burden of an Uncertain Future

I am forever being barraged by student questions—concerns about this or that in their lives. One worry that has been repeated by numerous people concerns our uncertain future. First of all, our future is always uncertain, and worry does not make it better. In fact, the training in this book is meant to prepare your mind so you are not emotionally dependent on external conditions for your wellbeing. Instead, you address the world—whatever the conditions—from a position of balance and strength.

I cannot tell you how to invest or where to put your savings. That is not my expertise. But I can help you prepare your mind for whatever the future brings.

My mission is to help people. As you go through this book, if you have any breakthroughs, I would love to hear from you and to know how I have helped. And if you let me share your story with others, it could help them as much as this has helped you.

Assignments: Beliefs Around Money, Part 3

Assignment 1: Belief Inventory

1. Set a timer for 90 seconds and ask yourself the question **"What are my beliefs on money?"** Then just write everything that comes to mind.

2. Set a timer for 90 seconds and ask yourself the question **"What are my beliefs on assets?"** Then just write everything that comes to mind.

3. Set a timer for 90 seconds and ask yourself the question **"What are my beliefs on liabilities?"** Then just write everything that comes to mind.

4. Set a timer for 90 seconds and ask yourself the question **"What are my beliefs on credit?"** Then just write everything that comes to mind.

5. Set a timer for 90 seconds and ask yourself the question **"What are my beliefs on debt?"** Then just write everything that comes to mind.

6. Set a timer for 90 seconds and ask yourself the question **"What are my beliefs on cash?"** Then just write everything that comes to mind.

7. Set a timer for 90 seconds and ask yourself the question **"What are my beliefs on investing?"** Then just write everything that comes to mind.

8. Set a timer for 90 seconds and ask yourself the question **"What are my beliefs on saving?"** Then just write everything that comes to mind.

9. Set a timer for 90 seconds and ask yourself the question **"What are my beliefs on bills?"** Then just write everything that comes to mind.

10. Set a timer for 90 seconds and ask yourself the question **"What are my beliefs on the job?"** Then just write everything that comes to mind.

11. Set a timer for 90 seconds and ask yourself the question **"What are my beliefs on business?"** Then just write everything that comes to mind.

12. What do you perceive as positive from your Belief Inventory? (Write "positive" directly after those items.)

13. What do you see as negative from your Belief Inventory? (Write "negative" directly after those items.)

Assignment 2: Inner Thoughts on Money

1. What is your innermost thought about your worth and money?
2. How has this belief served you? (List 30 benefits.)

CHAPTER 3

Understanding Wealth

Importance of Doing the Work

Not all of my students have been committed to do the work. I tell them right up front that I am committed to their transformation, but am not responsible for their transformation. There is an old saying, "You can lead a horse to water, but you can't make it drink."

Sometimes, you merely have to put one foot in front of the other and keep moving, no matter how difficult that might feel or how many distractions seem to pull you away. You have to want and need the transformation enough to fill every nook and cranny of your time with the work—especially doing the assignments.

I am merely saying that if you have not done the work, you are not robbing me; you are robbing yourself. I have enough work to do; do not worry about me.

If you were to tell me, "Doc, I'm really busy. I can't find the time to do the work," I would understand, but that is not the solution to this. If your body is running down because you need to eat, drink water or sleep, then you are forced to take care of that responsibility, even if you do it in small portions. Your financial future is waiting for you to take full responsibility for it. The dynamic here is no different. You either do the work or you don't. You either achieve financial mastery or you don't. It comes down to a matter of choice.

When you choose to take decisive action in the face of insurmountable barriers, you will find, more often than not, that you find ways to be more efficient. You discover new resources, or repurpose old resources to make your life suddenly easier. Another old saying comes to mind, "Necessity is the Mother of invention," and your decision to commit yourself to this work will show **the intention** that you are serious.

Measuring Your Progress Through the Work

Some of my students have amazing breakthroughs and realizations— what some of them call "epiphanies"—even after the first week of my six-week course. But everyone is different. One student was quite concerned that he had not had the types of breakthroughs experienced by some of my other students.

Please realize that this is an extended, multi-layered process. Some people have more junk to clean up on the first level, while others do not. All of the steps along the way are meant to cover every aspect of your financial mastery. Whatever is holding you back will be handled in one of the many assignments or in some combination of assignments.

And never dismiss an assignment which may seem deceptively easy. There is a deep power to simple concepts and a shallow use of those concepts will never tap into their deepest potential. You need to approach every assignment with the expectation of "unexpected value." That type of openness, or humility, allows you to discover things others might miss.

Another student raised a concern regarding the "positive" and "negative" labels applied to the items in our assignments. These judgments of positive or negative will be different from one individual to the next, based on their experiences. The assignments are meant to peel off the layers of your own core beliefs so that you can see more clearly the code by which your life program has been working up until now. So long as that code remains in darkness, you will not be able to have much control over it. Awareness allows you to make changes. What one person may take as a negative, another may take as a positive.

During the Belief Inventory, one student, on the topic of money, in general, wrote, "Important, allow you to grow, exchange, pretty challenging, managing it can be a pain, feeling empowered, ability to do what you want, only for people that work hard, makes you more of who you are, game of frequency, makes you feel inferior, and makes you not worth it."

Wow!

See the conflicts? This person is living with some conflicting paradigms around money. Discovering this can prove quite cathartic—a big relief that sets them free, to an extent. They now know what they have had to deal with most of their life.

The same individual had a markedly different list on the topic of savings—"freedom, ability to breathe, future wealth, ability to see your own growth, the kids' future, strength, value in self, not knowing what to do with it, storing of cash, increases my self-worth."

So, that individual has a lot of more positive associations with savings. It seems that they are going to be more inclined toward savings.

And even more revealing is the same person's take on budgeting—"Combining, a way to measure details, keeps you feeling trapped, essential part of a plan, makes you more trapped, stops you from looking at the big picture, keeps your business from growing, makes you have to trust someone else with your money, they'll control you and your life."

To this person, budgeting remains a painful subject.

There is much more to money than merely making it. There is keeping it, spending, managing it, budgeting it. There is also spending future money, called "credit" or "loans," and paying back for that credit or loans—or not! Each person has their own unique mix of pluses and minuses.

So, the subject of wealth and financial mastery is not as simple as most people initially think it is.

Confusion About Money and Wealth

In this chapter I will show you the truth about this thing called money and it will probably blow your freaking mind.

There are three components to money. They form a triangle. On the left side we have this thing called "attract," on the right side we have this thing called "manage" and on the bottom we have this thing called "retain." Each one of these has a different component around money—a different set of emotions which determine how you view money. They also affect how you live and everything you do with money.

Based on your Belief Inventory, if you believe money is simply a positive thing, you can say it is positive. And that sounds great.

If you look at it generally, like personal development gurus have done for many years, they may say, "Well you just look at your life and it will determine if you have money." But that is a shallow and largely inaccurate assessment. At the very least, it is not at all helpful.

There is so much more that we can determine from that.

Our money triangle—with attracting on the left, managing on the right and retaining at the base—can help us unpack a person's view of money.

Someone who cannot attract money is repelling it. Anyone who cannot manage money has an emotional delusion around it. And a lack of retaining money is because of guilt and shame. In other words, they do not feel worthy of holding on to it.

These are the three paradigms of money, or emotions around money making:

- Attracting or repelling
- Managing vs. "freedom of money" (delusion)
- Guilt and shame

Notice the words "freedom of money" I included. Your addiction to "freedom of money" is the reason you cannot manage money. You cannot keep it under control because, emotionally, you want money to be free. You cannot manage money because you want to set it free. Do you see? This is how emotion has created confusion, blindness and chaos on this aspect of money. Money management for most people thus remains a mystery.

Most people want to have a life of joy, happiness or success, but without the downside of it. They become elated with money rather than looking at the downside of it, too. Their view is out of balance.

Wealth is not a state of abundance; that is a delusion.

In order to understand this bald fact, we first need to understand the meaning of the word. And finding a common definition among my students is next to impossible.

One of my students defined wealth as "a culmination of things that allow you to be the person you're supposed to be. Whether that be taking care of family or creating a foundation. Wealth, to me, is the result you achieved in the process of life."

Another student defined wealth as "having the freedom to live your life and having everything you want."

Still another student gave the definition: "I view a wealthy person as somebody that, A, has the assets, but also has investments, and they might be involved in different things, sort of across the board, not just a job and whatever. They have the freedom to help their family and be a benefit to people, or solve problems if something comes up; they just truly have financial freedom. Have the kind of house they want, drive the kind of car they want, send their kids to the schools they want, that kind of stuff."

In other words, "financial freedom is wealth."

One more student definition: "An accumulation of wealth and riches whether they be monetary, spiritual, social, family..."

The root of the word wealth, *"weal,"* means "wholeness" or "welfare." The *-th* ending simply refers to the "condition of."

We have been programmed into thinking that it is all about money. Financial freedom is a myth. And wealth as money is a delusion.

Most people today figure that, if they do not have money, they are not wealthy. They end up putting a belief barrier on themselves that prevents them from ever being wealthy. If wealth is about money, it is only about money. If family is not a part of your wealth, then you are always broke.

How do you ever experience wealth? When you achieve a condition of wholeness. Remember? From the root word?

If we understand the root of a word, then we can understand what things mean, and then we can define how we live. We can define things, truly as a culture, as an organization, as individuals. If we each come up with our own definitions, then we begin to lose cohesion as a society. We lose our ability to communicate and to understand our direction in life.

If we look at the language—where things come from—then we can understand where things are. And most people judge their wealth based on their bank accounts.

Most people—not all, but most—judge their state of being based on their bank account. If this were true, then someone with money is happy and good with life, and can say, "I have everything I want."

And then, someone else says, "I never have enough money."

Unfortunately, this modern paradigm is built around the idea that when you have money, you will be happy, joyful or fulfilled. And if you do not have money, then you are left empty.

You can never actually attain "true success" on these terms. Most people, when they look at and talk about money, are in a state of elation—a state of imaginary "freedom." And this mindset is from a state of polarization toward the positive, and this polarization—this off-balanced condition—is what creates the chaos in their lives.

Most people, and their psyches, believe that wealth equals money and that this is associated with happiness. Well, let's debunk this myth right off the top. We all know people who are extremely happy but who do not have any money. And we also know people with lots of money who are miserable.

So, money cannot be the parameter we use to measure success and wealth. As I said, *weal* and *-th* mean, "the whole being" plus "condition of." The root word, *weal,* means "to heal," or "to align your inner self." You align your inner self to congruence. This is really about helping yourself align with love, but I will call it congruence for the purposes of this book; there are too many confused ideas on the topic of "love."

If you have the ability to heal yourself, you have the ability to create *weals* which are whole. Wholeness becomes a condition of being complete; it has nothing to do with income. Money is a component of life, not the source of it.

However, we tend to judge our lives by this term "happiness." We judge our happiness by this thing called money, which most people deem to be the source of their happiness.

Making Money and Gender Stereotypes

One of my male students brought up the subject of stereotypes around money. He said, "As a male—as a provider—I'm defined by that. I'm defined by how much money I'm able to provide for my family. And, I think, that's somewhat a stereotypical thing, at least from a male perspective, that I've always thought."

Being aware of such beliefs and common truisms (whether or not they are true) is a great thing. And, on the flip side, a similar thought pattern occurs with women. For instance, if a woman is making more money than her husband, she may judge herself for that because of the stereotypical things that have been placed onto our society. This is in great need of a paradigm shift.

You have to be more aware of the basic questions: "What have you been told about money?" "How do you make money?" You also need to be more aware of the common stereotypes around money—things like, "You have to grind it out," and "You have to work harder."

One of my female students replied, "I was kind of taught that a 'knight in shining armor' would take care of me, or as I call it, a 'Captain Save-a-Hoe,' would come in, but then I would have negative experiences with that."

Each one of us has our own unique set of experiences. These form the basis of our paradigms about life.

Your experiences create the paradigms of your future. They form the basis for what you are experiencing today. And you get taught this stuff— these distorted views of what it all means. All of these constructs—these moments of perceptions—are created at a very young age and they form the basis of what you believe to be right or wrong.

Levels of Income, Prosperity and Net Worth

If your self-worth is derived by the outside-in, then you will never have wealth. You will bring money in, but then you will lose it. You can sell stuff, but you will lose the income. It will be gone; you will not hold on to it.

One businesswoman student of mine voiced a concern that she was only making $200,000 a year, but remarked that everyone around her seemed to value the "always elusive" millionaire status.

Remember our money triangle? In that triangle, retaining is about self-worth. If you are concerned about how much money you have made, don't! Who cares? So, you made $200,000. Fine. By the time they take out taxes, you are down to $140,000. By the time you are done with your expenses, you are now down to $65,000 to $70,000. Okay great, but compared to who? Compared to the guy who is making $20,000 a year, you are a gazillionaire.

Three of my consultation clients voiced similar concerns, but they were already millionaires. Do you see? They are driving themselves crazy over the same attitude, but at a different level.

Let us say, for a moment, that you approach American billionaire Mark Cuban about having a million-dollar salary, and he is like, "What? Get out of here. I don't even have time for your low level of energy."

On the flip side, take a clerk at a local 7–11 convenience store. He is going to think your $200,000 per year is a ton of money.

This is all relative. The experience of money is all relative.

It is not what you make that matters; it is what you attract, manage and retain that matters because that is going to determine the net worth of your life. And your net worth is completely determined by your self-worth.

If you hold onto guilt and shame, you are giving your money away. If you have a negative self-worth, you will be in debt, and you will keep adding debt.

If you have a positive self-worth, and you feel like you bring service and value to the world, you will have a positive net worth. This is just how it works.

But if you live in the paradigm of other people's opinions of you, then you are never going to be monetarily rich. Also, you are never going to be wealthy. Because no matter what, you can be making a million dollars a year and it will not be enough. You will need someone else's accolades to make more money.

You will keep searching for more accolades, chasing for another person to say, "Yes, you are good enough." And that is where people falter. That is not just Primerica (the investments and financial services company); that is every network marketing company.

For that matter, this rule applies even to all of society. I know people who are a part of mastermind groups, and they say, "How much money did you make last month?"

I will usually reply with something like, "I'm good, brother. How are you?"

"Well, I made 97,000!"

"Great for you!"

And that is how some people talk. And please understand when that happens: It is not a reflection of their business; it is a reflection of their lack of self-worth. If they need to start the conversation with a focus on, "What I have," then they are in a paradigm of lack. And they don't have enough self-value to be real.

A student of mine, who is also a doctor, related a story from his own childhood. "I was 6 or 7 years old, playing in a sandbox, and I had a little red Ferrari car. I made this huge mountain out of sand with a roadway, and I drove up to my mansion—all of this in my mind, right? I don't know where I got that from. I have no idea. Now, I don't know if that is influenced by television, but certainly it wasn't from the group I was around because nobody had money. And the other memory I have is about a friend of mine, in that same age group. He had a piece of gold, and I was so excited about it.

'Oh! We are going to be wealthy!' It turns out it was fool's gold. And I was so, so disappointed. So sad. I don't know, but maybe there are some negative beliefs around money from that."

A great many emotions are built up over money and possessions at a very young age. We get such things from parents, siblings, other relatives and friends. "If you're rich, then you're good."

As children, we create these paradigms and beliefs because it is not the money we want. We want the emotion that money brings to us—that is what we want. That is the key to it. We perceive, when we keep searching for money from the outside-in, that it will bring us some form of happiness.

Relying on something external to yourself makes you at the "effect" end of the cycle of action. And, all too often, this makes you a victim. But when you work from the inside-out, you become the "cause"—you are taking responsibility. And if you do this well enough, you cease being a victim, entirely.

If you keep searching for money from the outside, it is really the emotion that you want because you perceive that the emotion is going to be more satisfying than not having it.

What does a million dollars mean? This is entirely different for every person reading this book.

For some—for me—a million is not enough. It does not give you enough options. My business cannot run on a million dollars. My payroll is over a million dollars. If I make a million, then what? I go into debt.

Do you see what I am saying? It becomes a relative experience.

But if anyone is searching for some amount of money from the outside, the real, but hidden objective involves the emotions created by the money or what that money can buy. The emotions are what you are searching for, because you feel unfulfilled on the inside. Because of that emptiness, you are searching for that emotion, and you think that something on the outside is going to give it to you.

That is why I say, "When you need motivation, you are in a deluded state." Inspiration is from the inside; motivation is from the outside. That is why you keep searching on the outside to keep you motivated—to give you the emotion. Then, you feel powered up for about 3 or 4 days, and then you fall and crash.

All the time, I hear people say something like, "I went to a motivational seminar and I feel fantastic." Two or three days later, they find emotional chaos kicking in, again. The outside seems to have betrayed them because they never addressed the root cause on the inside.

Motivation is from the outside; inspiration is from the inside.

I am hoping that, by the end of this program, you are going to be inspired to make money—not "have to" make money.

I hear from most of my new students language that includes "have to." But realize this: When you have to do something, you will only be forced into it. When you love to do something, you will be inspired to do it. "Have to's" needs motivation; inspiration leads to "love to's."

When you love to make money, and love to serve your clients, money follows. Money is a byproduct of the services rendered. Period. I do not care what you are doing; this principle applies at all levels.

Assignment: Understanding Wealth

1. How do you define wealth?
2. If you never achieved it, how would that be a benefit? (List 50 answers.)
3. If you achieved it, what would be the drawback? (List 50 answers.)

CHAPTER 4

The Attraction Strategy

Most people think that money is going to give them happiness. There is nothing further from the truth simply because our internal programs and paradigms are not built on happiness.

I wondered, where do our paradigms come from—the operating basis for our lives? Is it because we get happier from certain motives? Are we happier by taking certain action steps?

Some people create vision boards—pictures of the things they want or which help to define what they may consider to be the perfect life. They stare at their vision boards and all those things are supposed to show up by magic. You put those things out in the universe through your mind and meditation and the universe makes you happy. All you have to do is meditate and it just shows up.

Well, that is just not freaking true!

Personal development gurus use this and similar tricks to make you feel like you are in some fantasyland, but your brain does not work that way.

What I am about to share with you is going to have your jaw dropping. The more common ideas of abundance and fear are complete nonsense. When it comes to money, you need to throw out the old way of looking at things.

Money is a mechanism of value in your life. You need money in order to survive. That is all you need it for. So, the idea that you want money for some kind of fantasy—something that is going to bring you happiness—is a myth you allowed into your head.

When you look at money, and you have some trauma in the past around money, you tend to think from the standpoint of the future. The internal "logic" seems to go like this: The more money you have, the more you are going to be able to avoid the pain of this trauma from a lack of money. Somehow, this "money" thing will protect you. And while there seems to be some logic to this, people are invariably getting it backwards internally. Their emotions get in the way and they get off balance—reaching or flinching.

The bigger the financial trauma in the past, the more money you have to have in the future to bring you sufficient relief from this. That is the internal logic, but it is wrong.

Comfort Zone and Net Zero

I tried vision boards. I was committed, but they did not work. To this day, I still do not have six pack abs. The pictures were there, but I am simply not that guy. And I wanted to understand why they did not work.

We think we are going to move toward pleasure, but it is not true. Your brain, your body and your mind live in a state of comfort because you think you are here in this world for abundance, and some fantasy life of ease. But it simply is not true. It is not true at all. Instead, your brain is programmed for comfort. That is all it is programmed for.

You look at your life, and you say why am I not moving forward? The reason is because you perceive more pain in the future by going through the necessary steps to achieve your goal.

Let me give you an example. This will relate to a lot of you, especially the ones in sales.

Let us say that your bills are $4,000 a month. Most people will say, "I've got to make $4,000 a month." One month might end and you will say, "Man, I've worked my ass off, but I've only made $2,500." So, now you are behind $1,500 for that month. Next month, let us say you make $5,500, and you might say, "Man, I killed it! 5,500 bucks!" But I would say, "All that did was make up for the missing $1,500 for the first month. You end up with net zero." And in the next month, you make your nominal $4,000, and you are still left with net zero.

The following month you make $3,000. The month after that you make $5,000. And you oscillate around the mean of your household bills throughout the remainder of your life.

That is what most people do. But maybe not you.

Remember, earlier we talked about the mean or average. Here, we are talking about your "comfort zone." These two ideas are related. What if you merely changed the definition of your mean?

For a moment, say to yourself, "I don't have enough money because I didn't program it or plan it in."

Now, consider this: Most people do not ask themselves the question, "If I have more money, what am I going to do with it?"

Now, I am going to throw another idea out there for you to consider. What if you paid yourself another $4,000 per month? Now, your bills are $8,000 per month. Do you think you can go out and earn $8,000 each month?

If you value yourself, by the end of this book, you will.

If you do not value yourself, you are going to oscillate around your older mean. You do the work detailed in this book, and then you will put this other $4,000 into savings. If you do not do the work, you will be stuck with your old mean or average.

When I started to figure out that we really are driven to live in comfort, but usually tend to ignore this reality by painting in our minds these fantasies of money and the pain of not having money, then it started to make sense why we oscillate around the mean defined by our comfort zone. And your excuses for defining this comfort level are the expenses within which you live.

Without the changes you achieve by doing the work in this book, you will oscillate around your mean—your "comfort zone." You will stay right around the place in which you need to be comfortable. And let us be clear on this: "Comfort," as it is used here, is not that which is defined by your thinking brain, but by your feeling brain—your amygdala.

Maximum Evolution and Growth Happens at the Border of Support and Challenge

Maximum evolution and growth happen at the border of support and challenge. This is where self-transformation takes place—right at the edge of discomfort and self-awareness.

Most people seem to be looking for some form of "financial freedom." But this is a delusion. There is no such thing as "financial freedom." That is an emotional construct. Perhaps a more realistic term would be "financial independence." Now there, you can find a specific, definable number. For instance, if your passive investments are making more money than your active expenses, then you are financially independent. In other words, you do not have to have a job to meet your monthly obligations.

But, if you are looking for financial freedom, you are always going to be chasing that illusion from the outside because you think that more money is going to give you more freedom. This is not true.

The addiction to the illusory "freedom" that you think money will give you is what is keeping you trapped with money. You believe that the more money you have, the happier and easier your life is going to be. Certainly, money gives you options, but if you do not know how to manage those options, you end up losing the money. Management takes work. It requires your active responsibility. And that is not the kind of freedom most people seek. Responsibility and self-discipline set you free, but most people try to avoid the responsibility. They have it backwards.

There is a pervasive philosophy in our culture which goes something like this: "The more money I have, the more I can do whatever I want, whenever I want, and thus I have freedom." But you are not here for that kind of freedom. The more of this kind of freedom you try to create, the more discipline life throws at you to bring you back into balance. You get more bills, more problems, and other difficulties to hold you back.

If you only see the positives of money, and not the negatives, you will be blindsided by those negatives. Most people only see money as a positive, so they are rudely surprised by the things they do not see. Your addiction to money will eventually lead to a resentment of money. And if you are not fully aware that this is happening, you will remain frustrated and puzzled.

And whatever you resent you resist.

The addiction to money is what forces you to see the negative side which forces you to get off the money addiction so that you end up resenting money. In a way, this is very much like a romantic relationship that is based on false perceptions. And just as in any relationship, everything seems to start out in perfect harmony. But eventually, the delusions catch up with you.

You say, "We each have two eyes, we have two arms, and—oh my God!—we have two lungs! This is just amazing; we were meant for each other."

Six months later, you look at your life and our lungs no longer match up, our eyes simply do not see each other the same way, and you end up resenting the other person because the relationship was not based on love, but on an addiction.

Love is the ability to see both sides of an object or person. Any person who has been in a relationship for a long time realizes that their partner has both positive sides and negative sides. If you cannot see both sides, then you cannot manage the relationship. And whatever you cannot manage, you cannot hold onto.

The same thing happens with money because you are going to get the feedback to wake you up—to make you realize that there are two sides to money.

Those who will not look at the balanced sides of money will lose it. That is why one of the world's richest people, Warren Buffet, says, "You can't master money until you can master your emotions around money." This is what he is talking about. He is looking at the downsides. Bill Gates looks at the downsides of money. But if I were to ask any of my students what are the downsides of money, most of them would struggle to answer. And even then, their answers would likely be shallow ideas that do not help them resolve their imbalance.

One of my students replied, "I would say the more money you have it seems the more bills you have, and the more assets you accumulate the more money you pay in taxes."

But this is not what I was asking. Those are the "bills of money." That is where the money goes; not the negative of having money. Let us say a downside of money is that now you have to manage it. You have to make sure you do not lose your money. That is all about the having of your money. Most people will set their paradigms when they detach from their money—spending it, paying bills, paying taxes, etc. What I am talking about here is having—not spending—the money. What are the downsides of money when you have money?

Of course, you do not want to lose your money—your investments, your real estate property, and other assets. So, people tend to worry about losing these. That is one downside.

Another student offered his own answer, saying, "I'm going to say if you don't have enough of it, you're out of your comfort zone and then you get into that survival mode if you don't have enough, right?"

Again, it is easy for students, as they are learning this, not to understand the question. He said, "...if you don't have enough..." but that is a downside of **not having enough** money. The question involved a downside of **having** money. His reply revealed, instead, his addiction to money.

I clarified the question with an example: "If I gave you a million dollars today what's the downside of it?"

And immediately, he answered, "Managing it."

See how this "managing" thing keeps coming up? This is because we are afraid of managing something we view as so "important." We are afraid of losing it. All our hard work, plus a little incompetence, can give us a lot of heartache. Our lack of knowledge, plus uncertainty, gives us an undercurrent of fear. Anything we are afraid of losing, we have an infatuation concerning it. And whatever we are infatuated with we cannot manage.

Another common downside listed by my students involves other people taking their money through outright theft, embezzlement, a confidence game, or some other nefarious method.

Then, the question becomes: "Why would you bring money into your life when you would be putting yourself into a state of pain to get it, only to end up losing it?"

It seems only natural that you would not do that. Every conscious attempt to bring more money into your life would be scuttled by your desire to avoid discomfort. And this is why the Belief Inventory is such a vital part of your financial mastery; it helps to ferret out the sources of your self-sabotage. The more you understand yourself, the easier life becomes. This does not eliminate work; it merely makes your work more effective.

The Money Triangle and Fear

We have touched on the three sides of the money triangle:

- **Attraction**—Bringing money into your life.
- **Managing**—Budgets, cash flow and debt.
- **Retention**—Saving and holding onto money.

Money is built on fear—not abundance. Whenever you do not handle the three sides of money, you will create within yourself stress, anxiety, and other challenges. The lack of money is what challenges us most.

That lack, on a fundamental level, is all about fear of the future and a deep worry about how you are going to survive. Your amygdala—the primal core of your brain—is hardwired toward survival. You do not know how you are going to survive until the next day.

Consider for a moment the body's daily need for food. Do you ever worry about eating? I have been there. There was one time in my life when all I had was a single lemon to eat. When all I wanted was food for the next day, I was stressed! Anxious! I was nervous about how I was going to exist in the future.

We can be fearful about the future, but never about the past. The past is done; the question of survival is all about the future.

The first thing you need to concentrate on is protecting your future. If you cannot protect your future, then you are going to be in a constant state of stress and survival mode. We see that skyrocketing stress throughout the world today with increasing rates of child suicides, and people terrified of "climate change." We humans thrive best when we meet our challenges head-on.

Life insurance does not help you. When you are dead, money from life insurance benefits will not help you one bit. Far more critical for protecting your future are disability and health insurance. I am not saying that "death insurance" is wrong—and that is actually what "life insurance" is all about. What I am saying is that while you are alive, you need to protect your future so that the unexpected does not destroy your chances in that future. Helping out your family if you should die is a good thing, and that could reduce some of your stress. But surviving is far more challenging! Your death challenges your family, but if you have cancer, your family's challenges skyrocket because now the family not only has the normal, daily expenses, but they also have the medical expenses of keeping you alive.

I am not telling you what to do, but consider the relief you will feel in not having stress about your future. Health insurance, disability insurance, auto insurance and the like, can relieve the worry. A secure future helps you lose the stress and anxiety.

If I gave you a week's worth of food, are you going to worry about eating on Thursday? No, of course not. But what about eating next March or next December?

I talk to people all the time who are afraid of losing their homes. They are afraid of losing many things. So, whatever you do not protect, you have the fear of loss of that thing because it can go away.

Reduce Stress by Protecting Your Future

So first, you have to protect what you have in life. It does not matter how you ease the fears of the future. If you have enough money in the bank to cover your future, then you do not need insurance. But insurance is there to protect you in case of emergencies.

Assets do not make people go bankrupt. Emergencies do that. In this country, the number one cause of bankruptcy is not debt; it is medical expenses. But we do not plan for that. When we do not plan for our future, we get a feedback mechanism kicking in called anxiety. This feedback is there to wake you up and to tell you that you are out of balance. In a way, your lack of planning is an act of taking out more credit on yourself. That increases your risk.

Again, first, you have to protect what you have in life.

Achieve Tranquility with Security

Second is security. Every personal development system out there has taught that security is a bad thing. I challenge that belief. I am here to tell you that security is one of the more blessed states on the planet because when you are secure, you have peace of mind. That mental tranquility lets you feel safe about where your money is coming from, about what you will have to eat, about the fact that your kids will have a roof over their head, and that your kids will have food on the table.

And Now, You Can Achieve Abundance

With peace of mind as a foundation, you can then move into a state of abundance. You cannot create abundance from stress and worry. That does not work. When you are releasing cortisol, the stress hormone, all day long, you weaken your health and your mind. Your body becomes more susceptible to diseases. You may blame money as the culprit, but it is not money. It is you—your consciousness around money and related states. It is the way you think about money that is causing those conditions.

Protecting your future is a component of management. This will help you stay in a state of comfort, but this is not an absolute. It is not a perfect solution. A few people will move toward more pleasure, but most people will move toward the idea of pain or removing pain.

But what if you do not have money?

The Process of Reaching Financial Maturity

Security is where you mature. People can start a business right away. Now, do they hit abundance right away? Of course not! Like a child, you have to go through the challenges of learning and growing.

It is natural to struggle with these ideas when you are first learning them. One student asked, "How do I reconcile what instinctively I have been taught, and I am so prone to wanting to hold to be true?"

The words we choose to use will, quite often, reveal what is going on inside of us. In his question, he referred to "instinct," which is a fear-based mechanism. This comes directly out of the amygdala, the seat of survival instincts in your brain. What my student was telling me was that he was coming from a place of fear about money versus a state of neutrality around money.

I had challenged my student's choice of words, so he rephrased his question. "That's what I'm asking. How do I change from being in a position of fear to neutrality?"

You never want to lose fear of money. Remember, when we revisited the subject of the money triangle, I said that money is built on fear—not abundance. Money first starts with the game of fear. Money is about fear. Because you move from a place of pain, into comfort. You do not move directly into abundance.

The Top 2% Are You and I

Perhaps you have heard the statistics that most of the people in the world make only about $2,000 per year. Compare this to the citizens of

America and the so-called "civilized" nations—the top 2% of the entire world. The person reading this is part of the top 2%.

My student did not immediately see this and that is understandable. Most people are somewhat insulated from reality. He said, "Really? See, in my mind, I immediately went to those who have, as opposed to those who are starting to get. That is who I see as the 2%."

A few years ago, when my kids went to India, my son told me, "Dad, there are so many poor people here. I realize that we have such a big house. We have all this stuff. Compared to them, we are rich!"

Such a wise observation from a kid who was only 10 years old.

Poor, in America, means you have a home, a television, a smartphone and food to eat, even if it is from food stamps. Compare that to some places in the world, where if you can afford to get on ZOOM, on a smartphone, you are rich.

If you define "top 2%" only by the people who are making a billion dollars a year, you are always going to be "broke" by that meaning. And remember, wealth is not from the outside in.

By the end of this book, if you do the work, you are going to say, "I get it. I don't need it from the outside."

Another student, a single mother, spoke up on this topic of security. "Yes, so, piggybacking on what you said, that security is great. The gurus don't preach that—peace of mind, which takes you to abundance. And then you said security is a state of maturity. What I got is that I have lived in chaos literally my entire life. Like, I am talking about from birth. Growing up in the Projects. And it's always been like a high survival mode that you're in. ... I've had money. But even when we had the money, it was still chaos! It was like chaos everywhere. I don't even know what security feels like. And so I want peace of mind. I'm like, what's next?"

Protect the Future; Manage the Present

Security brings peace of mind. If you were to look closely at the state of consciousness, you would see what I am talking about. If your consciousness is in the midst of protection, neurologically, then you would be in a parasympathetic state—the more peaceful or relaxed side of autonomic activities. At this mental location, you sit in a state of security which is truly a state of balance. When you are in abundance, the way I am going to define it, life is not easy. Instead, you are in a state of support and challenge. Security comes through saving.

So, if you are secure, protect your future from the outside. If I were you, and I learned this the hard way, I would get insurance so I can cover myself no matter what happens. Get disability insurance. What if you cannot work? That condition would lead to cash flow issues. When this happens, some people look at their life and say, "I can't work. With a mountain of medical bills, I can't earn any money. I might as well die."

My single mother student from the Projects did not immediately get it, and this happens with a lot of students. She replied, "Then you're constantly living in fear all the time. All the insurances in the world! I'm afraid I'm going to trip and fall so I got fall insurance. You see what I'm saying? That's negative to me, no?"

It is the addiction to the positive that makes you think it is a negative. But it is not negative. I am not saying you have to buy insurance. If you have enough money in savings to handle any potential problem, then you will not need to buy insurance; your savings will cover your needs. All I am saying is that you need to protect yourself from whatever may happen so you do not have the stress of the future. When you don't have that stress of the future, you can actually manage the present.

I understand that this may be completely counterintuitive to some people. This may even be opposite to what you have been taught. I get it. Me too. And your head is probably going, "What the hell are we talking about?" Because if you only sit in the land of abundance in your imagination, you only need to look at statistics to bring you back to reality. How many people really make it to that level? It is a wonderful fantasy. You are more than welcome to believe it, but that will not help you make the transformations you desire.

There is one story of a boy who had to live in a bubble because his immune system was so weak that a mild cold could kill him. He had to protect himself from life, so he never really had a life. Throwing out our cherished beliefs can sometimes be terrifying. Sometimes we take calculated risks, but we also need to know our own burdens and limitations. These help us manage in the wisest possible way.

Life is full of choices. Protecting your future could look like a negative, but look at the viewpoint which holds that opinion. That is one of countless possible viewpoints. Another viewpoint is one called "responsibility." Some people erroneously equate responsibility with blame, but these are entirely opposite in intent. Blame is a negative attempt to shrug off responsibility. Taking responsibility is a positive part of owning the challenges of life. Protecting your future is a part of being responsible.

Imagine you live in a sunny, desert climate. You build a house with no roof. You like the sun during the day and the stars at night. You did not build a roof because this is the desert. It does not rain. But then it does rain—a downpour for thirty minutes—a freak monsoon-like storm coming out of nowhere. Now, everything in your house is ruined by three inches of rain. Building a roof would have protected your things. Now, you have been set back several thousand dollars, and some of your things may be irreplaceable.

And there are different kinds of "fear." On the one hand, there is needless terror and worry. On the other hand, there is a sobriety of purpose— a responsible intention to protect what you have built so that it remains useful. Do you see the difference?

That is reality. We need to get real with life. Because we want to understand money, we need to get real with our money. This is not a fantasy book.

You need to prepare for the things that might happen so that your family will not suffer needless setbacks. In today's world, you lock your doors because there is significant risk if you do not do that. But let us not talk about death. Instead, let us talk about life and taking full responsibility for that life.

Not preparing for what might happen is part of the delusion. Too many people want fantasy and freedom of money, but, in truth, it leads to chaos and resentment about money.

The 'Financial Freedom' Delusion vs. Financial Independence

Do not let your taking responsibility make you afraid to live. No, this is you taking responsibility so that you can live without worry and without the trauma of major life setbacks.

Statistically, people who have more money tend to live longer lives. This is because they have a reason; they have purpose. Those who do not have money have shorter life spans; they live in chaos and frustration.

On the subject of financial independence—not "financial freedom," mind you—let us say you normally make $4,000 a month from your job, which covers all of your monthly expenses. And let us say that you make $5,000 a month from your investments. You could quit your job because you are financially independent. Your passive income covers all of your expenses and then some. You can do what you want to a certain degree.

Whenever you become addicted to something in life, and you only see more positives than negatives inside of it, you are going to get humbled. That is inevitable. And that humbling event will force you to see the opposite. You will end up resenting what you formerly viewed as "positive;" you will end up seeing more negatives than positives. This happens with everything in your life. Life always seeks a balance.

If you become addicted to money, you have four feedback mechanisms to help wake you up. You have negative symptoms called anxiety. You have negative self-talk and negative thinking around money. And you have your friends and family trying to get you organized around money, usually your spouse.

When you are addicted to money, your spouse is probably the one saving the money, saying, "You're spending too much." Or vice-versa. And if those things do not come into reality, you will have some sort of universal force that comes into your life to balance your awareness of money. If you are too addicted and high on money, you will create chaos in your life to humble you and to lose your money. That is just how it works. Every single person has gone through this in one form or another.

Doctors know that people who are financially anxious will see more physiological stresses on their body. So, what I am trying to teach you is not a fantasy around money.

What happens to a sale when you don't need it? Any salesman who has been around for a while will tell you that you close the sale without hardly trying.

And what happens to a sale when you need it? It goes the other way! If you need a sale to protect you until tomorrow, that sale is gone. It's history! And, you now have to manage your emotions around that lost sale.

If you protect your future, you become more calm so you can actually create new sales.

One anecdote shows the power of this effect. A husband and wife were struggling with their business. They absolutely needed to close an upcoming deal or they could lose their house and much more. The husband had to fly to Las Vegas to meet with corporate representatives and had to close the sale on that business trip or his family business was sunk.

The wife was concerned that her husband was stressing out and wondered how she might relieve him of his stress. Perhaps she had heard of this effect of salesmen pushing sales away when they were vital. So, on the evening before the big meeting, she called her husband, all excited, to tell him that she had won the lottery and that the deal was no longer so important.

With great relief and a more formidable confidence, the husband closed the deal and returned to his loving wife. When he arrived at their home, she confessed that she had not won the lottery—that she had lied in order to reduce his anxiety. She had eliminated the "importance" factor, making it easier for him to close a deal that was no longer "vital" in his own mind.

In wartime, the heroes are not those who have no fear; they are the ones who know how to make their fear unimportant. The danger becomes merely information to help them navigate the future with competence.

Homing In on the Real Positive

If, as a salesman, you think of a sale as vital, all manner of physiological reactions occur in your body. This causes you challenges with the income you are about to make. Everyone I know has been like that in business. I definitely have. At the beginning, I did not understand this stuff. Nobody taught me this stuff. I would go home and look at my practice, and I would be like, "Man, the bigger the sales, the more it kept on crashing." You get elated one day, but the next it is depression about money.

Do not look at the elation as positive and the depression as negative. Both of these help bring you back into balance if you go too far one way or the other. The real "positive" is between the two where you have neutralized emotion—where you are in balance about money.

People want to live in fearlessness. But once you clear up one source of fear, another shows up. Instead of fighting against it, learn to manage it—to take responsibility for it as the fear shows up in your life. All the supposed "negatives" in life are merely information which can help you improve your life.

Getting insurance or a fat savings account can help you reduce the fear, worry and anxiety. This is you managing your emotions along with your finances.

Fear is meant to be managed—not eliminated. Anyone who tells you they do not live in fear is not alive; they are dead.

In my practice, I would interview people 80 years old and ask them, "What are you afraid of?" I wanted to know what their thought processes were. How did they live? What were their philosophies about life?

People 80 and older have this pervasive philosophy that, "I am responsible." The people who are under the most medications will say, "Others are responsible for me." This is a key distinction. Those with the greatest vitality are working from the inside out—responsible; those who are hanging on by a thread are working from the outside in—blame or shifting responsibility to others.

Self-empowerment is the answer and the more you empower your life the more you create your own longevity. The more longevity—the more empowered you become—in all areas of your life, the more you can extend health and vitality to someone else.

Protecting your future is the key for this lesson, whether it is the right set of insurance policies or several million dollars in savings.

Most people live day-to-day. If they have an accident or a serious illness, they could easily end up homeless. And if they ever build up a little bit of savings, they will usually spend it on something frivolous.

Patterns in Relationships

One of my students offered a brilliant example of this effect, but in a different part of life's overall wealth. "What you're saying is it's a delusion to think that fear will ever be eradicated, so manage it. So, if you look at it in terms of love, for example. 'Oh, when I find the right one, everything is going to be rainbows, happiness and joy and sex all the time.' But that's just not real and so, maybe those people can't be in relationships because they're living a delusion. They're not managing the relationship or their life."

And he was one hundred percent correct. The more you live in the fantasy of an idea, the more you lose it.

Many people think their relationships are supposed to be happy all the time, supportive all the time, kind all the time, only good all the time. And that truly is a fantasy. Relationships take work. They take effort. It takes time, strategy, negotiations, discussions and more—all these different things that it takes to make a relationship really work. It is not all about happiness all the time, kissing, making out, having sex all the time. You have to work at it. You have to get a job and pay your bills. All these other parts of life are in there.

In the early stages of a relationship it is all about happiness and anticipation. The second part includes things you did not want or expect, including resentment. Then you realize, eventually, how to love this person from both sides.

Managing money fits the same pattern. Instead of running away from the fear, the annoyance and the discomfort, you work with them. You take full responsibility for them, for they are part of the whole.

Expanding on the Money Triangle

Our money triangle has three sides—attract, manage, retain. These tie in to the topics we have been discussing—abundance, security, and protection.

Protecting your future, whether it be through insurance or a hefty savings account, helps you retain what you have built.

Security is all about proper management of your resources through planning and other actions.

And, naturally, abundance is all about attracting. This one side of our triangle sells great in the marketplace because everyone wants to be rich, but it leaves people broke because they do not look at the other sides of the money triangle.

When you think about it, money is a relationship. Whether or not you master your finances comes down to how you relate to it. What I am teaching, here, is how to relate to money. How you relate to money determines whether you have more of it in your life.

Assignment: Creating the Attraction Strategy

1. Do you have a strategy in place to protect your assets? What is it?
2. What is your strategy to create the first part of PSA, which is protection?
3. What are the benefits of protection to you and your family?

CHAPTER 5

Abundance of Pleasure vs. Abundance of Pain

Value of Work

So, how do we make more money? To understand how to approach the right answer, we first need to understand the nature of pain and pleasure and our reactions to each.

Whenever you are in pain, your sympathetic nervous system drives you to escape that pain and move toward comfort. Pain is an internal communication that some part of the body is being threatened. The fight-or-flight system is automatic in seeking out a solution to any potentially life-threatening situation, but once you achieve comfort, the need for change is gone.

Let me give you an example.

I have known my old college roommate for 25 years. He is an amazing individual and I love him to death. He is like a brother to me. But his lifestyle! He smokes three packs of cigarettes per day. He has McDonalds and Domino's Pizza every single day. And he normally drinks 12 Diet Pepsi's every single day. At 6 feet 4 inches, he weighs a hefty 310 pounds. By both height and weight, he is a big man.

Recently, his doctor discovered something abnormal with his heart. So now, he is doing all manner of things to change his health because his former comfort zone has become a source of immense pain—the terror of potential death. He felt an internal pain which inspired him to leave what had been "comfortable" before his doctor's discovery.

Making 'Comfort' Seem Painful

It is only when "comfort" becomes more painful than the future that you actually move out of that "comfort zone."

Otherwise, "comfort" is an attractor—a destination for your sympathetic nervous system. Once your bodily system reaches comfort, it stops looking to change its location.

A while back, when I studied all these wealthy people—from Jay-Z to Mark Cuban—I wanted to find out the common attitudes and behaviors that contributed to their success. What was their psychology around success?

And this is what I found: They believed it was more painful to live comfortably than it was to move toward being wealthier. To them, "comfort" became the new "pain," and the relative discomfort of constant change became their new "comfort." Daniel Coyle's *The Talent Code* touches on this idea where being comfortable with a little bit of unpredictability and chaos allows for accelerating your own learning and achievement.

Let us look at some other examples, because this can seem somewhat counterintuitive to many of my students.

Several years ago, a college student took a creative writing class twice. The first time, it was for an elective toward his computer science degree. The second time was for additional education on one of his many passions—an interest which had nothing to do with his degree program. He had found it easy to "suffer" the supposed discomfort of criticism in order to maximize his learning experience. In a way, he was grateful that so many of his fellow students were too shy to take advantage of this deeper opportunity to learn. The other students remained in their lazy comfort, never risking their egos by exposing their writing for comment. But this college student was decidedly uncomfortable at the thought of wasting an entire semester on the lazy standard of others—sitting back and hoping that they might learn something valuable by blind osmosis.

And this ambitious student had been inspired by the words of a professional writer and guest speaker at one of his writing classes. That professional had told the students that they would likely start to learn their own writing styles after they had written a million words or so. Most of the students in that classroom had been overwhelmed by the professional's statement, for they were still struggling with hundreds of words—not millions! And our ambitious student was made uncomfortable by the thought of languishing in the realm of hundreds of words written, instead of millions. He knew he had better get busy writing to reach his first million.

Now, let us look at a monetary example.

Let us say you make $10,000 a month, and that is where you are staying. But you may complain, "I'm not making enough money!" yet there you stay.

What if you found more pain in staying there? What if you found more pain staying in the land of comfort where you are right now? Will that move you toward some other direction?

In order to change your condition, you need to be sufficiently dissatisfied with $10,000 per month, plus have a vision of some direction to go, for you to break free of the clutches of that comfort trap. But, as before, this needs to come as inspiration from inside to drive change on the outside. And part of that change is the decision to change.

Still another example might involve your children. Let us say that you have no food for them and they look up to you and say, "Daddy, Daddy, Mommy, Mommy! I'm starving." Would you feel uncomfortable? If you are human, of course you would! But would you become motivated or inspired? Motivation can stimulate short term action and eventually fizzle out. Inspiration can create a lifetime of passionate action which compels you to change the fiber of your being. Remember, motivation is outside-in; inspiration is inside-out.

Motivation eventually fizzles because the mind and body return to their former comfort zone.

Inspiration can sustain you, if properly activated, because it creates a new, internal paradigm that redefines what "comfort" means.

You are likely sitting in a state of "comfort." Intellectually, you may call it something else, but viscerally, your body and your "feeling" mind view anything different as "uncomfortable."

So, what happens if your current "comfort zone" becomes more painful—sufficiently uncomfortable to force you into action? You will move toward something new.

Your dissatisfaction can be a source of inspiration, but the reward for your actions needs to be greater than the costs involved.

It is quite likely that some form of financial dissatisfaction led you to purchase this book. You paid "X" number of dollars for the book. Then you have dedicated "Y" number of hours to reading it, plus a certain amount of discomfort in going through the assignments. The lure for you is that your reward will be far more than the amount you are paying in dollars, hours and discomfort. You are counting on the transformation being a permanent part of your life that can change your average monthly income.

Virtually all my students have some form of difficulty unlearning the old and learning the new. One of them tried to explain to me her own feelings. "Yeah, I almost struggle with that a little bit because it does definitely make sense, but I think when I spoke to you months ago, I explained that yes, I need to do X, Y and Z, but the reality is I can only afford X, Y, and Z. You know what I mean? So, sometimes yes, the pain is so great, but I think before you make any changes you need to see that you're actually seeing changes in your income. Sometimes you are limited. You'll see a lot of the alternative things that could make a difference are so outrageously expensive, that it's limited to who can access them. And sometimes I find that kind of frustrating when I am in a position like I can't do those things, and I feel like that would make a big difference in my life. So, I am trying to get myself to that point, so that I do have more freedom in some of the choices that I wanted to make, you know?"

In all of that rambling, she revealed clues to her inner self. Her focus was on limitations—limited access and limited income.

Now, consider this: If I were to put a gun to your head and said, "Look! Come up with 20 grand or else you're never going to see your kids again." How many people would figure out how to come up with 20 grand? I suspect that it would be far more than without such harsh motivation. Suddenly, you find yourself dissatisfied with your limited thinking. Suddenly, you are thinking of possibilities and methods you would not otherwise have considered.

Beg, borrow, steal. The cost has to be great enough to provoke sufficient action. So, hear me when I say this: It is never a matter of a lack of money; it is always the lack of a reason to do it. It is a lack of sufficient pain to move you out of your lazy comfort zone and to move you to go and get it.

My student then countered with, "Sometimes though, I feel like it's a lack of vision."

But this is exactly wrong. If you have a clear idea in your mind of what it is you want, there is no lack of vision. You know what your goal is. The ideas for how you might reach that goal are a dime a dozen. The real cost is your decision—your commitment—to take action in that direction. Quite often, the effective ideas come after you start taking action.

It is not a "what" or "why" that is stopping you. Your barrier is, instead, a "why not," because, if I put a million dollars in your lap right now, you would find a way to do something with it.

As I have said many times, 5% of the population will say that they will travel through enough pain to get to their goals. Most people will live in a state of comfort based on their neurology. They will stay where they are unless a sufficient level of pain forces them to move.

One of my clients is an anesthesiologist who makes more than $700,000 a year, yet is flat broke. How is that possible? Many people who win the lottery are broke within a few months. In fact, the man who won a third of a billion dollars a few years back told one reporter that he wished he had never seen that lottery ticket. He ended up having less than he had before he had bought the winning ticket.

One-Sided Chaos

You are not here to experience the freedom that money can give you; you are here to experience both the freedom and the constraint. You have to have both. You do not simply have one.

So, the greater the delusion of the fantasy, the greater the bankruptcy. The greater the money delusion, the greater the money chaos in the long run. You will make enough to survive, but never enough to be wealthy because you do not value money. And if you do not value money, you will keep chasing it.

Your exercise in this chapter is going to be totally counterintuitive to what you think and to everything I have written, so far. I want you to find 50 drawbacks to having money.

If you think that having money is only good, then you are living in a delusion. Remember what I said on the management side? If ever you cannot manage both sides of a thing, you cannot manage it. The side to which you remain blind appears to you as if it were chaos. You cannot control it if you are so certain that it does not exist.

Management is about your emotions. To manage something is to have emotions about them. If you cannot see both sides of the emotion regarding it, then the emotion takes over and runs your life.

If it runs your life, you are now its victim—not an empowered individual.

Some people get lost in the credit and debt cycle. They think credit is good because they are addicted. They say to themselves, "I want what I want right now!" Later on, they resent the debt they had decided to take on. This becomes the chaos of failed management.

There is a documentary which came out a few years ago which said something like, "The more debt people create, the more freedom they lose."

Which is true. The banks want to put you in a state where you can have it all, now. But what is it about "having it now" that is so addicting? Well, it is the illusion of freedom. You have not earned the money, but you can have it, now. And now, you are a slave to the banks.

That is the addiction to easy freedom which has not been earned. You feel as though you deserve something, then you become trapped by the debt you created by not being able to manage both sides of money. If you cannot manage debt, it is because you are addicted to freedom and credit. And there are lots of companies out there wanting you to take on more debt.

If you cannot manage money, you will not have more of it.

I can teach you all the tools to attract and retain, to get rid of the guilt and shame, and all that stuff, but if I cannot get you to realize how to manage money, then you will have a lopsided skill set. You are not going to protect yourself in the future. You are not going to create security and then move yourself into abundance. Very rarely does wealth come magically overnight. Even if someone seems to become wealthy overnight, more likely than not, they have spent years and years and years building a business or selling an idea that has led to that abundance. It did not literally happen overnight. Such success goes through a systematic progression of protection, security and abundance—retention, management and attraction, from our money triangle.

True Freedom Comes from a Balanced, Responsible Approach

When you live in abundance on the side of "attraction," it is because you have security and protection for yourself to balance out the triangle. You know where your cash flow is coming in from; that is security. That is having a future. Only when you know where your money is coming from in the future can you really live in abundance.

When you live in abundance, your life will be filled with little things that add up to a big plus. If you think you currently live on a fixed income, you are limiting yourself by your self-definition. Imagine, people start taking you out to dinner more often. People will offer to pay for you to do little things for them. They will start to show up in your life because you are protecting yourself from the future. The illusion of "fixed income" starts to evaporate.

This is a consciousness which moves you into the next stage of true freedom, abundance and light—a place where it is not all stress and cortisol.

Business security happens when you have lead flow and cash flow that are both a steady stream. Until that point, it is a "newbie" business. With this state of consciousness in business, you have security and systems—you have cash and reserves enough to survive 5, 10, possibly even 12 years.

Now, you are talking about true freedom—the kind you create and about which you have full responsibility. This is not the thin veneer of fake freedom being pursued by most people. From the position of true freedom, you can take all the risks and do all the things you want because if you lose a little bit of money, you are not worried about it. Your survival is not threatened. You have managed both sides of money.

Abundance does not come by accident or wishing; it is created. That takes managing your emotions. But too many people want to get rich fast. Their minds are full of addiction to money. They tell themselves, "I can do it now. I can save myself all the time and energy and I don't have to work." What if you did what you love to do and didn't worry about the money because it keeps piling up. That is another fantasy. I could write an entire book on that one. But with the abundance of consciousness, built from responsibility and management, you now live in a place where you can do those things which are, for others, merely a fantasy.

Most people are so afraid of what they are going to do with money. They harbor a hidden fear: "What if they lose it?" They worked so hard to get their money, and like the man who lost most of his retirement benefits in 2008, they fear the worst. They have done something they resented all these years, and now, with the money gone, they have to do more of that shit—back to the job they hate. Their attention is focused on: "I can't lose this money."

And, while teaching this, I realized that this should also be an exercise—50 benefits of your current way of producing money.

If you do not value what it is you do now, then you are going to create resentment toward it. And if you resent it, then you stop bringing money in the door. I do not care about all the hucksters telling you how to get out of the job you hate. J-O-B is what puts food on the table. So, reexamine your feelings and decide to create new, more empowering feelings. In other words, chill out. Relax.

Be grateful for your starting point, otherwise you will end up sticking yourself there even harder. Resentment gives you more things about which to be resentful. Gratitude gives you more things about which to be grateful. Now, it does not take a genius to figure out which attitude produces the better results.

One pair of students—a lovely husband and wife team—had a question about my inspiration regarding this new exercise I mentioned a moment ago. He said, "So, the 50 benefits of the current way of producing money—and I'm asking this because my wife is going to have to get off the call. How would she approach that since her occupation is homeschool Mom, and taking care of our home? So, 50 benefits of the current way of providing money. She is providing a tremendous amount of value. Does she get paid? No. And I know you're going to get to that eventually, and will have some discussions around that, but in terms of that exercise, how would you recommend she approach that?"

Indeed, I will cover this in a later lesson. I told him, "Same thing. I want her to look at work as work. And then I will help you guys structure the finances around it, to be balanced. Because work is just providing value. Whether your fellow student, the nurse, is doing it, or another is selling life insurance, or someone else is selling AFLAC—it doesn't matter. They are each just providing value. So, she is providing value to the kids and to you; that is her work. And we have to figure out how she gets paid for it. If not, she will end up creating resentment by not being paid for her work. Does that make sense? And I say this out of love for you because now I know you, personally, as well. If you don't pay her, that leads to complications down the line."

The Promise: Reality and Results

I promised you reality. I did not promise you happiness. I do not sell happiness. My programs may not be the biggest, most popular on the planet, but my students are going to get solid results. My students are going to transform their lives, and you will tell other people about this book. I am going to tell you the truth, at least to the degree that I know it.

Now, I have already mentioned one of your upcoming assignments—the counterintuitive exercise about 50 drawbacks of having money. Then, there are 50 benefits of your current way of producing money. This second assignment was inspired by teaching the lessons in this chapter to my students.

The third assignment is, by far, the most important one. In fact, this entire chapter is based on this one concept—100 drawbacks for you staying exactly where you are financially.

Pain will cause more movement—more transformation—than any pursuit of pleasure.

Escaping the negative to get back to comfort is a more powerful force than leaving comfort for some potential positive. Most people will opt to stay where they are—in the relative safety of the known. If that safety can become painful, then you might become inspired to move beyond that prison of safety.

You will always move more from pain than you will to pursue pleasure.

I need you to hate your life at this current moment so you can go make money. When you do this exercise, you are going to look at it and say, "Oh, my God! This sucks!" Good! Because that is what is going to get you to say "I've got to get up and go sell." It is only when you feel enough pain in the midst of your "comfort zone" that you are going to find the inspiration within yourself to decide and then to follow through with massive action. You will say, "I've got to do this for my company and for my kids." And, again, let us be clear on this point: You need to work from inspiration, not motivation; from the inside-out, not outside-in.

Your nervous system is built with twice the intensity of pain than on pleasure. So, pain will make you move, but not necessarily pleasure.

For a moment, consider a dog. The nervous system operation is similar to that found in humans. If you put a treat in front of the dog, it may move, but then again, it may not. But if you kick the dog, it has to move. The treat is not necessary for survival, especially if the dog has eaten recently. But moving because of pain is directly connected to the dog's survival instinct.

Same thing here. I am going to get you to move to make more money.

And do not think in terms of absolutes. Most people, when they hear the word, "budget," they feel controlled or trapped. If they go over their budget, they feel like they are a failure. But do not think of it in terms of hard edges—of absolutes. Instead, think of a budget as merely a feedback mechanism or early warning system to keep you from straying too far. It is a governing mechanism for yourself, versus something that controls you and tells you what you can and cannot do. Life is full of variables and a constant need for adjustments and course corrections. Your budget is not an "all or none" proposition. Going over budget on one item is not the end of the world. The budget is there to help you; not to destroy you if you make a mistake.

Quite often, parents will work really hard so that their children will not have the pain that they had growing up. For example, another husband and wife team had started a college fund for their child. The wife had experienced a great deal of pain in her own life on this. The pain drove her to take action.

But let us say that the husband did not have the same pain growing up. If the wife tells him, "Honey, we are going to put another $1,000 in the college fund this month," then very likely he is going to say, "Okay," because he does not want the pain of conflict. He will want to keep the peace because the pain from her wrath is too great.

For your assignments, I recommend you do not have loud music blaring in the background. Instead, put on some meditation music or some of the symphonic classics to soothe and inspire your mind. And do the exercises for this chapter all in one sitting.

Assignment: Pleasure vs. Pain

1. Write 50 drawbacks to having money
2. Write 50 benefits of your current way of producing money.
3. Write 100 drawbacks for you staying exactly where you are financially.

CHAPTER 6

Fear of Loss

The student who needed to put more money in her daughters' college funds had a confession to make. She confided that she was overweight and was soon to turn 40 years of age. She had made a series of bad choices since she was in her late teens, and she admitted that she was starting to have health problems. Her mother had died at 56 and the thought of the same happening to her had become a source of severe mental anguish. Her daughters would be 21 and 26 years of age when she turned 56. And my student did not want to miss out on the marriage of her daughters and the birth of their children. So many things she would miss if her poor decisions resulted in her early death. Now, her so-called "pleasure foods" had become a source of regret and self-condemnation.

Concerning her death at age 56, if she were to follow her own mother, she would regret missing all of her daughters' future birthdays. I asked her, "What's another drawback of you not being around for your daughters if you continue to eat this way?"

"It's just they won't have anybody to go to if they need somebody."

"What's the drawback of that?"

"They will feel alone."

"What's the drawback of that?"

"A word that comes to mind is abandonment. It's not the same thing as being alone."

"Well, you are abandoning your kids right? You can talk about a father who leaves his kids because he found some hoochie to screw around with or you can talk about your addiction and your affair with food and how you chose to keep going down that path in order to leave the kids. It's all the same thing, just in a different form."

"Yeah, I was that kid."

"What's the drawback if you continue to eat this way and you don't survive? Are you going to teach them the exact same pattern?"

"Yeah. I don't want to see that."

"To live a life of being unhealthy."

"Yeah."

"But you can make different choices," I said. "And can you see how you starting to make these choices for your health is not only saving your life, but it's actually saving your daughter's life?"

"Yes, this is a good example for them."

"Where do your kids currently learn their nutrition?"

"They're not learning anything good. They're learning to just eat whatever."

"And if your kids eat whatever, what is that going to do to their grades? What will that do to their brain function?"

"It lowers it. They're not going to have as high a quality of brain function."

"Smarter or less intelligent?"

"They're going to be less intelligent. They're going to struggle in school."

"If they struggle in school, does that mean they're going to have less of an opportunity to work, for jobs or even business? You have to have a brain to be able to think and move. Right? Your brain is the key to consciousness, as I call it."

"Yes."

"So, in essence, you're teaching them how not to take care of themselves, how to struggle financially and how to struggle with thinking clearly."

"Yes."

"This is not just about their weddings," I told her, "and that type of bullshit. I hate when people say that because this is about their whole life. The wedding is only for one day. Life is a reality. Does that make sense?"

"I can see that."

"Good. So, you saving your life is far bigger than your life. I want you to realize that. It's saving their life. And the more you learn about health, the more you can teach them about health. The better food choices you make, the more you pride yourself on teaching your kids about what to eat, what not to eat, about intermittent fasting, all this stuff that you're teaching them because nobody else is teaching them that stuff.

"My kids," I said, "will not look at a McDonald's. They won't even look at it. And I joke sometimes, like you guys want to go to McDonald's, we'll go get some fries? Come on, like fries are good. Come on, dude. Like, 'No, Dad. We don't want that.' Okay. Cool. And I do it to test them. But sometimes I want one of their fries, I'm not going to lie. But I don't do it. Can you see that's far greater than a burger and fries? This is deeper. I want you to go. You have Netflix, right?"

"No. But I can get it."

"Go get it. And then go watch *What the Health?* Let it scare the shit out of you to change your life, and it's perfectly good. I'm okay with that. And then go watch, *Forks Over Knives.* It's all on Netflix. They're all free, there. All great, great documentaries. And you can argue with me and say, 'Well, it's propaganda.' I don't really care. If it makes you get healthier, I'll follow so-called propaganda all day long. You follow what I'm saying?"

"Yeah."

Health is a Primary Component of Wealth

Can you see how this is a big shift for you right now? Money will be secondary. You cannot make money when you do not feel wealthy. If you are not taking care of yourself, it is because you do not value yourself. If you do not value yourself, you do not have money coming in the door. So this is something to consider.

The conversation above took place when I was on the fifth day of a water fast. It is quite amazing what your body does when you give it a chance. The body needs no help. It just needs you to stop interfering with its natural operation. Stop screwing it up by putting the toxins in your body. That is my health rant for today. But this ties in with the topic of this chapter.

Though this is a course in financial mastery, the principles involved can be utilized in multiple areas of your life—health, diet, relationships and more. Even my students on the Align Mastery course say the same thing.

Oscillation Around the Mean and Your True Abundant State

One point of confusion on this entire topic involves the words we use and the meanings we have attached to them. Take, for instance, the term "abundance."

The idea of abundance in our oscillation around the mean is the peak from which we come crashing back in order to achieve balance. For lack of a better term, we might call this "fake" or "temporary" abundance. This is part of the cycle of boom and bust.

Using the sequence of protection, stability and abundance, you can build up layer upon layer, raising your mean to greater heights. You modify your "comfort zone" by some method of finding the old "comfort zone" painful, then using inspiration and responsibility for all aspects to change your state.

If you remain operating from the outside-in, then you will feel joy and pride at the peaks, and sadness and regret at the valleys. But I want you to achieve more. I want you to achieve the truer form of abundance, which is from the inside-out. When you achieve this inner state of true abundance, then it does not matter what part of the cycle you find yourself in. The things on the outside do not affect you the same way anymore. Inner abundance becomes your mean as it rises up. But even if the stock market crashes or the national debt bubble pops, you remain abundant on the inside. The booms and busts on the outside merely provide you with information; they no longer torture your soul with false elation and equally false hopelessness.

The Decision to Take Responsibility and Resulting Breakthroughs

The decision to take responsibility is such a powerful, inner force that it frequently results in startling breakthroughs. This kind of fearlessness, despite the apparent risks, can literally change your life. Time and again, my students tell me how they get unexpected breakthroughs once they decide to take one of my courses or shortly after starting their training.

Not long ago, I had a client who got off the call with me, decided to enroll in one of the courses—essentially valuing herself—and literally two hours later, closed a $200,000 deal that seemed to come out of thin air. For her, this was huge. She was completely flabbergasted.

I had another client, a software CEO, who had been working on closing a deal with potential clients for months and months and months. He did not seem to be getting anywhere with them. He started working on his own self-improvement through one of my courses, and, within 24 hours, those potential clients called him and said that they wanted to do the deal. Over the next 10 years this was going to be a $30 million project.

Fear of Loss and Recurring Clues

One of my students, who is also a doctor, mentioned that one clue which keeps popping up in his assignments is a fear of loss. He is keenly aware that it is his responsibility to provide for his family, but he harbors a lingering concern that if he fails, he could lose them. The fact that this idea or concept keeps coming up in his exercises can be a clue to something deeper he needs to address. This may help lead him to the root cause of his own difficulties.

Another student had a similar fear of loss. She was a single Mom who had lost her only child, then her mother, and then needed to take care of six siblings. First of all, she felt a deep resentment. It seemed to her that every move she made would cause her brothers and sisters to suffer.

And if she did not go and produce an income, she was afraid of losing literally everything. More than anything, she would end up resenting herself.

I asked her what it would mean to her if her siblings suffered.

"Well, hell," she replied, "I damn near feel like I'm suffering because I want so much for them that I put myself on the backburner."

Then I asked her what she was really doing by enabling them and not producing. She could not tell me; she did not know. But I told her that she was with them. She was giving them her time and her love.

The masses tell us that time is the thing of exchange. The masters say that time is for creating opportunity.

She told me, "When my mother died, it was like she had never spent time with us. We barely knew her. But it's like, the reason why I have them is because I always made time for them. So now, I'm like, now that I have you guys—it's like a tug of war with myself when I have to leave because I don't want them not knowing me or not feeling like I wasn't there for them. Like the things that they say now, like even though they miss Mom, but it's like, 'She was never here. We didn't know her. You were always our second Mom because you always made time for us.' So now, I'm like, I've got to go, time to grind, and they complain, 'Oh, you're always at work'."

Quite often, it seems that kids want the opposite of what their parents give them. That is a constant challenge for parents.

Nelson Mandela spent something like 27 years in jail and ended up leading his country. He is known as the Father of South Africa.

At one time, Mandela's son said to him something like: You led the country. You freed the country. You changed the world by leading all these people. And you are known as the father to all these people. But you were never around to be a father to me. The fleeting moments you gave me were too little.

Nelson Mandela replied: That's interesting. I'm the father of a nation. I have all these children in this country. Yet, you are the only one who received my special, one-on-one attention.

So, I told my student, live your mission in life and then you will inspire your kids. Do not let your mission be delayed because you think of guilt and shame toward your kids.

Assignments: Fear of Loss

1-a. If you lost all your money, what would you fear losing the most? (Example: marriage/relationships, material things, etc.)

1-b. If you lost "it," what would be the benefit?

CHAPTER 7

Chaos and Organization

Doing the assignments can stir up a great deal of mental chaos. Do not be afraid of this. Your transformation depends on there being a storm for you to go through.

Also, do not be surprised if your mind keeps going back to specific topics or details. For instance, one student was concerned that his assignments on money always seemed to funnel him toward social topics—friends, family and the like. His focus was on fighting with them or losing them. Your focus may be different. Your mind is going to lean automatically toward your highest priorities. When you dig past the superficial ideas, you get to the root cause of your chaos. And that is a good thing. Embrace the chaos. Be grateful for the clues, whatever they are.

One lady told me that she really values wolves. Virtually everything in her life revolves around wolves. Many of my students focus on sales or business.

When you judge your mind and consciousness on what is good or bad, that is when you create chaos. It is only the judgment of yourself that is creating chaos because you think you are supposed to live someone else's values.

Who you are is simply who you are. Your values are yours. When you stop living in your shame and actually appreciate who you are, then you will realize that you do not need to be anybody else. That is when you no longer have the chaos running through your head.

Well, the chaos is there to wake you up. People think that chaos is bad. Let me explain.

Whatever you value, you are going to organize. Whatever you do not value, you are going to embroil in chaos. This is chaos theory. This is not me. This is universal cosmology, physics and mathematics. Chaos theory resides in all of it. The theory is that everything leads to a state of chaos, but what we now know is that chaos is actually more organized and there is a reason for that chaos. Quite specifically, chaos effects lead to local unpredictability, but global stability. Yet, there are self-similar patterns throughout the system under consideration.

If you can see the value of chaos, and see the lack of value in the organization, you create a midline understanding, and then you have organization and chaos all going on at the same time. So, where are you chaotic right now?

Let us say, for example, that you are chaotic in business and organized in family. In these lessons, I am waking you up to a new style of business.

Now, you are going to find a business in your life that is going to balance out your family and create inspiration for yourself. This chaos is necessary to create that. If you did not have chaos, you could not create that. If it was all "happy go lucky," happy, organized, and everything was fantastic and great, you would never create a mission to accomplish more, would you?

Chaos is necessary. Every state of chaos leads to its own state of organization, if you are aware of it, and every state of organization creates its own state of chaos. How many people have noticed that when you finally organize something, something else goes to hell?

We live in an evolving universe, but we want things to be stagnant. We do not want things to evolve. We say that we want it to stay exactly like this because this is good; it is stable and predictable. Dynamism is going to exist the whole time. That is how it works. The universe is delta (the symbol for "difference"). It is always changing. This is a money course, and here I am talking about cosmology. What the hell?

When working on a list of drawbacks, digging past the primary, secondary and tertiary layers, you want to dig deeply enough to get to the specifics. If your quaternary layer is still too general, then go down another layer. What would be the drawback of that? Remember, this is like the doctor attempting to find the root cause. If a patient comes in saying, "It hurts," then you have to find out what hurts. What kind of hurt? Does it ever change? If so, what happens right before the change? Is there anything you do to make it change? See? Get down to the specifics so you can tell the difference between fracture and cancer, or between dislocated and bruised.

People virtually always start out general, glossing over their perceptions with generalities. For example, parents will sometimes say, "I love everything about my kids." Do you, really? Oh, you love cleaning up their dirty diapers? You love when they wake you up at 2 o'clock in the morning? You love that? You really, really love that?

So, what don't you love about your kids? Nobody loves all parts, if you are being honest and real. Every part of your life has two sides. There are sides to my kids I absolutely cannot stand. Of course, this is because they are human with human flaws; we all have those. There are things that I absolutely adore because they are human. Every one of you, even in your relationships, have two sides. There are things about your partners or spouses, your friends and family members that you adore. There are things—like, man, this guy is such a pain in the ass. But you keep that to yourself. You do not tell him that, even though you do not hide or ignore it. You only dwell on the positives, but you keep all specifics in mind.

Remember, just as you move toward gratitude when you are grateful, you help others do the same when you dwell only on their positive aspects. Yet, you never ignore or hide the negative from yourself so that it does not become a festering sore. To stay in balance, you need to accept both sides.

Also, when you have feelings of anxiety and are overwhelmed with your finances, know that this is because your finances, or your attitudes about them, are out of balance. Such feelings are a bit of a wakeup call to you. Listen to your internal feedback.

When you value your family more than yourself, you will send your money to your family. There is an element of guilt involved. When you think the family is more important, you will put your money toward the family, and not for yourself. The guilt frequently comes in the form of a feeling that you left them hanging. But what if you leave them hanging? That is guilt rather than realizing that they have to fend for themselves.

I am not giving my money to my kids. I have told them that point blank. I have told them, "I will give you the platform to win. I will give you the tools to think. But you have to create your life." This is because, if you give people money, they will not value it.

Again, I am not saying not to love and take care of people, but I am saying that this is part of the decision process for your own money management.

I remember when I was younger, I put more money into my life insurance than into my investments, and I eventually realized that I was out of balance with it. If I am not taking care of myself.

If you do not try to take care of yourself, the universe is going to give you feedback to wake you up so that you value yourself.

To value yourself—that is the whole game.

This may sound a little ethereal, and I do not mean to make it sound that way. But the more you value yourself, the more you are going to take care of yourself. Every personal development guru says, "Don't wait for a knight in shining armor." There is truth to that, but that means you have to take care of yourself, including financially.

Occasionally, I will have a student who wants answers, but remains conflicted about asking for those answers. One of them told me, "It definitely stirs up feelings for me and nervousness." When asked, "Why?" she could not answer me. She thought the obvious paradox was "funny," but clearly she was struggling emotionally.

Upon probing more deeply, she realized that she and her husband have different philosophies about money and she did not know how to overcome that.

I told her, "Now, there is resentment built up, and that's really what the frustration is. You have to expose this frustration and this resentment that's showing up in the relationship."

In an upcoming chapter, I am going to talk a lot about relationships and money, and I am going to blow your mind.

If you do not protect your future, you create chaos. If you are not saving money, that leads to chaos. That is why the rich say that you need to pay yourself first because you are protecting your future.

It is not easy to look in the mirror and say, "What I've been doing for 20, 30, 40, 50 years of my life is completely backwards." After doing the work in this program, you will be in an entirely different place in maybe six months, or perhaps two years.

The mortgage companies, the banks, the medical corporations—they win by keeping you closed off and not knowing the truth. You become a puppet in their process of profit and control, while you live a life of quiet desperation. In my program, success is alignment and mastery.

With the medical doctors keeping you sick, you start to realize that their industry is not about health maintenance. They make very little money off of your health; but they make a ton of money when your illness keeps going on and on. We have already lost the diabetes game in this country. We have already lost the health game. The disease maintenance industry has to keep you in the dark about these things so that they can maintain control. But that is not the way I work. I plan on making a lot of money, but I also plan on adding lots of value to your life in the process.

No matter what your current age, wherever you are in your life, if you can wake up now, you can always change. You can always transform yourself and make your life more meaningful.

You start protecting, controlling and managing effectively. You stop living in the delusion of this myth that life is all about being rich. Life is more about serving others. But the more you serve, the more financial wealth you gain. In a matter of five to 10 years, you can be financially independent.

Most people cannot handle the truth. They are afraid of it. Most people want a simple and easy solution. That is why so many in this industry promise these things, but it is all bullshit. So many people get hurt—scammed. That is simply not cool because all those people have worked hard for their money and they are trusting others to provide real help, but it never comes. Those people look forward to a better life. I take that very seriously. I take people's investments very seriously.

Earlier today, my staff and I had our regular meeting. One of them told me, "Dr. Trivedi, you went two-and-a-half hours on a call the other day!" Not that they were angry. They were surprised that I was just giving and giving and giving.

I told them, "That's all I'm going to do. I'm just going to give. I'm going to serve the heck out of the people who are in front of me. I didn't have to create a $700 product to do this. I didn't have to do this. I did this because I wanted to serve the people who I couldn't otherwise serve. I don't weed people out. I weed people in. How do I help you more? The more I can help you, the more you get from where you currently are to the next place in your life. Or maybe you say, "I don't want to do the work."

That is fine with me. My concern is this: Did I serve you in a capacity whereby you can go forward? Because it is not about the numbers. It is about the value of the service. And when the service is in tune and aligned, somehow, some mystical way, the universe brings more people into your life.

When you are authentic and as loving as you know how to be, good stuff happens.

Life's Trajectory

One of my teammates was with an elderly lady the other day. The story is heartbreaking. This 73-year-old woman is living on social security, no children, no family, three months behind on her rent and about to be evicted.

You can be pretty certain that at age 20 she did not look into the future and expect that her life would bring her to this point.

If you do not prepare for the unexpected, it hits you hard to make you wake up. This is the hard truth of reality. It is challenging. It is in your face.

You have got to face your own reality. You have got to face your own financial mess which comes from your own chaotic delusions. Only then can you look ahead and master it, or you can learn the lessons from your mistakes.

You can master it. You can change it. You can make the decisions. You can change the tone of where you want to go with your life because you have time. I do not care how old you are. You can be 22 or 65; I do not care. You can change the way you think, if you understand both sides of it and learn to manage it. So, whatever you get in life, you can manage. You can create true freedom for yourself. When you have money saved, you are truly free. When you have your future prepared for, you are free. That is the real "freedom." That is financial independence.

If this sounds like preaching, I am sure you will get over it. If this helps in your transformation, then it will have served its purpose. This is meant to inspire you to wake up from the delusion you have been calling your life. Once you fully wake up, you can take charge of your life, fully responsible for both sides of each element.

Getting Past Feeling Stuck

One husband and wife pair of students—I get lots of those—had a question about the wife asked by the husband because the wife was busy with their little baby. On one of the timed assignments, she wrote down only three items in the allotted time of 90 seconds. The wife was feeling overtired, overworked, having gotten no more than five hours of sleep a night for something like two years, according to the husband.

Sometimes people feel stuck. Take investing, for instance. They may say, "I don't know how to invest. I don't want to be involved. It all sounds too complicated."

Not long ago, I was talking with a Forex trader. I am not a Forex trader and I have never tried it. I have zero awareness on how to do that activity. I would not know what to look for or how to think about it. If Forex trading had been one of my assignments, I might have felt stuck. I would not have had sufficient information to discuss, or even to think about the topic.

But sometimes, your delusions can keep you stuck. You cannot see the delusions because you are not even aware that they exist. In a way, it is like a vacuum or an empty space; you cannot see it. Now, if someone removes an object from a room, you might know that something has been recently removed because there is a spot on the shelf where there is no dust.

In the delusion of "financial freedom," you can go through countless highs and lows and feel the chaos and frustration of not being able to change your financial means. But there is importance in having those experiences. You can now appreciate the value of money.

If you continue to look only at the positives, you will keep running into that chaos. When you embrace both the positive and the negative, you will probably feel a shift in your body. Your physiology will change. Sometimes it is like a lightness where it had felt heavy before. That is one effect of your transformation.

Quite often, people will say, "Oh, I never even saw that. I never looked at it that way." That is the most common thing people say. And when this happens, your entire physiology is mapping your consciousness. And when you stand upright and your head goes up more erect, it is like awareness kicks in and taps into the prefrontal cortex of the brain. It links into your mission so that you are actually looking forward.

Suddenly, your body and mind are linking you into your mission all of the time. You may not be aware of it, but it takes a little while to reset. Now the world has become different. Then the stress in the muscles evaporates. The body begins to change because you think you are separate from your body. Even though this is a book on money, most of this chapter has been about health and physiology because they are related.

Here is what I learned in practice. Very commonly, as people's financial chaos shows up, so does their health chaos. These go hand-in-hand.

I hope you appreciate me challenging you because most everyone else wants to tell you it will be easy. If that was the case, everyone would already be wealthy. You could read Napoleon Hill's *Think and Grow Rich,* then sit and meditate, and think you are going to be rich. But that does not work.

A friend who works in Hollywood has told me a great many things about the movie industry. For one thing, 50,000 people enter Hollywood every single year. But also, 50,000 people leave Hollywood every single year. Most of them come with the hopes and dreams of becoming the next Brad Pitt or George Clooney. Some might think, "Hey, look, if he can do it, I can do it. I've got that positive thinking belief. I've got it." But the real question becomes, are you willing to be him? Not just do what he did, but are you willing to be who he is? Most people are not willing to go that far, so they do not reach his level of success.

That is where the gap shifts. Because if it was just about doing as he does—just about hanging out with the right people—just about the right behaviors—who wouldn't want to be wealthy? Who wouldn't want to pop bottles of champagne, live a life of ease, luxury and happiness all the time? Look, I don't mind hanging out on a yacht with 14 hot blondes in bikinis all the time. I am cool with that. If that is what my life has to be, that is fine, but that is not reality.

The music videos show unrealistic lifestyles. Most of those guys go bankrupt because they do not know how to manage money, and they fall apart because of their highs and lows.

I am challenging you to see it for yourself. When you do this work, I promise you, life will change. Your financial world will change. Your life can have a completely different trajectory.

I have seen it happen. I have seen people in the bottom of the bottom— the dumps of the dumps—transform their life in a year; their income soared. That is what I am trying to give to you.

If you want just happiness, go watch a motivational video, go watch the latest comedy movie. They will make you laugh. But if you want the truth on how to live an empowered life, that is what I am all about.

Assignment: Chaos and Organization

1. Organize your monthly income. Where does the money go, currently?
2. 50 benefits of paying yourself first.

CHAPTER 8

Protection

Breaking Past the Ordinary

Every once in a while, a student will reach a point where they become a berserker—a fearless warrior—a madman mowing down a jungle of chaos. They find an inner energy and commitment to do what may have seemed to them impossible a month earlier. My students paid good money to take my course. When a student realizes that they could end up wasting all that money if they take the easy way through these exercises, they wake up to a state of decision, determination and responsibility.

One such student told me, "I'm not living up to my full potential and I'm cheating the people closest to me. I say I'm grateful for things with my mouth, but my actions are incongruent. I don't keep my word because I'm overly emotional. I have to change now, not tomorrow. Then I wrote back a couple hours later. Said, fuck that, I'm cheating myself. I've limited my options, and with those limitations I go to men and I give them the power, instead of taking control and disciplining myself. If I relinquish control— even a part of that control—then a part of me always has someone to blame. Victim!"

Then she added, "Because once you did the 50 drawbacks—to say, okay, cool. I can do 50 more. We all kind of worked on it together at four. So, I can do 50! When it was 100, I just kept on going. I didn't wanna cheat myself and I was kind of getting frustrated with the exercise and frustrated with myself.

Like, you may not feel good but it's medicine. Medicine doesn't taste good, but, you know, you feel good afterward—or feel good after a good workout. And so that's how I was looking at the exercise. I don't know about you guys, but I don't want to just waste a couple hours a week doing this and not getting any results. Like that's not the shit that I'm here for. I had a lot of clarity from doing the exercise. It took much longer because I wanted to do it right and actually get something from it.

"I decided to go ahead and reactivate my real estate license because that is a passion of mine. And really, once I decided to do that—because that's authentic to me—it has all been coming together, Doc. Like seriously, I got my first listing already. And it's just flowing. So, I'm super excited and just excited there's already results. And I'm just excited about, you know, what else is to come from being authentic and not living up to somebody else's standards, or whatever. So, I'm done."

The Delusion that Money Makes You Evil

Another student told me, "It took me a long time to do this assignment. I mean because I think I was more scared of what was going to come out of it."

It is interesting what some people consider to be a "long time," especially in this age of instant gratification. Is it really so very long? A student spends a few hours and feels emotional about all of that time used up. It only took me 23 years to research and to put this together. In the grander scheme of things, 23 years is the blink of an eye.

The student added some clarification to her earlier statement. "It was the courage. We had to build courage. But I just didn't realize how scared I was of becoming a bad person for wanting money. I'm still very emotional about it."

Whenever you come across an implied assumption like this, you have to challenge it right away. While the emotional bias is still fresh, jump on it and wrestle it to the ground. So, I asked her, "What is it about getting money that you think is going to make you a bad person?"

"I don't know," she said, "There's something about it that scares me."

"And what is that something? You'll be a bad person, then what?"

"People aren't going to like me?" she asked. "I don't know."

"You'll end up in Hell, right?"

"I guess. Probably."

There is a lot of that going around. We are going to talk about that toward the end of the book—about the layers and dimensions of consciousness. I am going to end this book in such a manner that you cannot come back afterward and attack me.

But seriously, there is a lot of guilt around the topic of money and receiving.

So, consider the possible answers to this question: "What if you become a bad person?" While you consider how you might approach an answer, let me ask you another question to give you a broader perspective. "How good is a person being broke? How can you serve anyone else if you are broke?"

Not a pretty sight, poverty.

Picture this analogy: You are on an airplane traveling in the stratosphere. Next to you is a young child—a niece or nephew, daughter or son, or perhaps a grandchild. Suddenly, alarms sound and little plastic masks drop from above you. The cabin has lost pressure and you will need additional oxygen very shortly. You fumble with the mask dangling above the child and attempt to put it over their face, but they fight against you, frightened by the sudden noise and the change in lighting. The next moment, you slump in your seat, oxygen-starved and your child starts to shriek before they too pass out from oxygen deprivation. This is a case of compassion without wisdom. The wise man would place the mask over their own face first, ensuring that their near-term future is secured. Only then will they attempt to help the child or others.

You being broke is serving nobody, yet your internal constitution is about service. You being broke means that you have not served anybody. So, if you think that by being broke you will be a good person, and by having money you are a bad person, this creates a great deal of mental chaos because it conflicts with the simple logic of reality.

There are a lot of people in that same, guilt-ridden boat. And it is perfectly okay to sit in that emotional boat and get pissed off at the incongruity of it all. When you master your own finances and create wealth, everyone around you can benefit. You become a garden of prosperity making everyone else's life better. It is only when you stay disconnected that your personal prosperity can become stagnant and spoiled.

Chasing Money vs. Protecting the Future

A business owner student of mine did the 100 drawbacks of staying where you are with money. At the end of his list, he ran into an old habit he called "disposable income"—on a regular basis, spending something like $300 on a hockey game and refreshments. He realized that he could have, instead, spent that on protecting his future.

"Which is really tough, you know?" he told me. "Just to find a percentage to put away for retirement was difficult to face. I didn't get pissed off as much as I needed to. It made me look more into myself. Asking myself the important questions, and saying, 'Hey, wait a minute!' Geez, you know. You've got to be honest with yourself. Because, I mean, let's face it—people will do just about anything. The good person will get up and go to work every day—go to work, and they're chasing money. Whereas there are other people who just don't want to work, and they'll do what it takes—rob, cheat or whatever. So, there's the good and the evil. Where do you draw the line? Between one bad result and the other? What the hell is it that I need to do to look at it and make some changes, you know?"

I asked him, "So, when you did the 100 drawbacks of staying where you are with money, what came up? What was the emotion at the hundredth point on your list?"

"Holy shit," he replied. "I'm screwed. I mean, I gotta get myself together, you know what I mean? I got to get it together and really kick some ass. Be smarter, work harder. I used to waste a lot of money. Disposable income. I used to go to NHL games all the time.

"Credit cards! I only have one left. I got rid of all the others. They're just a waste, you know. The banks are going to get compound interest. The two words that I hate. So, I try to pay cash."

I could tell that he was quite emotional about the banks getting compound interest on his purchases. I told him, "I'm going to interrupt that belief pattern. Compound interest is not only—"

"Well, yeah," he said, cutting me off to clarify his point. "I mean I just don't wanna—I just don't feel like making a purchase and then having to pay for it three times over, you know?"

I reminded him that "compound interest" can have both a positive and a negative side. The positive side gives people benefits by increasing their money—savings accounts and similar investments.

Should we be angry at credit card companies for being clever about compound interest on outstanding balances? Anger can be good if it helps you decide to take responsibility. Even guilt can be good for a few seconds, if it helps you sober up and tap into your own power. But could you be grateful for their cleverness? Could you merely decide not to play their game, yet learn from their ingenuity?

Transformation and Valuing Money

Superficially, we all "value" money, but it is a shallow—even fake—valuation. Most people have a distorted picture of what money is. They are not in balance. They do not appreciate both the positive and the negative. And they are trapped in a "comfort zone" which they may think is insanely uncomfortable. But the latent mind feels a kind of awkward, emotional balance with the status quo. That assessment is held in place, in part, by a lack of awareness of these other elements—the positive aspects of what you would otherwise consider negatives.

Only by embracing the wholeness of money—the real meaning behind "wealth"—can you see the deeper value of money.

What one of my students told me, recently, touches on the beginning of her own transformation.

"I'm writing my 50/50, 100 lists. And I think what I'm realizing, like, with my current situation—I'll share my current situation of making money. Like a month ago, when I talked to you, I was really wigged out because you know the reality and the pressure of having to make money differently than I have in the past was there. And then seeing the shortfall and everything. Really being afraid of the future. But I would have to say that in the last month things have changed a lot for me. And I'm starting to really think differently. In fact, I think I'm starting to attract things that I wasn't able to before.

"I don't know. I'm just feeling a lot more confident about my ability to make money. And the more I like what I'm doing—which is a benefit of producing money right now—the more I like it overall. And seeing that I like it, and seeing what I'm capable of, I'm happier with myself because I really resent having to work for somebody for a paycheck. And I've resented that for a very long time. I didn't realize that that was a real thing for me. And I was very afraid to step away from the safety of a paycheck. But it got to the point where I had to.

"And so, I'm starting to see that there's other people that respect themselves enough and believe in themselves enough to, you know, be confident about what they can do to make money. And also, I am seeing that there's a ton of responsibility associated with making money and being in business for yourself. And I'm just realizing that I've taken the easy way out for a long time. So now, I'm on this growth thing. I'm like being stretched like crazy and I'm really getting serious. I actually started a budget for my business and a budget for my family within the last week. And my husband doesn't understand any of this. I'm like, that's okay; I'm gonna just do it. And I have to do it. And so, I'm seeing where our shortfall is in my real estate business, but I'm also seeing new and unexpected opportunities. I just came across a chance to list a commercial property this week valued at $800,000. And I'm really excited about that. So, I reached out to my broker, who's not excited at all because he does this all the time. But I'm excited. And so, I see things changing for me.

"And I know that I'm not making a ton of money right now, but that doesn't mean that this year is not going to be dramatically different than the way it ended last year. And so, I'm just seeing a change. And the dreams of having more than enough are returning to me. And there's a lot of respect for people who are wealthy. They handle themselves differently. They think about themselves differently. They also think about their money differently. But they're able to produce because they don't accidentally become wealthy or successful in anything they do. It is not that. It's so interesting to see that there is some real serious thought behind all of this stuff."

I told her, "Some people learn this knowledge; some people grow through it; some people get taught this; and some people don't. Some of us have to take the hits and get beaten and let life teach us. And then we finally learn it, and get it, and understand it. How many people realize that after doing this exercise the way you are looking at spending money. You are thinking twice before that hand goes into that wallet."

The intrinsic value of money does not increase as you do these exercises. Your internal assessment of its value—that is what changes. Unless you value money you are never going to have it. Period. End of discussion.

There is no way you can have money if you do not value it. This last exercise was specifically designed to increase your value of money.

Some of my students got angry when they completed the last exercise. They hated me, even if only for a few minutes. They felt like absolute Hell. And that is good. That means the transformation was happening.

I want you to realize that if you do not take control of your financial destiny, nobody will.

Assignment: Protection

1. How will you protect your "future" life while you are alive?
2. What do you feel is worth protecting?
3. Why are you going to protect your future? (30 benefits)

CHAPTER 9

Management

Stuff happens! Life is unpredictable.

One of my students and I were talking recently about a gentleman we know—a friend of a friend. He is 66 years old and got laid off from a job, but had a little bit of money saved up. That was a couple of years ago. Since that time, he has been trying to find work without success.

In a relationship, when two people are committed to one another, they work together to take full responsibility for that relationship. But this is not easy, especially when one of the partners is not providing value to the relationship. A lot of anger and resentment builds up toward that person. We are talking here about conflict.

If the other person is just sitting at home playing video games or watching TV, I do not care if they are male or female, it does not matter. You will cause a lot of resentment.

So, this individual is 66 years old. He has no path; no purpose. Nothing. Now, he is working in a car wash—a car wash!—getting the cars ready to be detailed.

Do not get me wrong. Kudos to the guy for going out and getting a job and doing that. I am not saying "no" to that. I respect that 100%. But I am not looking at that. I am not looking for anyone reading this book to end up at 66 or 70 or 80 years old to be working at a car wash.

I want you to master your money so that you do not have to do that.

A week ago, one of my students and I were arguing. She was getting really pissed off. Everyone was getting pissed off. Such emotion can make you think as though you are living in fear. And I told you early on that money is more about fear than it is about success. It is about preventing the pain in the future so that you are allowed to live today.

Money is a value exchange, but it is also a method of survival. If you cannot understand that, then your future is in jeopardy. If you do not see both sides of money, you are going to get smacked across the head to wake you up.

When you do not have a strategy to protect yourself, your body will give you feedback to wake you up to protect yourself. It is trying to get you congruent and aligned in order to do that. Your body and your circumstances will be trying to wake you up, to see exactly what you need to do to move forward.

Sometimes it is helpful to look at things from a different perspective. This can trigger realizations you might not otherwise have seen. Here, I am going to throw a different spin at you.

What if you lived backwards?

What if you lived for 100 years, but you looked at your life from that 100-year mark? How much money would you need at 100? At 90? At 80? And at 70?

What if there was nothing moving forward and everything moved backwards? Are you ready for the future? Let me ask you that question. Now, you are the deer in the headlights. These are the types of questions which run through my mind all the time. This is what I think when everyone else is sitting around laughing at television comedy shows and having fun. This is how I think. I love it. What do you think about that?

How long are you going to live? Do you know? Of course not. You have no damn idea. Nobody does. So, what if you prepared for 100?

And do not be too surprised with this idea. Medical science keeps increasing the average life expectancy with better understanding of diseases, old age, stem cell regeneration and more. Two centuries ago, life expectancy was on average about half what it is today. Some doctors predict that the first person to live past 150 has already been born. And this is not about drugs and medication, but real health maintenance.

The most common reason for resenting money is that an individual would have to manage that money. Because they do not understand both sides of money, they feel chaos every time they look in the direction of having more money to manage. That resistance to chaos—to having to work to manage money—pushes people back into their comfort zone—the place where they do not have to work so hard.

Management requires the ability to see objectively both the positives and the negatives of the things being managed.

And yes, there is a negative side to money. When you see anything only one-sided, you are being delusional. Your certainty toward the positives is blinding you to the negatives. And, naturally, this can happen with things you typically think of as negative in quality; you can blind yourself to the positives.

There is a quote by Henry Ford that touches on this type of blind bias. He supposedly said something like, "The man who thinks he can and the man who thinks he can't are both right." What the Ford quote lacks is the wisdom of seeing both sides, but the bias of which it speaks is very true. Now, imagine having the bias of the "Can do" individual added to the ability to see both sides of all resources involved.

When you become delusional to one side—negative or positive—it runs your life. It creates chaos, anxiety and stress in your life to wake you up, to get you back to reality. Because the more anguish you create behind that, the more delusion you have. The more chaotic your life is going to be.

But now that you start to see the value of money because you are starting to see that it is neither positive nor negative. You start to wake up.

I do not merely give you the assignments. I do all of these, again, as well. I sit there and do all of these things. After all, I have to get to the next level.

But how am I going to do that if I live in the satisfaction of being okay with where I am at right now? If I live in satisfaction, I am not going to push myself to the next level.

If you see more positives in money than negatives, it is going to consume your life. When you only see positives, you are going to get feedback in the middle to show you the negative zone. The symptoms in the body—anxiety, stress, depression, chaos, confusion—will help guide you back. All these things are there to wake you up—to let you know that you are completely deluded with money.

For some people, this imbalance even stops them in their businesses because the greater the delusion of money the less the income grows. So, the less the business actually grows. Now, managing money is all about these two sides.

Credit Scores

What is the purpose of a credit score?

Some of my students have given me some interesting answers.

"With an awesome credit score I can then borrow more money. With an awesome credit score—honestly, I see this little mark that I've managed what I have. I'm really all about my credit score."

"It's a measure of your creditworthiness—your ability to pay back debts."

"How about it's a measure of your self-worth. Is your work good enough?"

"It's how financial institutions gauge how well you manage money so they can determine if you're worth the risk."

"It's something that's necessary if you can't pay cash. If you don't have enough money to pay for something, then you need to borrow."

Now, let me throw some interesting perspectives at you just to get you to think a little bit differently.

People are welcoming the idea of credit because they think they are worth it. That is a positive feeling. They resent their debts because they do not want to give the money back. And this is a negative feeling. When someone goes into a state of pride because they think they deserve something they do not have, that is called credit. And then they resent the credit because those people want their money back.

So, your credit score is the gauge which shows whether or not you stay in fair exchange. It indicates the ability to manage money. It is your feedback mechanism to see how well you manage money. If you do not manage your credit score, you reveal that you do not know how to manage money.

When you value the debt, you stay in fair exchange. If you do not value debt, you create emotion. That emotion keeps you in a state of pride, thinking that you are worth more than you actually are, and it keeps you in resentment, thinking that you do not like having to pay back what you borrowed. Instead of the more desirable self-value, you are stuck with pride and resentment.

And we just stack up the debt, deeper and deeper.

Our government is doing the same thing. They keep stacking up debt because they think they are worth it. The representatives in government are stuck in the same delusions—certainty of pride and ignored resentment to take responsibility for what has already been borrowed.

Our society is being torn apart with this chaotic, consumer mentality. Though people do not openly say this, their feeling says, "How dare they ask for their money back. Those bastards."

But then we say it is easy to erase all of that; we have done so much pride building that we declare bankruptcy and force them to forgive all of this chaos. So, this allows us to continue to do it again, and again, and again—never learning from our mistakes.

More and more people are trapped in his chaos. That is why bankruptcy lawyers keep advertising on TV.

There are three parts to our money triangle—attract, manage and retain.

Most people have a difficult time in the management section because they are emotional about it. A kid graduates high school, applies for a job and wants to make $30 per hour. But what has he done to warrant that? Because of this entitlement mentality, we take away the ability to value anything.

This chaos is behind the insanity of minimum wage. It used to be that a small business would be willing to hire a kid who knew nothing and had no skills with which to add value to the business, but the owner could pay a tiny allowance while the kid received an education in responsibility. As the kid learned to add value, the owner might increase their meager wages. And the kid had to realize how lucky he was to get paid while also getting an education. That is what an entry level job should be. A kid just starting out does not need a "living wage."

And think about the internships which used to exist. A college graduate makes zero dollars per hour for an education in a competitive field far more valuable than the university degree which they just received. The entitlement crowd demands that the intern be paid minimum wage. With all of the government interference, minimum wage costs far more than that more visible amount. Some college graduates will have paid over a hundred thousand dollars for their degree, but demand minimum wage for an even more valuable education. Perhaps the companies offering internships should call it what it is and charge big money for the education. The college graduate did not make minimum wage when they attended their college classes. Why should the internship be any different?

When we truly value something, we see both the positives and the negatives.

If you cannot master the management of money, you cannot have it. Warren Buffett said that if you cannot master your emotions, you cannot master money. If you cannot manage your emotions, you cannot manage money—you will end up losing your money.

Part of that management is the principle of fair exchange I discussed at the beginning. Giving and receiving need to be balanced. If you are biased toward giving, make sure it is only to the degree that you "wow" your customers or clients; for example, marketing samples. Go too far in either direction and you throw everything out of balance.

A lack of ability to manage emotions around management prevents you from keeping money. Because if you are afraid of managing it, it is because you either have too much of an addiction to money, or too much of a resentment toward it.

Assignment: Management of Money

1. What is your Financial Independence Number?
2. What is your strategy to attain this?
3. What is the biggest fear of having to manage money?
4. What emotions come up when you have cash in the bank?

4-a. What does that feel like?

4-b. What can you compare it to?

CHAPTER 10

Gratitude Toward Money

Whatever you resent you resist. Let's put this another way: Whatever you resent in your life you are going to push away.

Lots of wonderful people picture themselves as magnets, attracting money and other good things into their lives. The Law of Attraction is their mantra. But let me debunk this nonsense.

If you are attracting one thing, you are simultaneously repelling something else. A magnet has two poles—north and south. The north pole will attract one pole of the second magnet but will repel the other pole of that second magnet.

Isaac Newton told us that for every action there is an equal and opposite reaction. This entire universe is built on such opposition. From this set of phenomena, we have balance in our world. And whenever there is momentary imbalance, nature will seek a return to balance—like hot air rising and cool air rushing in to take its place. Heat seeks to find equilibrium.

So, when you are in a state of attraction, you automatically have to repel something else.

If you are attracting money because you value it and it feels good, then ask yourself, "What am I repelling?"

Normally, we do not want to look at the downsides of any situation. We do not want to look at the other side of success. But the truth is, if you are attracting money, you are repelling something else.

The masses want you to believe that the attraction of money is good.

In physics, if something is attracted, something else has to be repelled. It is like a magnet. So, what are you repelling? Understand that your emotions are emoted ions. I will not be discussing the details about ions, but I will briefly say that human physiology is made up of ions. Your ions dictate who you are. At the most elemental state, we are nothing more than positive and negative ions. Positive and negative charges and polarity. And that is it.

Law of Attraction versus Law of Repulsion

So, people want to say that if you get something that supports your desires, it is positive. It is part of the Law of Attraction.

If it is negative, it is part of the Law of Repulsion. But no one talks about the Law of Repulsion.

What is the Law of Repulsion? It involves all of the things that you are resisting and pushing away.

If you have a positive association with money—you feel it is supportive—you are going to want more of it in your life.

We call this pride. And we call this parasympathetic.

The more money you have, the more powerful you think you are. The more success you have, the more joy you have in your life. And it is wonderful and quite easy to sell that.

The more negative things you have, the more you are living in the Law of Repulsion. What are things that are taking money away from you?

This is the Law of Repulsion. It compels you to say, "That's bad. That's negative. That's not good. That can't be the Law of Attraction. It's got to be a negative thing. That can't be worth it. It's got to be a bad thing." And that you might also call "resentment."

Most people today live in the Law of Repulsion instead of the Law of Attraction. Most people stop themselves from creating any sort of success in their life because they think money is supposed to be only a positive thing. So, if you have a positive addiction to credit, pride, and money, your life ends up with debt, chaos, and resentment. These negatives are only there to wake you up so that you understand the value of the whole.

Because of the imbalance to which most people cling, they will go through cycles of highs and lows. For a while, you might say, "Man, this is so good." But then you will ask, "Where did it all go?" And this is where your resentment comes into play.

Because of your imbalance, you are going to oscillate around your mean. And that is why they say there is no one season in life.

As you resent these opportunities—and they are, indeed, opportunities—you keep trying to stay in the one-sided life which creates an expectation of chaos. And that expectation leads to your depression. So, you judge yourself based on that.

You judge your life based on a one-sided delusion, thinking that this is the way life is. But it is not. This is your gift. As you do the exercise for this chapter, you are going to realize that the gift is resentment, not pride.

You have plenty of people out there who are trying to teach you to stay only in the good or the positive. But if you do not learn to master the whole, then you are going to go into the oscillations of up and down, which creates more chaos in your life.

The Dark Power of Resentment

So, the assignment this time around is for you to clear some of your resentment.

Consider for a moment any story from your life involving both money and resentment. Maybe it was a trauma. What was the trauma that you had with money? Maybe it was bankruptcy, or losing money in the stock market.

In 2008, I was some kind of super genius, losing roughly $270,000. This held my business upside down and stopped me from making money. Do you think I might have had some resentment toward this?

I am trying to bring money back into your life. In this chapter, you are working on the attraction phase of our money triangle because whatever you resent you resist. You need to clear up the past trauma which keeps you secretly resisting money. Find the episodes where you think you have lost something of monetary value—either money or something for which you paid a good deal of money. Maybe you loaned someone money and they never paid you back.

Now, consider all of the jobs you have had. Were there any of those jobs where you felt trapped—where you hated the job? You needed the job because it gave you the money you needed for food, shelter and other things, but you resented the source of that money.

But look at this dynamic: You resenting the job which allows you to pay your bills, to put food on the table and to live your life.

And now, consider this: You being grateful for the job for allowing you to make money, to pay your bills, to put food on the table, and to allow you to survive and live.

Now, it is wise to find inspiration in your current location on the path to your success. Quite often, the apparent hardships you experience are exactly what you need to achieve the goals to which you have committed yourself. But if you resent what is happening in your life, you are no longer moving forward. You might self-destruct because you resent what is giving you the money you currently require to survive, and you resent the lessons life is making available to you.

Another prime source of resentment is divorce, and frequently this involves the perception of lost money.

If you have invested and lost money, that will cause you resentment. Whatever you resent you resist.

Some people resent social security because the government now tells us that the program will become insolvent in a few years. Young people are paying into social security but they may not be able to get anything out when they reach retirement age.

And every once in a while, the economy goes wild with inflation and the dollar loses value. People can no longer afford things. This happens when the government goes even more crazy than usual, raising taxes and printing lots more money to pay for programs they cannot afford.

One of my students related a story from his own personal experience. His father died when he was really young and his mother remarried. But then the stepfather passed away in a work-related accident. The worker's compensation claim could have helped his family for quite awhile, but his mother blew right through the money so that it lasted only a few months. And he deeply resented her for being so irresponsible with the money and not protecting their future. Quite likely, she felt guilty for losing her second husband and the guilt forced her to give away the money. This is the nature of guilt.

The Law of Moral Hazard

Yet another source of resentment is loaning others money. Everyone to whom I have ever loaned money told me that they would pay me back. They never did! But you can change that outcome if you include with the loan the Law of Moral Hazard.

Consider the following facts. If you do not pay your mortgage, what happens? You get kicked out of your house. If you do not pay your electricity bill, what happens? Your lights do not go on. And if you do not pay your cell phone bill, nobody can call you.

Because of this Law of Moral Hazard, you tend to pay the bills which will cause the most hurt if you don't. If you do not pay, you lose! This gets you to pay them on time, or to negotiate with them so you can cure a late payment.

Some people are too trusting, which may well be another way of saying, "They are too lazy or shy to do what needs to be done." A friend may borrow $5,000, $50,000 or even $100,000, and they might say, "Well, they're a good friend of mine. They're going to pay me back." You may as well just pour that friendship down the drain, unless you put some moral hazard in the gate leading to that loan.

Such a moral hazard is defined as putting a contract in place telling them that there is a due date for when the loan is to be paid back, with interest. If they do not pay you back, a penalty kicks in to put their finances in even greater jeopardy. This is why banks and other institutions usually ask for some kind of collateral. If they do not pay back, they lose the collateral, which is frequently more valuable than the amount of the loan.

If you do not value your own money, they are not going to value your money, either. In our society, money runs from those who value it the least, toward those who value it the most. The one who values money the most has the most of it.

In a company, who values money the most? Is it the CEO or the janitor? Believe it or not, it is the CEO who values money the most.

If you value money, you move up the ladder to create more money. If you do not, you will lose money.

Your resentment toward money is preventing you from attracting money because you have the Law of Repulsion activated.

With each event in your life, you create in your mind a perception which you interpret—you decide to give it a positive or negative association. The aggregate accumulation of all your associations will affect how you see the world—whether you associate a positive or negative feeling with the things which cross your path. You resent something in your past related to money and now you have a hard time attracting money. You are going to get just enough to survive.

That may be a jab in the gut. How many people realize that they make just enough to survive? And when you do that, it is because you have built-in resentment toward money. A deep-seated, instinctual part of your mind knows that it would be crazy to want any more money because of the resentment locked into place.

More Examples

One of my students told me that she still had resentment from when she was in her late teens. "Something that I didn't realize, I still hadn't gotten over something that happened when I was in high school. My Dad forged my grandmother's signature after my grandfather passed away, and took $25,000 out of an account for my Mom and her brothers. Spent it and ended up spending it on whatever. And ended up cheating on my Mom and they got divorced. We lost the house, then filed for bankruptcy and all that comes with that. This was all before I went away to college. And I didn't realize that all of that still bothers me as much as it used to. And it's definitely something that I need to deal with because it has controlled my whole financial life since those things happened."

Another student resented his past, but for an entirely different reason. "Just a realization that, when I was young, I made more money than I make now. And now, I'm kind of stuck. And a lot of this is coming up now. And that's making me angry. I don't like it at all. And, I guess, I've always known it, and I have been scared to make a move because I failed in a business several years ago. My last big failure was about eight or nine years ago. I almost lost everything. And now it's making me paralyzed. And that's pissing me off."

Gratitude Is the Gateway

Money comes in gratitude. That's it. Gratitude is the gateway to the income that you desire. Anything other than gratitude activates the Law of Repulsion. If you do not find gratitude it will hold you back.

When you do not have gratitude, these other emotions create the Law of Repulsion. Gratitude is the gateway to the income that you desire. If you do not have gratitude, you do not have money. Do you want money in your life? Then get grateful for all of your life.

All the self-help gurus want to teach you to be happy. That is not what I am trying to do. First, I want you to get pissed off—so angry that it wakes you up enough to say, "Hold on. Why am I angry? Let me find the benefits to why I'm angry. Let me get clarity on this thing called money, and around this situation."

When I was 26 years old, I was in a $330,000 lawsuit. I did not have a dollar to my name. From my first practice, I went into a lawsuit. Some guy sued me and I lost everything. But hold on. I did not have anything, so there was not much to lose.

I did not know what to do. I did not want to fight. I had just graduated chiropractic school, but the guy who sued me gave me the best business lesson I ever had. After I went through that nightmare, it taught me to become a businessperson. It taught me to understand money. It taught me to understand business.

When I was 30 years old, my associate doctor was hit with a sexual harassment case. Another great lesson I learned about managing a business. Systems, policies and procedures in my practice went up to another level.

If I had not found gratitude inside these things, they would have consumed my life because I would have been emotionally deluded by it.

Now, realize this: If you are ever attached to anything or any situation through pride, you will end up with resentment when that pride is ever assaulted. Gratitude nullifies resentment.

If you sit and dwell on what others did **to** you, then you are deluded. Your pride is clouding your perception. You are dwelling in pride and victimhood. To change this, consider the notion that they did those things *for* you. Another way of describing pride is "entitlement." This is the attitude people have when they show off their cars and houses. When a person is all about seeking admiration from the outside-in, they are about to crash.

So, keep your attention from the inside-out with gratitude to others no matter what they do. You can learn from every situation. It can make you stronger and smarter, but the real gift is your use of gratitude to keep your inner self aligned with your desired direction.

Assignments: Gratitude Toward Money

1. Write down 100 Gratitudes for your current financial situation.
2. How has this been a benefit to your life?

CHAPTER 11

Expectations

Your mind works in images. You know this; you have been taught this.

That is why some people put up these stupid vision boards. Yes, even I have done that. But they put these vision boards up because they think that the visions pinned to the board are going to come about. That is absolutely great! Fantastic! But it does not work that way. If anyone achieves startling success after a vision board, it will not be because of the pictures pasted on that board. Success comes from something changing on the inside.

Those people think that the one second of admiration poured over their vision board is going to dictate the future events of their lives.

Okay, let us say that you buy the Ferrari. Is it the fact that you have the Ferrari, or is it the fact that you actually got to sit in it and say, "It's mine!" But what happens after you get the Ferrari? The following day it is just a freaking car—an expensive chunk of metal with a huge price tag.

Now, time is not an image. The time stream is always unfolding—or perhaps even unraveling. The timeline can go this way or that way, but it never stays the same. Time is never stagnant. It is always on the move. Yet, these images from the vision board are what the mind perceives—the objects of desire or what is loved.

What people typically do is this: They have this image in their head and it defines who they are. They are attached to that image and to its meaning— prestige, status or other forms of pleasure. Every time they compare that mental image with the current reality, that disconnect leaves them feeling depressed. They end up resenting themselves for falling short of their ideal image.

And remember: What you resent you resist. If you want that Ferrari, but you resent yourself for not having it, then you are going to resist getting it.

To the degree that you do not match your own self-image—whether it be the owner of that Ferrari, a husband who provides well for his family, a loving wife who takes great care of her family, or whatever else is in that self-image—your own self-love goes down. Other things go down as well, including self-appreciation and gratitude.

Your ability to have money matches your ability to love yourself. As your self-love goes up and down, so too will your ability to have money.

Your unmet expectation is what causes your suffering. And this expectation does not necessarily have to come from you; it could have been placed on you by someone else. The expectation could come from that gap between your mental image and your current reality, or it could even come from something you have seen—perhaps by a clever bit of advertising or by how someone else was treated.

In a very real sense, the actual you gets lost in all the scrambling to attain that elusive mental image as your reality. And even though the image in your mind may seem "internal," it originated external to yourself, so it is not going from the inside-out, but remains outside-in. This creates chaos and suffering in your life.

When you compare your life to that of someone else based on money—and even I have done that—you end up letting that external fact depress your self-worth. You judge yourself as unworthy because of your lack of accomplishment. "I'm not there! What is wrong with me?"

You might stay up late at night, looking at yourself in the mirror and asking, "Why am I not good enough? If I'm not good enough to do this, maybe I don't deserve this. Maybe this is not what I am supposed to do."

The secret to attracting money is to love yourself—not resent yourself.

We have all had challenges, but stop comparing your life to 's. Period. As soon as you compare yourself to others, thinking that they are better, you start to resent yourself.

On the flip side, if you think you are better than them, then you are in pride. And remember: Pride is akin to victimhood in that both are looking to the outside as a place to shift responsibility. Responsibility should only come from the inside-out. Pride seeks acknowledgement from the outside while blame seeks to burden someone else on the outside for what you have allowed to happen. Both result in self-resentment. Victims frequently find it hard to take responsibility, especially when they confuse responsibility with blame. They are not the same thing.

When you are stuck in the attitude of resentment, you are going to push money away. You will end up judging yourself because of it. And, if you judge others, then money is going to run away from you, as well. You cannot love and judge at the same time. When you let go of such burdens, then you can love what is.

What if you are broke and have nothing? I remember the day when I had a lemon to eat, and I was like, "Damn! I have no money." I wanted to blame everybody. And I did. I was so good at it, and it was so easy that I could blame everybody, it became clear very quickly that such an approach did not work. It did not solve anything.

And then I took responsibility and started loving myself. I started appreciating myself and saying, "What the hell was all of this trying to teach me? Why was I resenting?" That is when I started to understand and when I started to discover what actually works.

Some of my students bring with them an old belief that tells them that self-love is selfish or prideful. Think about this carefully for a moment. Sometimes our words are clumsy and inadequate to describe exactly what we need to discuss. The type of self-love to which I am referring is not the self-importance and arrogance of the boastful. Instead, it is the kindness toward self that you might have to your own son or daughter, to your mother or father, to a sibling, or to a dear, lifelong friend.

Such true love is a synchronicity of complementary opposites. True love sits in the middle of the highs and lows—at fair exchange.

But when we only want love to be an addiction—hedonistic love—we have the delusion that it is only good and never bad, always happy and never sad. And it is that from which I am trying to break you—to wean you off your dependence on that delusion.

As you go through this material, your workload will increase. Like lifting weights, you start out small and gradually keep adding on. So, with this new knowledge you will be creating a list of everything for which you judge yourself about money.

And if you were as wealthy as you thought you wanted to be by now, what would have been the drawback to you?

It is time for you to love those other people who have screwed you over with regard to money. But this is also to get you to love yourself for putting yourself in the exact position where you can now love and appreciate who you are.

You do this exercise and money just shows up. It does.

So, you think you should have been rich and famous, and making $1,000,000 a year? That may have been the fantasy you bought into. What is the benefit of not achieving that dream image of yourself?

You have to open up your resentment and take a good hard look at it. You have to open up all of your old wounds because no one else wants to. They want to sell you shallow happiness. I don't. I would rather train you to master your life than to have 30,000 people in an audience, just to keep you and them happy with empty promises.

When you do the exercises in this chapter, if you get to the point where it seems impossible and you feel you cannot finish, know this: You are choosing to play into the victimhood game. And that would be your choice. I will not coddle you for it. Instead, I would merely reply, "Go to work. Find the benefits. You can do it. I'm 100% certain of it." If you really do the work earnestly and diligently, then you can find the benefits of someone who did not pay you back $5,000.

Finding the benefits of a negative situation can seem quite difficult, at first, especially if you are locked into outside-in thinking. Blame, resentment, lack of forgiveness—these are hard habits to break. And the real work is in finding that empowering attitude which transforms you from someone who resents into someone who is grateful.

If someone has cheated you out of money, then quite likely you are stuck in the mode of attracting people who will cheat you out of money.

One student commented, "Yeah, I saw that shit ten years ago. I was like, damn I did it again."

I told her, "You're going to continue until you learn to love it. I'm trying to teach you to love it so that you can actually let it go. So, you're going to say, 'I hate that person, I never again want to work with someone like that.' Six months later, 'Oh, this person is just like that. Oh, man! I'm not working with them.' But then, the next person is just like that. That's why it's wise to say, 'What did I learn from each person?' This is so that you can attract and love them rather than push them away and keep attracting challenges into your life."

When you do the assignments, the objective is to get to the transformation layer. This is achieved by quantity of answers, peeling off one layer after another. As I said before, every individual is different, and the requested quantity is an approximation based on the average student. But the real objective is not to match that quantity—not if you want to move on from being challenged with money—but, instead, the objective is to get to the transformation which will send up flares within your physiology. You might get a tear in your eye, or a chill coming down the spine.

You do the work, here, and I promise you that you are going to walk out of this and say, "Holy cow! I feel so different. My physiology, my body, the lack of resentment." Everything is going to change. You are not just increasing your money with this activity; you are changing your entire life. By following this formula and doing the required work, you are rewiring the entire nervous system. Your physiology is going to change, your heartbeats are going to change, your blood pressure is going to change.

Whatever challenges you have—even diseases—will resolve by doing this work and by the resulting physiological changes.

You may get the extra $500 a month or $10,000 per month, but you are doing something far grander than that in doing these exercises.

A female student started one of my programs and confessed that she had lupus—an autoimmune disease. When we were done, she no longer had lupus.

If you want to see results, whether it is on a thyroid condition or an apparent money ceiling, the work that I provide you is transformative because your resentment is stopping you from keeping your physiology from functioning properly. If you want your blood pressure to come down, then stop being angry at the person who betrayed you.

If this were easy, everybody would have money. Everybody would be rich. The rabbit hole goes pretty damn deep in my world, but it brings you out to the other side, full of gratitude and wealth in the broadest sense of the word.

Assignments: Expectations

1. What image have you drawn out of your life? List all of it.
2. What is the drawback of having said image? (25)

CHAPTER 12

Ego vs. Value

As always, every student is different. They will have their own sequence of breakthroughs because of their unique set of experiences. Unpeeling this onion of confusion, as you do the work, could generate a great deal of clarity in your life. You will start to see how all of the experiences, behavior and beliefs are tied together.

One student shared these thoughts to describe what he was experiencing: "I'm allowing myself to delve within my deep-seated feelings and that oscillation which Dr. Trivedi talks about. I experienced that almost 24 hours a day because I am allowing myself to understand the fears versus the pride. All of those things are starting to come together and I feel good. ... I am getting to a place where all the external things are starting to make sense. It's almost like being reborn, you know. You're letting go of everything that you thought you knew, and like a sponge soaking up all of this energy."

Another student had this to say about her own breakthroughs: "I can't speak for everyone, so I'll just speak for myself. So, when you see the somber look on my face, it's because I'm having all these realizations. Dr. Trivedi is shaking up my entire world. I mean, it goes back for years. My career in Primerica kind of started me on the whole self-improvement kick. And I am having to unlearn a lot of that. One of the biggest things I've seen since, like yesterday, it was hard for me to go home. I was working so much! And I'm like, 'Where the heck is this coming from?' And this was so different—I want to say, even 'motivation.' It was definitely an inspiration, and I haven't felt that in years."

Still another student gained clarity from a mix of life experience and the benefits of this work: "So, my buddy had some health problems and had a GoFundMe about two weeks ago. Probably a week before he passed away. And the first thought I had was, 'You know? This guy's 65 years old, having health stuff, and he's trying to raise money just to live off of.' And I'm like, 'Man, there's no way I could do that. I can't! I refuse to let that happen.' And this was after the first week of doing this work. It was a big realization. And then we went through the exercise with the 100 drawbacks of staying where we are. And things are making me realize that any comfort that we may feel is a total delusion. So, we're going to his funeral tomorrow, and I think it's all going to keep hitting me—like, man, now is the time to get your stuff together."

This is a sobering realization for anyone to have and, sadly, many of my fellow chiropractors do not wake up to this reality until it is too late. The delusion of many chiropractors is that they think they are never going to need modern, mainstream medicine. That certainty remains constant until they are rudely awakened by a need for such medicine. And the big drawback is that they had not prepared for that possibility.

Chiropractors always talk about this healthy, abundant life. The truth is, most of them live a life based in fear. This is why they keep drinking themselves into stupors. And eat junk, and generally do not take care of themselves.

Some of my fellow doctors have told me, "I don't need medical insurance. I don't need to do any of that." Until they need it! That is the stupidest thing in our profession.

The seasons change and if winter is coming, then prepare for winter. We know that stress kills. We also know that the effects of stress are cumulative over time. And part of the reality of anyone dying poor is that they are burdened with the embarrassment of being where they are financially. Poverty, lack of preparation, worry—these add to the deadly levels of stress.

And if an individual sees more benefits in dying than staying alive, he is, more likely, going to die.

One young man with a wife and infant son had found himself doing his assignment a little before midnight and had misread the instructions, so had not yet turned in his assignment. "The first one was good—100 benefits of mastering managing your money. I came up with a lot of good stuff. The second one was really intense for me. I didn't do the 30 benefits of each event. But what I did—and I can add more to that—I went through all of my records from the past decade or so and found probably 100 traumatic events, including business and finance. Some of these I had barely even remembered. It was very intense—very emotional. And I put at least one benefit next to each one of those. At one point, I hit a massive breakthrough where it all made sense. I realized that everything that had happened over the past ten to 15 years happened for a few different reasons. At least this was my conclusion by doing the exercise. And it was actually like a spiritual awakening. I ended up in Los Angeles. One of my business partners at the time was in town and so I got connected with a Rabbi there. That was a huge turning point in my 10-year learning period. I really feel like that was the purpose of all of this stuff that I went through. Where I'm at right now, with my wife and child, I feel like all of the trauma that I've gone through is for those two purposes. And I basically fell to my knees and was crying when I realized that."

It is great that he was able to see that, and to become humbled to the universe because the universe is trying to teach each of us the lessons we need to learn. And it was also gratifying that he got to experience love and gratitude through the work. That is what this work is all about.

Remember: Gratitude is a gateway to income. If you don't have gratitude for your life, you cannot have money for your life. This is just how it works. With these lessons, you can create a gateway for more into your world.

You do not need to put the money resentment events of your life in chronological order. Instead, start with the biggest one—the event with the greatest impact. Start with the biggest ones and work your way down toward the little ones. This gives you the biggest benefit right up front and makes handling the remainder a little easier.

Suffering and Self-Image

Too often people will wallow in their hurt—their suffering. Take for instance cheating in a relationship. Women are more likely to create a support group in order to suffer together. This is an inverted form of compassion—something we might call "sympathy." Interestingly, guys would likely never create such a group. Instead, they are more likely to say, "Let's go to a strip club and hang out and meet a bunch of other women." That is how guys move on. I am being gender specific in this because I'm just trying to give you a different parallel. But when your wound has not been loved and cleared—which is what I'm trying to teach you here—you keep attracting it in different areas of your life.

Many of my students will tell me their stories and I will have zero compassion or sympathy for it because I am not interested in suffering with them. Instead, I am interested in transforming them.

And while some students share stories of betrayal and such, others reveal feelings of guilt over their own pride of ownership. Last year, a friend of mine made $1.7 million. I told him that he is likely going to pay something like $500,000 in taxes and I recommended that he talk to an accountant and an attorney who specialize in tax matters. But then he told me about going to a mall in Florida where he spent $4,500 on a vest. Imagine that! This is how he is spending his money. And that's cool. Easy come; easy go.

The reason anyone feels guilt is because they do not have a true appreciation and love for who they are.

When you do not have love and appreciation for yourself, you do not want to have the best things in life. You feel guilty because of that. You find yourself saying, "I don't deserve that."

Before I learned these lessons, and I did not know how to make money, I had all this guilt and shame. Because of those hidden, dark feelings, I would not buy Gillette Fusion razor blades. They were expensive—$50 for a supply which might last me four or five months. At Costco, I could get disposable razor blades for like, $2.99. I would not buy a nice razor blade and every time I shaved, I would cut myself.

After clearing my own guilt and shame, I bought Gillette razor blades—the Fusion razor blades. It may sound ridiculous, but it was a huge win for me. Just to simply say, I no longer have the shame. I deserve to have the best shave I can get. It sounds so small, but when you are in the hole these types of victories are what help wake you up to realize you are starting to value yourself. It is not that the boats, cars, and yachts that make you say you love yourself; it is what you can do on a day-to-day basis.

There are a couple of ways we can look at pride. There is the pride of ego, and then there is the pride of value.

When you have self-love, self-pride and self-appreciation, you want to experience all that life has to offer. But you do this in fair exchange—loving yourself, knowing that you can do it in a state where you are loving who you are. This is because you provided value and service, and you appreciate who you are on the inside. So, there is pride from appreciation, but there is also pride from ego.

Breaking Past the Inertia of the Story

We each tell ourselves a story. This is our current reality. This is why we are at where we currently exist. It is just a story and we can rewrite that story.

One student told me her story about growing up in a single wide trailer park home. None of her family ever had much money—her brother, her Dad, her stepdad. Her husband grew up in a farmhouse and currently her husband, her two daughters and she live in a very similar house, minus the land. So, they are not currently rich. Doing the exercises, she kept running into the question, "Who am I to deserve that?"

I asked her about the size of the house in which she currently lives. She replied that it is about four times the size of the trailer in which she grew up.

Then, I told her that my kids were in India last week, and I told her that they were taking pictures of monkeys. And they were sending me pictures of monkeys. Then I asked her, "Ever see monkeys roaming around in the trailer parks and stuff like that?"

She replied, "I just wonder, compared to my family and my friends that I grew up with, how do I deserve…"

I interrupted her, "You are serious. As smart as you are, you really don't know?"

And she showed me a picture. "This is a reindeer. I'm turned into a little kid and I just curled up in a corner all right. But they're called Caribou in Canada, no frigging idea. So, go ahead. You were telling me about trailer parks and a monkey in a house."

By now, she is starting to become confused.

I replied, "Oh, but now, what's your story? I don't understand. You told me this story that you grew up this way, then you lived in mobile homes that could show up in an Indian zoo. Like, what was this? I'm totally lost now. You got to really tell me this whole frigging thing again because I'm lost. I'm confused."

"No," she replied, "it doesn't really matter."

"Oh," I said, "So, who does not deserve wealth?"

"What everybody else is doing," she said, "shouldn't affect what I'm doing."

"So, I have a different question for you: Who are your girls not to deserve wealth? Bam, that's right across the kisser."

"Yeah," she replied, "because if I don't create it for myself, they won't have it."

"But you had this story of a monkey and a reindeer in a trailer park with four mobile places. So, if I ask you what's the story, now? You see monkeys and reindeer, don't you?"

She laughed. "Yeah, we have some reindeer in the backyard."

What I had done was interrupt her story. I had gotten her to change her story. This used the Neuro-Linguistic Programming, or NLP, technique. The work you are doing in this program is not NLP; I merely use that technique on occasion when it is required to help someone interrupt their story.

Now, she needs to look at the benefits of growing up in a trailer park. Rap star Eminem did it. In fact, he made his money off of telling others how he grew up in a trailer park.

Assignments: Ego vs. Value

1. Write out 50 ways your pride has prevented you from making money.
2. Write out 50 ways you have provided value to other people.

CHAPTER 13

Managing Emotions

Finding the Right Mindset

Very few things in life stir up emotions quite like money. Because of this, we need to be able to manage our emotions, otherwise we become stuck in chaos. In this chapter, we will learn a great deal from student questions and confusion. Pay close attention to the details of how each point of confusion is resolved.

We start with a mother of four: "Okay. This is for assignment #3. I was a little confused about the last question where it says, if you were wealthy, like you want to be now, what would be the drawbacks to you? When I started it, I found myself writing things like, well, if I'm where I wanted to be, then the thoughts that I have right now, they are not going to be the same. I found that I had to change in order to answer that question, and then I just couldn't answer it anymore."

"So, let me ask you. If you were wealthy, how much money did you want to make? What did you want? When you think—I don't know how old you are—whatever, you say, 'I want to have this much money'."

"The goal was $20 million."

"Okay, $20 million. If you had $20 million in the bank right now, what would be the drawback to your life?"

"That—I don't know how to answer that. The stuff that I was—"

"No, no, no. Please answer my question."

"I don't know what the drawback would be."

"That's fine. That's why you're stuck."

"Oh."

"Are you married? You have kids?"

"I do. I have four kids. Married. My two older kids are in college."

"What has not having $20 million been able to teach them?"

"Oh, I see what you're asking me. I guess to show that I'm actually managing it well. Is that what I'm supposed to be doing?"

"I just want you to answer the question, please."

"To pay for my kids to go to college, that would have been done. Not having it, I haven't been able to do it. My daughter's going into the military so she can pay for school."

I asked, "She wouldn't have been in the military?"

"She probably wouldn't have gone that route. No."

"What's another benefit of not having $20 million?"

"Well, alright," she replied with hesitation. "How is it a benefit of not? I'm sorry. It sounds positive and then negative at the same time."

"Okay," I said firmly. "If you had $20 million, there are two questions I'm asking, trying to get you to realize it. I'll just go back to the first question. If you had $20 million, what else would be a drawback to it? You wouldn't have been able to teach them how to manage money effectively? Would you have been as resourceful in your life?"

"Say that again."

"Would you have been as resourceful as you are in life?"

"I would have if I was able to accomplish that. Yes."

"You would, or would not have?"

"Huh?"

I repeated the question: "You would have, or would not have?"

"I would have, if I had accomplished that. That would have meant that I would have been able to manage it well to get to that point."

"Eventually," I replied. I knew at this point that I needed to approach this from a different direction. "Let's say that you just got $20 million—gift, inheritance, whatever. The fact that you didn't, is the question. The fact that you didn't have $20 million, what did it make you do? What did you gain in that? Did you gain a closer relationship with your kids because you had to work together as a family unit to become more frugal in certain things?"

"Grew up that way," she said. "It was more of a habit."

"But did you get to do that with your kids and teach them that as well?"

"Yes. I did that with them as well."

"And how is that going to benefit their lives? Is that going to teach them the value of money if they want to create it for themselves?"

"To be more frugal?" she asked. "Yes. I believe so."

"If they become more frugal, are they going to be able to manage it better?"

"Yes."

"Is that going to lead them to be able to create more ability to invest and do things more effectively so they're not emotionally chaotic about money?"

"Right," she replied. "But those are positives. They don't sound like drawbacks."

"I didn't say that. I'm saying they're benefits that you got from *not* having it."

"Gotcha. Okay. Oh!" Her face brightened. "Okay. Now, I'm understanding."

"It's the same question. I'm just asking it in a different way. If you had it, what would have been the drawback? You wouldn't have gotten to do all these things if you had $20 million." I paused for a moment. "What do you do now for a living?"

"Financial services."

"Are you doing Primerica? Are you in Primerica?"

"Yes, and I'm a real estate agent."

"Okay, fantastic. Do you think you'd be able to serve your clients the way that you do?" I paused again and then offered an answer. "No, because you wouldn't be serving your clients; you'd be sitting on a beach in Tahiti and drinking cocktails like everyone in Primerica wants to do. I just want financial freedom so I can sit on the beach."

"No," she replied. "I'm going to go in a little different direction, but I hear what you're saying. Yes."

"But would you be in Primerica? Would you still be working if you had $20 million?"

"I believe I would still be working. I have a dream of building a school for little kids, and it's something that's continuous. So, yeah. I would still be working. But would I still be in Primerica? That, I do not know. I would probably do many different things. A lot of different things."

"What would have been the drawback of that if you're not in Primerica? Would you have the same relationships that you have right now?"

"Maybe as far as soul relationships, yes, but as far as the same type of people, maybe not. As far as the same type of relationships, yes because I value my relationships with individuals. It doesn't matter what they're doing. It's more so how we would help and support one another from the inside out, so the relationships, I believe, would be there. I used to be in the fitness industry and law enforcement and the military, all of those relationships, to me, are very valuable, so it doesn't matter what they're doing. It still exists."

"We've spoken before, haven't we?"

"I was having trouble deciding if I wanted to go the Primerica route. I think we talked about that."

"Yeah. The question becomes, what would be the drawback if you had $20 million? What else would be a drawback to you? Do you think you'd be as inspired as you are today? Here's what I can tell you. I'm not saying this is an absolute. Most of the time it's not. Most of the time people are not as inspired to go do something when they have money. Because you may have a mission, but here is also something that I do know, and I remember our conversation as well. If you are inspired by your mission, you don't have a challenge with money. I'm not saying you do. I don't know that. I'm just saying that if you are inspired in what you do, you master money automatically because what you want to do and create is more important."

"I understand and that helps," she said. "Now I have to change all ten of what I've already written on the assignment, but it's all good. Thank you."

As you can see from this discussion, some people find the concepts—the mindset—counterintuitive. It takes some struggle to find the right viewpoint. And that journey to learning requires humility—a willingness to let go of old ideas.

Stuck in Resentment

One female student was needlessly struggling with an exercise. The real reason was a little deeper than the obvious.

"So, in doing the traumatic event, I'm seeing some commonality across all the events. This seems like too much because like Brett did 100 and I'm like, 100 and then 30 for each one, and I'm like—this shit is depressing. I'm not sure." She paused for a moment. "Okay. The question is in order for this assignment to work and for us to see the value in doing it, how many traumatic events should we be putting down before the transformation kicks in? Because I'm like 100 and then 30 for each one? Because a lot of the benefits are like repeats. I don't know if they're going to count toward the total I'm supposed to do."

"You don't need to do 100 as Brett did. Brett just wants to be an overachiever."

"Okay."

"You can go through your brain and find out what the key trauma is. Brett wants to do this because he wants money. He's addicted to money, which is his infatuation. And this is why he's going through all this chaos with money. So, he's got to go through all of these and realize all the chaos he keeps bringing. He still has to realize the drawbacks of money. Once he brings the infatuation and the addiction to money down, he'll see what he's doing. But he wants money and he's trying to find everything that is in the way in order to get it, which is great. I'm not judging. Hey look, the more you clear out, the better you're going to be. I'm not saying it's good or bad. I am simply challenging the notion that you don't have to do 100. He's going to be doing a lot of work on it. That's cool. If he wants to get the most out of this course, that's fantastic. Good for him. But you don't have to. You can do the big ones which come to mind."

"Okay. When you say 'big ones,' are those the ones where you lost the most money?"

"Whatever you consider to be the 'big ones.' Did you notice that specifically I never said how many? There is a reason why I didn't say how many. Because for someone, it could be one that could be so freaking huge that it could stop their life. For others, it could be five. When I went through this exercise, right off the top of my head, I could think of probably four or five big ones—my divorce, the lawsuits, when I first got into practice, the practice closing down. Okay? And I've worked through all of that. But those are the big ones. Like when I was a genius in 2008, and I perceived that I'd 'lost' in the stock market. There is no real, exact number. I'm going to guess for most of you it's probably in the seven to ten range."

"So, the last question. One of the reoccurring things for me as far as traumatic events, under the category of me like supporting someone else, one of the traumatic ones for me was I supported an ex-boyfriend in his journey to RVP. I was like—" She hesitated.

"And then he left you hanging alone."

"Yeah."

"Let's create a support group around today's discussion."

"No!" she said emphatically. "I don't want a support group. I'm just like, why do I keep repeating the same self-abuse? What about my childhood or where do I go to search that I keep supporting people and then they like—boom—blow up or their business takes off and I'm like, I helped them when it was grassroots, when it was nothing, whether it was financial support, or just physical support of one of the workers or whatever and just volunteers or anything, I'm like, I have supported so many people in different situations, lost money, time, or whatever, and I'm like, why can't I just throw that energy into myself? It's so weird that I can jump on anybody else's assignment and help them win, but I'm not winning for me."

"So, what's your question?"

"I'm trying to figure out where that comes from?"

"Well, it comes from a lack of self-worth because you value someone else. What you realize is you're going to make a decision for which you see more benefits than drawbacks. You obviously saw more benefits in helping him because you thought you would get more gains in that process. And so, you trusted. You were addicted to a potential outcome and you thought that you were going to get more in that benefit, and you were addicted to the outcome of it. So, you gave of yourself, thinking it was going to be one thing, but now that sonofabitch left you. He got what he wanted, and you got what you wanted. But now you have to resent it. It's part of the cycle. Why you keep doing that is because you keep valuing other people and other things rather than loving yourself. When you learn to love yourself, you keep yourself in fair exchange. Why you keep doing that is because you're repeating the same pattern of trying to do something.

"Okay," I said, pausing for a moment. "Now, I'm going to say something you're not going to like. The delusion is that you think that you're doing it for them. The truth is that you were also getting benefits. That is why this exercise is crucially important. What were your benefits? When you see it, it's like, 'Oh, yeah. I did get some good stuff out of that damn thing.'

"How long were you dating this guy—this RVP gentleman?"

"Nine months."

"In nine months, you took him from nothing to RVP?"

"In nine months, I was very crucial in him going. Yes."

"Would he say that, or do you say that?"

"He would say the same."

"Okay. So, what was the benefit to you of helping him?"

"I saw another part of the business because I had made his activity more than mine. I just saw more, dealt with more. That's about it. I'm like, I'm trying not to be negative about it, but I'm really working on it."

"What's the benefit? Just answer the question. But don't worry. I got you. Do you see how difficult it is for you to find the benefit of it?"

"Uh-huh."

"Which is why you're stuck. Remember, I said way back, unless you can manage both sides of something, you can't manage it correctly. Management is the ability to manage and govern yourself and manage the emotions around something. If you can't manage this event, how do you think you're able to manage money, because money is made of events? This is what Warren Buffet was trying to say—the wealthiest guy on the planet, or at least one of them. So, what's another benefit?"

"Actually, I'm thinking stuff."

"Okay. Did you get to go to meetings with him?"

"I did."

"Did you get to go and join in the meetings and have fun with it?"

"Yeah. I was privy to information that other people didn't have."

"Really. So, you got more insight and information. Are you still in Primerica?"

"Yeah."

"So, you also understand how—if you really wanted to—you understand how to build the business. Or are you too busy resenting this bastard?"

"Yeah. That resentment is strong."

"What's another benefit that you got out of the relationship? Did you guys have some sex?"

"Yeah. Was that really a benefit though?"

"Obviously, you got benefits in doing that, right?"

"Yeah, but I'm just trying to stick to the business."

"No, no, no. Your benefits are not going to always be in the same place. Your life is holistic. If you only try to find it in Primerica, you won't see it. The relationship itself—you got benefits in staying in that relationship, not just building his business. You guys came home together, you cooked together, you watched movies together, you did all these things that you believed to be powerful which benefited and served your values in the relationship, which is why you stayed there because the relationship was of a higher value to you than Primerica was. Does that make sense?"

"Yeah."

"So, you're denying yourself the relationship which is the real part you stayed with. You didn't do it to build Primerica. You did it to build a relationship."

"Yeah. I was trying to be a great partner."

"Thank you. That's why I went to sex because I knew the extreme part that you wouldn't want me to talk about in public, so I went to it first. You were trying to be a great partner. A great partner means that you have to give away your whole soul and everything in your life and now you've become awakened. This fucker came along and taught you the delusion of putting yourself in someone else's life and to start to empower your own life. Is that right?"

"Yeah."

"Does that help you now realize that in future relationships you're going to keep a little bit of distance, but at the same time, stay in it and love yourself in the process of loving the relationship and not to give all of yourself away?"

"Yes. I'm working on giving less of myself."

"Interesting. He's teaching you to love yourself and for you to love who you are, so you don't go through this process of giving yourself away again. Is that right?"

"Yeah."

"Has that helped you understand who you are and taken you on a journey of self-development for yourself?"

"I'm trying to understand this part of me that always is like a doer and so if I come to any situation, I'm hands on. You don't even have to ask. I'm like, when I'm not that person because I'm holding back, trying to learn from past situations, I feel like I'm not being myself."

"Sure. Has it taken you into the journey of learning who you are and introspective questions to understand who you are?"

"I'm still trying to understand that because I'm like, if you take away everything I've always done, I'm always known for being a doer."

"Has it taken you on a journey to ask yourself and learn who you are? You are in this course to learn who you are, aren't you?"

"Yeah."

"So, it's gained you spiritual insight to understand yourself and knowledge of the self?"

"Painfully, yes."

"I didn't say it was pleasure for you. So, has that given you the ability to learn who you are? How is that going to benefit your kids? You have four kids, right?"

"I have six siblings that I care for."

"Six siblings. That's right. How's that going to help them, when you get to learn yourself and become who you are in this process, how is that going to help these six siblings that you have the responsibility to raise?"

"Helping them to become more self-aware and not falling into market falls. Not being another repeat of me."

"So, they get to learn and stand up on their own two feet because of this?"

"Yeah."

"And if he stayed with you and took you into Primerica and made you an RVP, what would have been the drawback to your life? You would have thought life was easy, that it would have been perfect, and you would have given away your soul in the process?"

"No," she replied. "Being his partner wouldn't have. ... An RVP partner wouldn't have made it perfect. There are still challenges at that level, seriously."

"So, what would have been the drawback?"

"At that level, even more of myself, even more. They say you can't give more than 100%. It would feel like giving 200%."

"Which would lead you into your own chaos. This is what I'm saying. I'm just taking you five steps down the line of a relationship. When you keep giving more of yourself, as you were doing, and weren't taking care of yourself, would that have led to more chaos in the relationship?"

"Yeah."

"Of course, it would. And would that mean, just because he became RVP, that you have been enthralled and loving of your life because of it?"

"Nope."

"But the kids learn how to love who they are and to understand this journey of really appreciating their life."

"I'm trying to understand."

"If you didn't get to learn who you are, do you think the kids would learn who they are?"

"No."

"If you were a Primerica RVP with this guy, everything would be a fantasy. It would seem wonderful, and everything would seem fantastic, but you would be one rude awakening away from a reality check. Do you think the kids would like it more living in delusion or in reality of how life really works?"

"For the delusion, they are so pissed at me. 'Why didn't you just stay with him?'"

"So you further the delusion for them?"

"Yes."

"And isn't that the responsibility that your mother put in your lap when she passed, to take care of them, to teach them how life really works, to be their mother from here forward?"

"Well," she said, "the sad part is she didn't think that I was going to be the person to get them. The person she thought would get them, didn't, and then I stepped up to the plate."

"Oh, interesting. So you decided to step up to the plate and take responsibility and learn who you are so you could teach everyone else."

"Having them has forced me to know more about who I am because children are brutally honest and they will remind you of your shit faster than anything, like how are you going to tell me what to do when you just did it? So, you know, I'm like damn, trying to be an example."

"So, do you think if you hadn't gone through that, do you think these kids would be able to learn who they are so they can grow up to be the individuals that you really are inspired to take them because they're your #1 value? It always has been. Being a mother is your #1 value. I remember our earlier conversation very distinctly. Now, does that make sense?"

"Yeah."

"Can you thank the sonofabitch for leaving you so you can actually be a Mom and teach these kids how to really be real?"

She shook her head. "Thank him?"

"Yeah," I replied in a matter-of-fact tone.

"Not today."

"Do the work and you will. If you can't say thank you to him—I'm telling you this—if you can't say thank you to him, you have more work to do."

"I know. I know I have more work."

"And that's fine. You can go do it. That's fine. I get it. But until you have gratitude and true love for all the shit that you've gone through, you can't move past it. People will tell me intellectually, 'I get it. I understand it. I believe it. I trust you.' No. That's not it. Until you say, 'Thank you for breaking up with me, and teaching me my life,' you don't have it. Because if you own it just intellectually, it will still run your neurology. If you can say, 'Thank you,' like Brett did, humbled to his knees, that's what I'm talking about. That's what I'm saying. Sound good?"

"Yep."

Gratitude for evil done to you is not easy. For most people, it is near impossible to understand. But once you get it, you will gain a freedom few people have ever known.

Resentment Fueled by Addiction

Sometimes I have to knock a student off of their pedestal of comfortable addiction. I never do this to be mean or to be a jerk. I do it to trigger a realization or transformation.

"When I was doing the last homework, I realized I was looking for happiness in the business that I'm doing, and it was causing me to resent the living shit out of it, like I hated it, and at the same time, I also realized there were so many other areas of my life where that was popping up. It's why I got so pissed off. I didn't want to go do it anymore. I actually wanted to distance myself and do it a lot less, almost dissociate myself from it in a way. Does that make sense—the idea that I would want to do it less—to say, 'Leave it the hell alone. But why? I guess I want to know."

"Why what?"

"Why do I want to do it less? Do I need to do more to be inspired to go do it?"

"Your addiction to it is what's causing you to resent it."

"Right."

I said, "Just stop being addicted to it. Find the drawbacks of it so you don't have to be addicted to it. Govern yourself. Master your own mind. Don't let someone else from the outside matter. If you don't master and govern your own mind, someone from the outside is going to come govern you and master you. So, find the drawbacks in it yourself. Until you see the downsides of whatever it is you do, you're going to remain addicted to it. And most people are addicted."

"You're the complete opposite, right?" I asked. "You want to do your thing so badly that you can't see the challenges which the world is giving to you all day long. Your anxiety is your feedback to say, 'Wake up! Stop and be balanced with this.'

"All of my students came into this program saying something like, 'Oh, my God! This will be amazing! This will be the greatest course ever.' Have I fucking deluded you, yet? Have I destroyed that perception? Shattered that idea? The more deluded you were, the less work you've done. I know that. But those of you who are doing it, are you starting to see gratitude improve for the work? Are you starting to see some gratitude for yourself?

"Are you starting to see gratitude for me? Not, 'Oh, my God! Here's Dr. Trivedi,' but fuck, okay, why does this guy swear so fucking much? Because

I take whatever it is and make things real. So, when you look at the life to which you are so addicted—'I've got to do this. I've got to do this. I've got to do this.' And this is the greatest fucking thing ever, all right. I knew this with you two years ago, kid.

"So, what's the downside? What's the downside to the customer of you hawking your services? You might say, 'What? Downside? But everything's positive all the time.' Let me ask again: What's the downside of you doing this business?

"Because there are no positives or negatives—no highs or lows—there is nothing. It just is. Until you break the addictions to what it is you think you want, you will never get it. If you're going to keep saying, 'I want to see more positives in this business,' whatever you do, you're going to see more positives, until you get inspired and you see both positives and negatives.

"I work my ass off, believe it or not. It's not just easy, sitting here doing this. I work my fucking tail off. It's got highs. It's got lows. It's got challenges. Would I do anything else? No. I wouldn't because I love it. I love the highs and the lows. If you only see the highs in a situation, and you can't manage the lows, you're deluded. You're deluded. If you only see the lows, and not the highs, you're deluded. You can't govern something when you see only one or the other. This is the same thing when we're talking about money. It's the same conversation that we had the Tuesday before in Module 2. If you can't govern an area, it governs you. If it governs you, it runs your life.

"Just like this other student was talking about. This guy that she's talking about runs her life. She was infatuated. She was addicted to this relationship. Now that she's been taught the lessons because she over-gave of herself—because she was addicted to it—she is now taught the hardships of it. It's just the mechanism of homeostasis and balance, not only in your body and your mind, but in life in general.

"If you're so addicted to your company and what you're doing, you're going to fall flat on your face with it. That's why, if you remember, two years ago I said don't tell people coming into your world that it's going to be only good.

"I tell everybody that comes into my world the truth—that this is going to be a lot of fucking work. I didn't come in positive, excited, or happy. I said, 'Let's get to work.'

"There is a reason you guys came in like this. I went fucking right here, right off the top because wherever you were, I was going to bring you back down to reality, out of your delusion.

"Another thing. The more you resent what you're currently doing, the further the other thing is going to get away from you."

"Yeah," he replied. "I noticed that."

"Again, look, it's not easy. I know that I'm totally shattering what most of your belief systems are and everything you've been taught. I get it. All these people that you've been looking up to in your world who have all been preaching happiness and sunshine, and here's this crazy Indian doctor showing you hard work and transformation.

"However, here is my argument. Do my work and tell me you don't see massive transformation right away. Compare that to reading books, still reading books, going to seminars and sitting under a tree contemplating your navel. Do my work. See if you experience the transformation. See if you get a complete transformational change in how you feel and what's going on in your life. If you do that, cool. That's why people come to my work.

"There is a lady who emailed me at the end of December. She came to the Creation seminar. She created her map for the upcoming year. She said, 'I wrote down 30 things, and 20 of them have already happened in 15 days.' When you understand it and get it, you don't have to circle around the chaos of trying to fight your way through life. I don't think you need to do that. Trying to be positive is only going to lead you to be more negative. Cut it out. Be real. Be authentic. Be a human being. Because you're not always positive. Here is what's going to happen. The more positive you are to the outside world, the more negative you're going to be to your girlfriend, husband, wife, parents, kids, all of that stuff. You're going to yell at them, snap at them. They don't deserve that shit. Be authentic. Snap at them when you need to snap at them, but love them when you need to. I'm probably really nice to my kids because they'd probably kick the shit out of my clients. There is probably some truth to them.

"The more you try and project to the world that you're one way, the more nature tries to find balance by giving you the opposite way. As soon as your public world goes one way, your private world goes the other way. That's what I'm trying to teach you guys.

"What many of you see is a Facebook world. What you see is not always what's real 100% of the time. What's going on outside is not what's going on inside. It's going to be contrary and the opposite.

"That's why I can predict most of your lives when you tell me about this one thing. Okay, let's go inside and find out what's going on. That's why I can't be all bubbly, cheery, happy. It's the same thing. I'm the messenger, but that's reality. What I'm trying to tell you is to start being real to yourself. Start loving yourself for who you are, not because you can make billions of dollars, but so you can actually live and breathe, look at this anxiety and look at yourself in the mirror and say, 'Hey, man, I'm a cool dude if I make billions or if I make $50,000. I'm just a human being; I'm good either way.' Because it's not the billions that are going to make you successful. It's you becoming you that's going to make you successful. Does that make sense?"

"Yep."

"I did it for years, trying to be somebody else—trying to be all these personal development gurus, trying to be all these other leaders in my profession. And the more I did that, the more I hated my life. The more I got away from who I really am, the more chaos I brought into my marriage, into my home and into the lives of my kids, my parents, my friends and my brother.

"I'm telling you this, trying to make all this real to you. And now I'm waiting on a call with Mike. He's going to yell at me and holy shit, we've got to get to work.

"And let me share this with you: My brother told me when I was 30, 'Dude, you've got to calm down that ego a little bit.' I didn't listen to him. I didn't understand what he was trying to tell me. Does that make sense? And so when I got it, I had to let the universe teach it to me, and I'm trying to save you that headache so that you can actually just be in your own skin and govern yourself. Make sense?"

Assignments: Managing Emotions

1. Write 100 BENEFITS to mastering the management of money.

2. Find the stories in your life about money that you resent (i.e. an actual event, a trauma, bankruptcy, lost money, loaned someone money, fired, divorce, investing, stock market, your job, stolen money, bad business deal, etc.). Then write 30 BENEFITS for each event.

3. Take any experience you perceive as a negative judgment around money. Then write 30 benefits to that event. (Judgment example: my Mom is cheap.)

4. If you were as wealthy as you thought you wanted to be by now, what would be 30 DRAWBACKS to you?

CHAPTER 14

Fantasy vs. Reality

One of the big rewards for me is knowing that I have helped a student through a powerful transformation. Here is how one student described her own breakthrough: "I wanted to share the last call that I was on. I did an exercise with Dr. Trivedi and was able to clear some resentment with my husband. Over the weekend, I was looking at our finances and found some things on a credit card statement that I didn't know were there. I saw that my husband had done it and it was kind of interesting because I wasn't upset. I wasn't angry. For the first time, I was able to look at it from the perspective of, 'All right. No worries. We'll clear this up, and get this taken care of.'

"Before, I would have been really angry and really resentful, and so I handled it completely differently. And even just how I'm communicating with him has been completely different. Just more patience, more understanding. It was pretty awesome. I'm surprised and I'm so proud of myself because I didn't feel that resentment. I was just pretty calm in the process. So, I thought that was a great win."

Another student told me, "Okay, so I've always had a problem struggling with my finances. I've had a few things that came up in the past couple of weeks that I actually feel better about how I approached them. When things were coming up, I found different avenues than what I would normally do to take care of them. I'm actually in a really good spot right now. I'm feeling much better. That's amazing for me because normally I'd probably be curled up crying in a corner right now."

Still another student attempted to share what he thought were breakthroughs. In a way, they were, but they also revealed a barrier. He said, "For me, I think I've really realized that I'm actually not as horrible with finances as I've always thought I was. I've kind of stumbled into this default, sort of like doubt that I have about really everything. I have a default doubt. I think that stems from just having these addictions to how things are supposed to be—how I am supposed to be. And so, every aspect of my life— because I happen to be a part of it—there's just this doubt. Going through all the different exercises and seeing that my life has progressively always improved financially, things really aren't so bad. It's been really kind of cool. I have a little star and a statement saying triple-D—done with default doubt. I think that's my new motto."

I attempted to clarify my own points.

He asked, "Are you doubting what I'm trying to say?"

"Exactly," I replied.

"I think I always think that I'm supposed to be something that I can't be," he replied. "I mean I don't really know what other word to use. But I always have sort of a doubt that I'll be able to achieve it. I can apply it to anything, really. I can apply it to singing. I can apply it to tennis. There's always this backdrop of that I'm not going to be able to be what I need to be to make it all work. I can't win a tournament because I can't be something I'm not."

"Okay," I replied, "But doubt assumes that you're not going to be something outside of you. It presupposes that you have to be something other than you."

"Right."

"As soon as you become anything other than you, you're comparing who you are by an expectation of someone else. The question that I ask you is this: Who are you subordinating to?"

"I think," he replied, "it's to the expectations of my family when I was young... if that's answering your question. I think that I was a broken child. I was the child that didn't meet the expectation of family. And so, no matter what I did, I couldn't be that, and I tried and tried and tried. And there was always a question."

"Who specifically were you looking for?"

"Well, the earliest memory that I have that something was wrong with me was from my uncle. Oddly enough, I posted a picture of him on my Facebook page today. But you know, in the early 70s, I was a little kid and I remember him telling my Mom that something was wrong with me and they had to fix me."

"And what was wrong?"

"Everything started there. I wasn't like my brothers. I'm not even 100% certain what the complaint was at that age, but it slowly became about my sexuality. It slowly became about not being one of the boys, basically."

"Sure," I replied, "And the reason I'm asking you this is because I suspect that a lot of that has to do with it."

"Oh, I think everything does."

"As soon as you try to become something other than yourself, you can never match into that because now you are subordinating your life to some other expectation of someone else and you always feel a sense of remorse and guilt toward who you are. And what that does is it forces you to give money away."

"I agree," he said. "I agree and I see that. I'm very generous so when I have money, everyone around me is going to have money because I'm going to just buy drinks and everything."

"I don't want you to do that. I don't want you to buy everyone everything. I want you to let them earn it. I want you to take care of you."

Because of this conversation, I had my staff arrange a one-on-one call with the student to explore this area more deeply. And we broke past the "triple-D," as he called it. The transformation allowed him to let go of the expectations of others and allowed him to live in his own reality instead of their fantasy.

The more we break those down—those internal expectations—things are going to change even more.

One lady had mixed feelings, but in a good way. "I'm in Module 3. That has really brought out a lot of emotion, a lot of anger, and realization at the same time. I'm only part way through some of the things that you asked us to do—the 30 of all the different money issues I have. I went through the first 30 and my body hurt. So, this morning I was cursing at you about that. I was just like—oh my God—this hurts!... But I love it at the same time. So, I love you at the same time because I'm feeling the freedom starting to come out of it as well. Thank you! My celebration is just that I'm working through it and it feels good."

This stuff is supposed to hurt, but then you burn through it. Your entire physiology—the knots, the tension, the anger—all this stuff should have melted in your body as you have gone through the most recent work. If not, then you have not gone through the work all the way. I can tell you that for sure.

The work is going to bring up all this anger and resentment, and you are going to find your blood pressure is going to boil. You are going to get hot and angry, and then you will start finding the benefits.

I have had students call me an "asshole" or the "devil." But now, once you do the work, you release that energy. You release that anger.

You do not have to achieve that release. You can hold onto the tension and the anger, and you can have a hard time with money. Hold onto that emotion and that challenge, or you can let it go.

What I am trying to show you is a science to let it go. You do not have to sit and meditate 14 times a day, and then realize that you are still stuck with the anger. I know about meditation; I'm Indian, and I have been doing the meditation thing since I was a kid.

Another student shared with us her own release of guilt.

"My celebration is actually not for me, but for my Mom because one of the things I felt guilty for was how when I was in college, she would just give me money to pay my sorority dues. She would give me money for rent— money that I know that could have gone toward something else because my parents had recently gotten divorced. She was a single Mom, working, going to college full time. But then I realized that the benefit to her was that she was able to be the Mom to me that she never got from her Mom. Her Mom, my grandmother, was schizophrenic growing up throughout my Mom's life until she became medicated when my Mom was probably in her 30s. Then finally she had a Mom. But she never had someone who was supportive. My grandpa was always the supportive one in her family. I was able to give that to her by accepting that money that she would give to me to help me pay for things and to help me to get through college.... I don't have that guilt anymore."

One student, a businesswoman, was having difficulty with a prior lesson. "I have actually been going fast. I feel like I needed to. Like, I got stuck on the previous lesson. I think I was stuck on that lesson. I don't know if I'm the only one. Maybe it's the perfectionist in me. That is stifling. I don't really have a question about this lesson because I'm still stuck.... I think it's just brought up a lot with me and with my business. I'm kind of overwhelmed."

This type of thing happens because the work—the assignments or exercises—bring the reality to the surface. The students come to realize that they had been hiding in reality—living in a masked world. I come along, and get you to do this work, opening up reality for you. And reality hurts sometimes. The truth is, it stings because it seems better to live in a fantasy. It is better to live in this land where everything feels good. This also leaves you disempowered and chaotic.

You can continue to live there, but I am trying to give you a path to a place where you can empower your life. I never said it was going to be easy. I did not say it was going to be fun.

What the work does is, it opens you up to reality so that you can make money.

Even though students are running into discomfort, many of them also notice new money showing up in their lives—random stuff. Someone may buy you dinner. You may get new business. New customers are coming in that were not coming in before. Random things, like financial opportunities, are coming up. If you are doing the work, they are showing up in your life. I have lost count of the times a student could not show up for a scheduled lesson or meeting with me because of job interviews or meetings with new business clients. Me, get angry that the lessons are working? Not at all! I remained thrilled by the levels of success.

Many of my students come in pairs—life partners or a parent and young adult child. One man—husband of the woman who had cleared her guilt from her college days—had his own breakthrough.

"I've always had in my mind," he told me, "what I thought my life should look like, you know—whether it be financially or defining success. This stuff kind of wiped that out, where it's causing me to think about who I am. What do I want the future to look like? What does that look like for my wife and I as a couple? What does it look like for our family? I think it overwhelmed me a little bit. Well, not a little bit; probably a lot. This has to do with the traditional male's perspective as being a provider—husband or male roles versus partner's role in terms of being the primary income earner."

His concerns, of course, involved the topic of the next chapter— relationships and money. As I said before, each person has their own focus of attention—their own barriers. So, it can be an added struggle to get through the early assignments until we cover the topic which addresses their own chief difficulties.

This one student and his wife have a rather unique lifestyle when compared to the majority of people. The wife stays at home, schooling the kids, while the husband is up working, providing, and doing all of that. In today's world, it seems that most families are two-income households and the kids go to public school. And their unique way of doing things is going to bring a different dynamic in the relationship with regard to money and economics.

The reason he felt overwhelmed is because he had lived in a fantasy the whole time and no one had ever asked him to look at reality. He did not have a strategy. The physiology of his body was freaking out about reality while his mind remained in a fantasy. This circumstance forced him to become very afraid of his future. And that is a good thing. This made him become more aware of protection, security, and abundance—our money triangle.

Another thing many of my students notice early on is that the pace with which they spend money slows down. They become more critically self-aware on the topic of money. They begin questioning old certainties and this new humility allows them to become more aware of things. They are no longer blowing money on stupid junk.

The fear helps to bring you back into reality. You realize that you have got to start saving money for the future. The fantasies that you build will lead to some pretty wild highs and lows, but they will not free up your mean— your average; they will not help you so you can be more real and affect real change in your life. Instead of getting yourself a Ferrari or a Bentley, you get a freaking Ford. You no longer need something on the outside to feed you on the inside.

By stepping away from the fantasies about money and getting real, you increase the value of money. Now, you are looking at it and saying, "Money is this thing that helps ensure my survival and gives me more life. The more money you put in your pockets, the longer life you are going to have. This is a fact.

People who do not have money become disempowered. People who have more money, have longer, healthier lives. Money gives you options to be able to do things for your life right now and into the future.

Do the freaking work. If you do not do the work, nothing is going to happen. That is my motto. That should probably be on my gravestone. Do the freaking work.

Assignment: Emotional Stability

When it comes to protection, security, and abundance,

1. How are you creating your security plan under your current way of thinking?

2. What does security look like for you?

CHAPTER 15

Relationships and Money

Fair Exchange in Relationships

Money. The #1 cause of divorce.

The #2 cause of divorce? Do you know what it is? Sex.

We are going to have a very adult conversation about sex and money.

This is going to seem almost mercantile, but it is going to break the delusions that you have around money because it is going to make you feel empowered. A significant number of people have been in a relationship and have felt disempowered financially. They end up feeling trapped.

What happens when you feel trapped? You begin to resent the other person and the relationship starts to go downhill.

Women are absolutely brilliant at this. When you start to resent the other person, what do you do? You withhold sex. This is how it works. I am not saying anything that you do not already know.

When you withhold sex in a relationship, the other party gets pissed off. This is because you are not now connected and sex is the factor that connects people—makes the man the man and the woman the woman.

Talking in this way may not be "politically correct," but please understand the intent behind this lesson. We are talking about primal energies—masculine and feminine. I am merely talking about types of energy. You can call them "testosterone" and "estrogen," if that is going to make it seem more palatable. For this discussion, I am going to use "man" and "woman" just to make my point.

What happens in a relationship dynamic when one person begins to resent the other? It causes people to be resentful. When people become resentful, they withhold sex. They withhold connection—withhold talking to people.

When this happens people feel that their values are now not supported. And when their values are not supported, they go look for their values to be supported in other areas, and in other ways.

Men or women. It could be with affairs. It could be having an affair on the phone with simple flirtation. Some people are having affairs through the use of their phones.

When you get attention and support from that other area, this relationship that is supposed to be about love, support and challenge, now becomes only one of challenge. When the relationship becomes only a challenge, how much do you really want to be in that? You don't. You resent the other person. You resent the idea of being with them. You resent who they are. You resent being around them. Then, you just get pissed off and then the fighting begins.

Basically, I just gave you the modern-day relationship. That is the modern stereotype.

Some people in this stereotypical relationship may say, "All well and good, but I don't love this person anymore." But that is a lie; you do love them because you are still with them.

You may remember that one of my students shared the story of her husband using their credit card on some items without telling her. She could have been angry, but she chose not to be.

How many people have shared bank accounts? They share everything. But this whole sharing thing is not really very practical. Because you all bring a different service level to the table. Your value is not determined equally.

Back to primitive times people shared food. But what was money in the past? Sharing is not caring. What was money in the past? Where did money come from? It was yak; it was cattle. That is how they started the notion of exchange. Money in the beginning was cattle to feed yourself.

Later, the exchange involved coins. They said, "We can't really transport cattle as easily," so they went to gold and bartering.

Bartering started first and they traded yaks. And then they went to gold. And then they said, "Gold is too heavy," so, then they started going to different coins. Eventually, they said, "We can't carry all these coins," so, they went to paper. Then, after it went to paper we realized that even this was inconvenient, so they went to this thing now called electronic. Now, it is all at the speed of light. I can quickly pay any of you in minutes and seconds. We can give you a credit card number in seconds.

Money has evolved. The speed at which it can be transported has also evolved. In the past you did have the philosophy of the hunters and gatherers. You had the hunters going out for food, but today it does not work that way. That worked in the testosterone world where it was about literally going out and killing for food.

When you are killing for food, there is a certain biochemistry which is not used very much in today's world. Later, trying to barter with cattle and yaks was very impractical. Civilization has evolved, but our consciousness has tended to stay in the old world of testosterone—the past around money and relationships. Many people do not evolve into today's 21st century economics.

Money is about emotions. You have your own emotions and in today's world, since about 1967 or 1969, women have been working from a different dynamic—one of liberation because of the birth control pill and contraception. These have empowered women to have free choice not to be tied down to a family. They have free choice to do with their body what they wish. If they want to have a career, they can go do that.

Today, there seems to be a movement—from my perception, at least—which is skewed in the other direction of women's empowerment; a movement where men are disempowered.

There is also a movement today that says women cannot make as much as a man and I disagree. Women choose different roles and different schedules, but there is nothing stopping any individual woman from working the same long hours in the same dangerous career and making as much or more than any man. If you are talking averages, women choose easier careers, but again an individual woman does not have to be average.

We now live in a period with androgynous relationships. Compare this to the hunter gatherer mentality. We see, now, that each human being is looking to gain their own value. In a relationship, you have two parties. You are going to have the masculine side and the feminine side. The masculine side is going to be focused on mental, financial, and vocational, and the feminine side is going to be focused on social, familial, and physical. The two of these make up the whole and the whole is what creates the relationship. It is the essence of any relationship because the parts that you disown are the ones that your partner has. The things that you love to do are the ones that the partner does not love to do.

So, the feminine side of a relationship is the side of estrogen, and on the neurological level, the parasympathetic—free flowing, the creative, the artistic, lovely, supportive side. About 75% of women and 25% of men are going to focus on this side.

On the masculine side is the side of testosterone, and on the neurological level, the sympathetic—the challenger side. About 75% of men and 25% of women are going to focus on this side.

You need both of these sides—the type of energy involved—to exist in a relationship for that relationship to work.

Contrary to popular belief, the essence of a relationship is not about happiness. A relationship is about completing the parts of the whole that are missing—taking responsibility for the unfulfilled elements. When a relationship is in its wholeness, it is in a state of harmony.

When both parties are in fair exchange is when the relationship is in the greatest amount of harmony.

We just want to be who we are and to be loved for who we are. We want this rather than trying to be faking it and inauthentic—rather than trying to be somebody we are not.

But more often than not, we are trying to be somebody we are not because we are afraid of being who we are. This big lie creates chaos.

One couple had a shared account from which they handled the mortgage on their house and property taxes. For everything else they had separate accounts. Despite the conventional wisdom of keeping everything together, they experienced greater financial growth by separating their individual finances. And, of course, they have experienced greater happiness and an end to arguments over money.

Another couple have a different dynamic with the wife taking charge and driving the family forward, while the husband remains rather laid back.

The more women take charge and the more authoritative they become, the more testosterone they build up in their physical body. What happens as female testosterone rises, so does the risk of breast cancer. Look at the women who get breast cancer. They are not the feminine women who defer to a man's authority; they are not the ones who get breast cancer. It is the masculine women who do. This is because, as the testosterone rises, it gets out of balance with progesterone. Please understand, this is not to say that every "take charge" woman is going to get breast cancer. But the chances increase when a woman throws her physiology out of balance.

How many men like fighting with their women? Not a hand will go up because men defer conflict, believe it or not. They fight on the outside. They are testosterone driven. They fight on the outside, but they want peace in the home. That is how it normally works. Women will love to fight with their man just to get their way.

That may seem to be a total stereotype. I know that relationship topics are very sensitive. But you have to understand the energy dynamics within a relationship.

My take-charge female student explained her own background: "My Mom and I are a lot alike, and my Dad was very passive and laid back. My

Mom ended up with breast cancer and she had it twice. She was a single parent and had to be both sides for me and my three older brothers. She had to be the nurturer and she had to be the disciplinarian. She had to be really, really tough. She provided for the family, but my Dad didn't give child support. That's what happened."

There is much more to that dynamic. The single mother's dominance forced him not to pay child support. If she had been laid back, he would have come in because relationships are a dance. This is what I am trying to share with you. Relationships are a balance.

But in the balance of a relationship, you have to be able to nurture both sides.

In that relationship dynamic, as one person is going to value some things, the other person is going to value entirely different things. They are going to value the opposites, and when that happens, that is what makes the relationship a whole. This is because the relationship is not about happiness. It is about wholeness.

The myth of happiness is what creates divorce and causes a relationship to break apart. We need to understand that a relationship is not really about happiness at all. It is about showing us the sides of ourselves that were disowned. Only then do we get to understand, appreciate and love ourselves because a relationship is not about the other person. It is actually about ourselves. The more love we give to the other person, the more we give to ourselves.

One student commented that she is not in a relationship. I told her, "Your relationship is with your dog. I'm actually dead serious. And your children are the parts of yourself that you disown because they're the parts that you're not paying attention to, they're the things that your kids will express. Let me say it another way. At the moment of the sexual act going on, the parts of your life that you disown will be the things that your children will own for you to learn to love them because life is about love. What does this have to do with money? Everything. I'm telling you, it has everything to do with money."

She said, "Then my children... Oh, I get it. Those are the parts of me that I... Do they come up in other relationships, like the office?"

They most certainly do.

"Because," she replied, "that's my community."

"Yep," I said, "They will be in different areas of your life. Great job seeing that."

In the beginning of a romantic relationship, the sex is a real high, say in the first six months. We do not see the downsides of our partner; we only see the good sides. At the point of the sexual activity, the things in that couple—in that relationship—that are not seen—the downsides—are what the kids will come out expressing.

The parent is expressing all these dynamics, and the kids are expressing all the other areas of their life.

Let me give you an example from my own life. I completely, completely, completely hate soccer. I hate all the running. I feel like it is entirely idiotic running after a ball, going in circles. I played soccer when I was nine years old. I thought this was the stupidest sport on the planet. I played baseball and I was good at baseball. I almost reached AA. I hated soccer with a passion. So, what do my kids do? They love soccer. They play it all the time. Not just one season at a time. They play indoors, and they play outdoors.

And then what do I have to do when I want to spend time with them?

I tried getting my kids to play baseball. My son played for a season. Now, I coach soccer as well, and now I have learned to love the game. I actually enjoy the game, and I once hated it. Because the universe is about polarity and whatever you hate, you are going to create. How am I going to connect soccer to sex? Because it is a part of my life that I had disowned.

Let me give you another example. If there are two people in a relationship and both of them do not really value money, their kids will come out valuing money big time. I can tell you, Warren Buffet's parents had zero value of money. That is why Warren Buffet became a master at money. Because it is going to be the opposite of what you see.

When a relationship loses intimacy—your partner withholds sex—you start resenting yourself. There is also financial resentment because the relationship is out of fair exchange. Any relationship which is out of fair exchange will breed resentment.

Money is about having self-worth, feeling valued and bringing value to the table. Every individual wants to bring value to the table, and if the value is coming to the table then what they do is they realize that they are providing. Because every human being has an innate need and desire to give value, to serve and to be valuable.

Consider the stereotypical Mom who makes meals for the family. She will make certain that her children eat no matter what. That is her value. That is how she brings value to the table in the family dynamic.

Similarly, the stay-at-home Mom who teaches the kids is bringing additional value to the family dynamic.

Every individual has a set of values and when they are bringing that value to their relationship, to the table, to the family, they want to be rewarded for it. If there is no equitable exchange rewarding them for the value they add to the relationship, then there is an imbalance in the relationship. That imbalance creates negative emotions, and the emotion then breeds resentment. The individual may think, "I'm doing this and I'm not getting paid. I'm not being rewarded." When someone is not feeling rewarded, they foster resentment.

A guy can start to resent his partner and himself when there is no more intimacy for an extended period. He will resent his partner because of the perceived lack of fair exchange, and he will resent himself because he does not feel worthy. "She doesn't want to be with me, so there must be something wrong with me." I had to learn this firsthand. I went through my own hell, my own struggles and my own challenges. I was celibate for four years, and not by choice.

Pride leads to resentment. Anything to which you become addicted you will eventually resent. In a relationship dynamic, if you have an expectation that is not met, it becomes a fantasy which you have created. Because of this disconnect with reality, you feel guilt and resentment toward yourself. You also feel guilt toward the family. You begin to ask questions, like, "Am I worth it?"

So, you judge this state of existence because of an expectation and a subordination to something outside of yourself. Instead of looking at what is really going on, you have this filter of expectation which turns reality into a fantasy. One or both partners in a relationship could be doing this.

Women in traditional marriages tend to want protection, security and abundance. If the man cannot provide these, then the woman starts to resent him for this failure.

In one class, 13 out of 14 women placed tremendous value on security. A much smaller percentage placed high value on abundance. That is based on oxytocin—a neurochemical process in their body. It is a protection mechanism. From the evolutionary development of females, an oxytocin release binds the female all the way up to the age of 10.

The reason, if you remember when I started this discussion and I was talking about evolution, this is why I was doing it because evolutionarily we talk about relationships and it's an oxytocin release in a female which binds the mother all the way up to the child's age of 10. It can be the ugliest kid on the planet, but they are beautiful to that mother, no matter what. That is motherhood. A father has a similar bond with the child until the age of 3. Then, the chemical bond changes.

In our modern society, people are easily confused because their physiology is saying one thing, but the demands of society drive us in a different direction. This leads to people being confused about their relationships.

Assignments: Finding Value

1. List out what your day looks like and what you do. Then write the market value of that task next to it.
2. If you had to buy this service, how much would you pay?

CHAPTER 16

Dis-Empowerment

Do not be surprised if you have started to feel psychosomatic discomforts—pressures and pains in the body—from the work you have been doing. These are mind-generated pains.

One student felt a major physiological response to the things about which I have been talking. She felt as though she was having an attack of appendicitis. Let me be clear, however—sometimes pain can come from a real, physical problem. So err on the side of caution and consult your physician.

My student had a sharp pain in her lower abdomen on the right side.

I told her, "That's male, so you've been sharing money and all this trauma is coming up because, as you just said, this explains your divorce."

When you disempower yourself financially, the trauma can sometimes come up on the inside of the body. It could force the bowels to purge. The body could be physiologically releasing stuff. The work you do could wake you up on a physical level in an attempt to bring you back into balance.

The short-term effects of this work are not always fun. In fact, they can occasionally be downright uncomfortable.

But know this: Even though the mind can powerfully affect the body with echoes of past trauma, if you ever experience excruciating pain, then treat it as a physical problem which needs to be addressed by a physician. Again, err on the side of caution.

If the discomfort comes and goes as you work with this material, then it could merely be a result of your trauma from your relationship with money.

Another student who had gone through a five-year ordeal that included divorce described what she felt: "I know when I talked to you, you said you felt like I have a huge resentment toward my husband because of the divorce and everything. I feel like we didn't really fit, or that my husband was the one that would withhold sex all the time. That was a huge struggle for us. My thing was protection; this was paramount to me. I felt like he didn't protect me or the kids. But then when I started to go through the divorce, which was a five-year process through two states. It was just unbelievable. He kept telling me, 'I'm going to take you down,' you know, like 'I'm going to destroy you in this process.' He was so angry that I was like this, but I couldn't live like that anymore. When you said that I resented him, I'm like, 'Oh, no. I don't really resent him,' but I think the resentment was all about the reality that this person who was supposed to love you and protect you, ultimately tried to destroy you."

I remember when she said all of this, her face changed. So did her tone of voice. She admitted that talking about it made her want to cry.

All women need to understand this: If you value protection and you are not protecting yourself, you are, instead, disempowering your life. You do this by expecting someone else to protect you. The very act of disempowering yourself forces your partner not to protect you. You are going to bring about abuse into your life in order to wake you up so that you will empower your life. The suffering is a wake-up call—a guide to teach you.

I am making this statement, helping thousands of women go through rape, divorce and other abuses. I have seen such tragedies way too many times.

If you value protection and you do not protect yourself, you are asking yourself to be disempowered. You will attract a man who, in today's world, we call a "narcissist." That is narcissistic syndrome. The narcissist is there to wake you up from your altruistic nonsense.

You need to release the inevitable resentment, even when the guy is trying to take you down. And this next part goes for guys, too. If your partner tries to have you locked up based on lies, get rid of the resentment immediately. Love the other person for what they try to do against you. Resentment will only pull you down and make you even more of a victim to their drama.

Do not hold any anger toward the other person, no matter what they do to you. Let their actions teach you and uplift you.

If you do not get this, and continue to hold onto your resentment, your physiology will show that you have not yet understood this. You will have symptoms that show that you have not yet handled this. Your blood pressure will go up. Your heart will pound; the pitch and volume of your voice will rise.

If you are interested, I teach how to release the resentment in my Align Mastery course.

But let me say this. If you cannot come up with 20 benefits for each trauma you experience, then you will remain trapped by it. The very act of writing out benefits has you taking responsibility for the trauma. I know that can seem counterintuitive, but understand this: When you take full responsibility for something, you can no longer take the viewpoint of the victim. Victimhood becomes impossible. Blame is dis-empowerment; responsibility is empowerment.

This is an important point to remember: You can redefine any trauma. You can give it new meaning. A trauma will seem destructive so long as you cannot see both sides of it in your past.

You can call any event a "trauma." You can call it a "rape trauma," or a "molestation trauma." If someone took your burrito at Taco Bell, you could call that a trauma. "Bitch, you took my burrito!" Anything on which you cannot objectively see both sides I would classify as a trauma.

One female doctor, a student of mine, admitted that she invariably attracted either an abuser or narcissist in order to help her awaken her altruistic side. She said that she would always be the one to give away money in order to earn "love." By this she wanted to help them take care of their problems. But this was all because of her own hidden guilt.

She said, "Yeah, I can see that too. When we wake up to our blind spots, this is how your body will give you some symptoms. Like, I honestly have not had a physical abuser to wake me up to my altruistic side, but I sure gave the money away."

"Seriously?" I asked with some impatience. "Are you frigging kidding me?

"You're right," she said, "I don't know why I forgot."

"This is the mess that has held your life back for 30 years."

"All right, yeah," she replied. "Okay. Again, only until I really look at that altruistic side and I know I'm doing it so that you love me, I'll give you money so that you'll love me, that kind of thing."

"So you can be accepted," I said, "but that's not love."

The narcissistic person comes in to wake up the altruistic person so that they value their own narcissistic side. We live on two sides—dichotomies. Our bodies and our minds are made up of two sides. You have a parasympathetic and sympathetic side. Your mind is made up of both sides, a light and a dark.

Please understand. Many of my students have trouble with some of this material the first time through. I recommend that they re-listen to a lecture, or, in this case, re-read a chapter. The second or third time through the material, it will seem a bit more familiar because you are not the same person who you were the first time through.

Support and Challenge, Plus Fair Exchange

An individual has seven values. They have all seven parts of their life and they want to be loved for every part of their life. However, a relationship splits up those values and separates them. A relationship puts one side together with this other side and that becomes something we might call "love." But that is only the physical side of things. That is dopamine-based love—that is only "support over challenge." When the relationship gives you "challenge over support," then you may see that as hate. The truth is, in a relationship you have both.

In a relationship you have both "support" and "challenge," equally, for that relationship to grow dynamically. How do you create that? Let me explain.

Let us take two parties—a couple in a relationship. You can respect the other person for who they are. For instance, one wife may have a set of values consisting of physical, social and family, more so than does her husband. Spirituality? I am not even going to put that in there because it is really a form of service in which you give. Some people may say that their form of spirituality is God. I do not have a problem with that, but I do not include God in this. The other values are mental, financial and vocational.

One student's father went to work, and he gave the money to the mother to pay all the bills and take care of all the household expenses. So, based on that, the father had a high value of working, instead of a high value of money. He also had a high value of family. He may have had a moderate value of social status, whereas her mother probably had physical, mental, spiritual, and financial.

The student confirmed these and she said, "Yes, even though she was a larger woman, she was pretty active for her weight. She tried to take care of everybody including the setting of doctor's appointments. She still tries to micromanage those today. And actually, the doctors are surprised she doesn't have diabetes or blood pressure issues. She's just a larger woman."

What happens in the relationship dynamic is that people just want to be loved for who they are and loved for their values. But then money comes into the relationship. In this relationship you have a set of expenses called life.

Let us say that the male goes out and makes $100,000 per year. Let us say that the female is at home, but she does not make any money. But what do you do with that 100K? If a man thinks that the 100K is all his, he is delusional. Divorce puts things in balance very quickly and it makes you realize what is equal in fair exchange. That is the purpose of divorce. That is why people fight in a divorce because it is about money.

You have shared expenses. Let us say that the household expenses are 5K a month, rent or mortgage of say $2,000 and then the other bills of say 3K. Then you have these rugrats between the two parents costing about $1,500 a month. Add these up and you have $6,500 a month to make the household live.

Here is what happens. The woman puts a lot of work into the family, but she does not have any money. She feels like she is working, working, working, but never being rewarded with money. She has to go over to this guy—her husband—and ask for money. By doing so, she feels disempowered. But really what she is doing is running the whole show. You have to look at it like a business. This is not my idea; this is from Albert Marshall, professor of economics at University of Southern California. I think this the smartest way I have ever seen it handled.

If you do not handle this properly, you will be forced to face this problem in divorce.

So, in our example, the man makes $100,000 per year, or $8,300 a month.

What services is the woman providing to the relationship? List them out: Childcare, dishes, teaching, laundry, shopping, housework and likely much more.

Now, hold on gentlemen. As these women want to list theirs, you also do a hell of a lot of work, too. I do not want to take away from what the man does so well.

For the woman, whatever the replacement value of these things are, is what the female gets paid. The husband, from this 100K, pays for these services.

Calculating this per month, that is $8,300, minus the $6,500 expenses, leaves $1,800 per month. Let us say the couple splits the leftover amount to pay them for their individual contributions to the relationship.

When you rob someone of dignity, accountability, and responsibility, you disempower their life.

If you want to make more money, you bring more value to the market. This is just how it works. Men, if you are sitting at home and not bringing anything of value to the relationship, you are not going to get paid. The universe is not going to pay you if you do not bring value. If the man wants to go make more money—say $10,000 per month—then he has got to go out and provide more value.

In any relationship, each person, when they do not feel as though they are being properly valued, may not express their beliefs or disappointment. They may hold a quiet belief that they have to suppress their beliefs and have to settle for what is the current reality. But eventually they begin to resent it.

A wife who decides to homeschool her children may have many good reasons to do so, including controlling the curriculum, decreasing the stress of both students and parents. But let us say that a teacher is making $40,000 per year with 30 children in one classroom. That amounts to a little over $1,300 per student per year. So, if a couple have two kids, that comes to $2,600 per year for their children's education.

The wife needs to be rewarded for her own work. After the shared expenses, the couple needs to come to an agreement on the amount each partner makes. How you are getting paid—how you are getting rewarded—has to be some agreed-upon arrangement. If you are not being rewarded, you will start to resent the other person. Resentment is where relationships fall apart.

Assignment: Dis-Empowerment

1. Who do you perceive is supposed to protect you? 30 Drawbacks to them protecting you
2. Line up everything you do in your household. (Past or present relationship)
3. Find the market value you bring to the table.

CHAPTER 17

Empowerment

Wisdom allows the male and the female both to be self-empowered and self-loved. Each partner can earn and do with what they value and bring to the table.

Some people set unrealistic goals, but it is not the size of the goal which is wrong. Unrealistic goals are those which do not align with your core values. Most people set goals that aren't connected to their reality. I had a client who reminded me of this, but if she had really wanted such things, she would already have done them. Instead, she wanted a secure business where she could provide a comfortable lifestyle for her and her family, instead of chasing the big dreams.

"I do," she told me. "I get it because I totally agree with that. I'm not looking for all the stuff. I just want peace. I want, yeah... That's what I'm looking for—is just safety, security, and peacefulness, you know."

"And live the life that gives you the experiences that you want to be able to experience."

"Yes, exactly," she replied.

It is called security. It is what women want. Women want security. Men want pride and abundance because testosterone wants it.

So, couples need to split the expenses of the household in a manner which seems right to each partner. Each person should have their own spending money after expenses. And if you insist on having credit cards (which I do not recommend), have separate accounts.

Each partner should not have to justify their spending to the other. To do so disempowers the other person.

If husband and wife run a business together, then what does each person bring to the business? How much would you have to pay someone else to replace their job function? And do not calculate from the gross income of the business. You need to subtract taxes, expenses and everything else it costs to run the business. You need to start from your own individual paychecks.

Inside a couple's relationship you are going to have two things happen from this knowledge. First of all, you are going to realize that you are not as high and mighty as you thought you were financially. Secondly, you are going to realize the actual value that you bring to the table. And do not get distracted by gross sales numbers.

When you see that, you are going to say, "Oh, okay. That's really what I'm worth. That brings you to a state of objective reality—where you are financially.

Want to do more? Go provide more. Go create more.

Treat your home like it is a company with regular meetings. When you create this structure and you organize your finances in this fashion, you are going to create more money because money goes where it is most organized. This is the law of negative entropy. I am attempting to teach you how to control your resources, manage them and empower each other to do these things.

Do not disempower your relationships and become emotionally chaotic. Instead, empower your lives, have more of it, and attract more of it into your lives, so you do not have negative emotions.

If I wanted to spend $400 on a shirt, I do not have to ask anybody. But if I have to ask somebody, how do I feel about my life? Do I really have control over my life? Think about that. You don't. If you have to ask someone permission, as a male, as an adult, even as a female adult, it makes no difference, whatever. You feel disempowered by such a requirement.

How empowered are you when you have to ask to spend the money you make? You're not. You are disempowered.

This is a wakeup call to say, hold on, my money is not organized.

Take for example a couple with a fairly stereotypical relationship. She wants security and wants to invest money for the future. But he wants to buy a new car because a new car is cool. It makes him feel better—more like a man. He is an alpha male with a fast, new car. And she wants security. Who is going to win? The one who has a higher value on money. They will dictate where the money goes.

You and your partner need to value each area of your life independently and to empower all of it so that you can empower your life with the money you have, and you both can be empowered and love each other long term because of it.

Two individuals who are empowered financially, in all areas of their life, create the sustenance of a relationship. A couple that is disempowered to one another creates resentment, guilt, shame, and a lack of value. Then, they stay in the relationship, not because they want to, but because they have to. And that is not a relationship of love, empowerment, inspiration and intimacy.

When I was reading *Atlas Shrugged,* it literally changed the course of my life. I am not going to lie; it is a painful read in the first 238 pages. After that, however, it glues you in. Ayn Rand wrote it in 1957. A brilliant, brilliant book, but there was a line in it that made me dig into relationships so much further. It defined for me what an empowered relationship is. Let me paraphrase it for you: An empowered relationship is one where the other person has the choice to get up and leave any time they want to, but they choose to stay in that relationship.

I thought, "Damn! That's impressive. Most people live in relationships that they have to; they are trapped.

Here, I am trying to share with you, at least from the best of my knowledge, how to create empowerment for yourself to be in that type of relationship that has love, intimacy and connection. Powerful. It is an important part of the relationship dynamic. It is not everything, but it is a big part of it.

Empower Who You Really Are

One of my students was concerned about traditionally male attitudes in a female having adverse health effects.

"For the testosterone-driven women who are out here trying to be independent and everything else, what tagline—you don't have to go really deep—but what would you say to them to get them, for nothing else, to calm down for health reasons? Even though it's great that you want to win, and you want to have a lot of things, you know health wise it can be challenging if we continue to drive on those hormones."

First off, any woman who feels that they have to win, realize that that is a competitive, testosterone-driven state. Instead, come from a place of love, not winning. Do not come through competition; come through creation. And moreover, honor the female in you. If you keep trying to fight when your body is geared for love, you create chaos.

Start loving the things that are in your life and the things that you have gone through so you can start coming from a place of appreciation and understanding both your feminine and your masculine sides. I am a very masculine man. There is no question that I am. But I also embrace my feminine side very strongly, as well. I am very nurturing, very loving, very giving, too. I dance between both, but my predominant nature is more of an alpha—more of a testosterone-driven guy. We are both. But it is not about winning; it is about loving.

Some women feel as though they are locked in the competitive environment, but they are finding it extremely stressful.

One woman working in multi-level marketing described her problem this way: "Okay. I work with every leader in the program. All of them! I literally got off the call with someone who's going to go over a million dollars this year. He's like, you are twisting my head inside out and he goes, you're right because it's all bullshit. I'm telling you what's real. If you want to drive to be in the numbers, you can, but let me ask you ladies a critical thinking question or an alternative thinking question: How's that working out?"

And some of the women in the class responded, "It's stressful," and "I'm tired. I'm tired."

So, consider this: If it is not working and you keep doing it, and you are saying, "Okay, it's not working," then you have got to use your intelligence. If you want to be a leader, then start thinking about what is real. Say what is real, namely that this is not working. Tell yourself, "I've got to do something different to create a different environment."

If the multi-level marketing program some of my students were in really worked, why are there only 86 who have hit a million dollars out of tens of thousands who are trying? My own students are having far higher rates of success.

One of my students had tried for 13 years to break out over 200 grand. After four weeks with me—boom!—done! Coincidence? I think not.

Another student made an additional 700 grand in 11 months. Accident? I don't think so.

I can get very heated on this subject because I am trying to empower you with what works.

Some of my students have been to therapy and realized after a week on this program that they no longer needed therapy. One of my assistants had some freaking diseases—bam!—in 45 minutes, gone. Another student had lupus—gone in one day. One single Mom had thyroid issues, gone. Still another student had cancer, but no more. I do not care what other people are doing. I do not care what they are saying because their approach has extremely rare success, if any, and this work is providing regular miracles.

How do you lead a team like this? Start by getting your team to be grateful for where they are currently at. Start teaching people how to live to be humans. It was Aristotle who said this: If you teach people how to love and be human, you will have more money than you know what to do with.

Sports Beyond Competition

One of my male students wanted to know how to win at sports if he is not competitive. "How do you apply that to sports? Because I'm a competitive tennis player. I want to win tournaments and I put myself in situations where, you know, I don't, yeah, I love my opponent, but I don't want him to win. I mean I want to win. Sometimes they are assholes and so now I really want to win, and so you kind of get caught up in all that. How do you apply that to sports?"

You have to detach from the emotion. Winning is a fleeting moment in time. The next time you will have a loss. And this will vary around your mean, just like your finances.

Roger Federer is the greatest of all time, not because he focused on winning, believe it or not. He focused on the game. He focused on adding value to the game.

The great Tom Brady does seem to focus on winning, but, in actual fact, he focuses on performing at his best. Again, adding value to the game.

I recommend that you read Tom Brady's book. His reward is the winning, but he is not attached to the winning. He loves winning and thinks it is great, but he is not attached to it. It is all about him being able to perform and play the game and be in it, but not attached to outcomes.

People who are masters love to do what it is that they are doing. It is not about the result. As soon as you become attached to the idea of the result of the victory—or the loss—you detach from both the game and the love of the game.

If your self-worth is dictated by whether you win or lose, you are in emotional chaos. Instead, if it is just about loving to play the game, then winning becomes a bonus. This mindset changes the dynamic.

For instance, I have worked with basketball players and I literally teach them to detach from the shot, and then they start making shots because the emotions of chaos are no longer there. We are emotional creatures, but emotions create chaos.

If you approach any competition with love for the process—the activity—then winning is a bonus. But if you approach the competition with the attitude of "loving to win," then you set yourself up for some major hurt when you lose. The disappointment can create some major depression. So, do not be attached to the outcome; merely love adding value to the activity.

More on Female Empowerment

"As a single woman, how do I embrace both sides of myself and not be too masculine when I'm trying to provide for myself and make sure that I can stand on my own two feet and just trying to figure this all out because I know if I don't do it right, I'm going to attract the wrong kind of relationship in the future."

Do you think Gisele Bündchen, the Brazilian supermodel, could make $90 million if she was masculine? Of course not!

Any woman who is concerned about building up too much testosterone to do her work should try something different for an entire week. You will watch yourself go through a significant change. I promise you. Ladies, put on heels. Be feminine. Watch the energy of yourself change. Your dynamic and your physiology are going to change. The frequency at which you work is going to change. This is going to change how you present yourself to the world, how you feel about yourself because you are going to be much more present in your biological state. Try it. I could be totally wrong, but if not, you are not going to lose anything.

So, embrace your femininity, just like men, embrace your masculinity. Do not always try to agree with the woman like you are trying to avoid conflict. Stand up for what you think.

Women may say they like to be right, but when asked if they like a man who always agrees with them, they said, "No!" Women like a man who can stand their ground and say, "No." This is what I think is right, some sort of a backbone, right. Of course, you do because that's the testosterone. That is how it works.

Do men want a woman who is always agreeing with them, or always challenging them? The answer is that they want a woman to support and nurture them; they get plenty of challenges from other guys. But a little challenge from your partner is a healthy thing to keep the man's ego in check. The woman should not be completely docile.

There is a balance of support and challenge that has to show up. If you are only passive and supportive, that is not going to work. If you are only challenging, that is not going to work, either.

Altruism, Expectations and the Art of Saying 'No'

A student had a great question about always having a giving attitude. "I've been doing all the work and I realize that I'm altruistic and giving. I also realize that it's not in balance. So, how do I stop without ... or how do I train the people around me not to expect me to do everything for them all the time?"

The answer to her question is simple: Just say, "No!"

"Okay, like, I just stopped and it's creating a lot of disruption in my life. Everybody wants to know what's wrong with me. I feel like it's going to work itself out, but I feel like I have to be strong to make it through this. I just want to make sure I'm doing the right thing because I find myself getting angry at people. They're wanting more than I want to give right now."

"They will have a disruption stage," I replied. "They have a phase in their life where they're looking at it and they are used to being able to get under your skin. They found it comfortable walking all over you and, now that they can't, they're pissed off."

She said, "And so, I also feel a lot of anger around it, like maybe sometimes I'm angry at myself, sometimes I'm angry at them. But how do I get through the anger?"

"Anytime you expect someone to respond differently than they did, you will tend to get angry or uncomfortable. You're attached to the outcome. So, when you expect some different results than what happened—that didn't match your expectation—it's called anger. If you expect them to respond in a certain way and you react, then that anger is on you. That's your judgment."

"Then," she replied, "I'm getting angry at myself that I've allowed it to happen. I'm like, I don't know, I feel just a lot of anger."

"Good," I replied. "What's the benefit of you getting angry at yourself and that you've allowed it to happen?"

"It's going to change," she said. "I'm making sure I'm committed to the right thing. I feel like I'm being disrupted in order to change, and it's out of balance."

"What's the benefit?"

"There's a lot of benefit. Everything that I'm looking to improve should improve, but I just want to make sure I'm on the right track."

"Just answer my questions. You're asking me to tell you that you're on the right track and when I'm done with you, you're going to realize it for yourself. Me saying it does not help you. You realizing it for yourself is everything. If I say it, I'm wrong. If you say it, you're right. So, tell me: What's the benefit to you in being angry at yourself?"

"That I want to choose a different action."

"Okay," I replied. "What's the benefit of that?"

"That I'll do better and have better relationships or results—everything that I'm looking to improve on. I'm doing something different to go for those things, instead of just sitting back and allowing it to happen and not being happy about it."

"So you're going to make different choices?" I asked. "Let different expectations create a different result for your life?"

"Right."

"Good," I replied. "What's the benefit of that?"

"What I've been missing or what I feel like I've been stuck on should come. That is what I'm hoping for. I don't know. I haven't made a—I'm making the changes, but I'm..."

"Don't look for a result," I said. "Just look for what's the benefit that's happening right now. As you're getting pissed off, what's happening? You're starting to wake up to who you are, aren't you?"

"Yes."

"And you're realizing that the standard that you've been living by is not really fair to you, right? How you have been allowing yourself to be treated isn't working, right?"

"Yes."

"You're starting to empower your life."

"Yes."

"And you're starting to make different choices and create opportunities. You probably notice that you are even making and saving more money and taking care of yourself better, aren't you?"

"Yes."

"And you're starting to love who you really are."

"Right. Totally. I'm more myself."

"Say that again."

"I'm more of myself. Yes."

"Then why in the hell are you asking me if you are on the right track because you're being more like yourself. Sweetie, that's the whole game."

"Because it's disruptive right now. Everything's a big mess."

"It is a mess because they're used to you being someone they can stomp all over, and now, you're standing up. It's all good because they're going to get empowered by you becoming disruptive. So, what I'm trying to say to you is that if you see the benefits in the disruption, you won't be caught in the chaos of the disruption."

Each and every one of us needs to learn not to be so afraid of a little chaos.

Exercise

Try this out: List out what your day looks like, what do you do and the value of each activity in the marketplace. Go find out.

I do not do laundry. I have zero interest in doing laundry. I have a wonderful lady do my laundry for me. Over the last Christmas, she was in the hospital. Not only do I love her like part of the family, I needed her help. Her husband texted me and I was honestly scared.

It is more valuable for me to be sitting on a call with students, teaching them, than it is for me to be sitting there folding laundry. How cool would it be if I am sitting down on Tuesday nights in here folding my socks when I am talking to you? That is never going to happen.

So, find out what you do in the market space and what it is worth. What would be the replacement of that? It is a wise exercise to do. If you sell, what do you sell? How much is it worth? And the focus of your attention should be on the highest value tasks.

The more you do that, the more you are going to empower your life. The more you go through this, the more you are going to be worth. You will find out who you are and what you do. And the more you do this, the more money you are going to create into your life.

Assignment: Empowerment

1. Treat your household like a company. Calculate what you're actually worth. (Gross – Expenses = Net Income)
2. What will you do to provide more value to your "company" (household)?

CHAPTER 18

Spirit and Matter

Narcissistic vs. Altruistic

We have been looking at the topic of money throughout this book. We have seen how emotions come into play and where they create chaos in our lives. In some respects, expectations create chaos around money. And now, we look at money from yet another angle. This is where many people believe it is better to be altruistic than narcissistic.

For those who do not know exactly what that means, let us establish some working definitions—how we will use these terms in the upcoming discussions.

Altruistic versus narcissistic examines whether or not a person is a doer or a haver. This is also an examination of whether a person is in guilt or in pride on a given topic. Your ego prevents you from having resentment in your pride. Your narcissistic self goes into the state of entitlement.

Altruistic: This is typically the employees—the doers.

Narcissistic: This is typically the employers—the havers.

We need both in society. Many people want to hold onto the idea that it is better to be in business than to work for somebody else. And that is perfectly okay. Many people want to be in a job rather than being in business. That is okay, too.

What I want you to understand is that there is no right or wrong to your life. It is what you choose to do with it. But if you do it out of a state of pride, thinking that you deserve something, then you are going to create the opposite.

If you do it in a state of altruism, thinking that you are only going to help, then you are going to create the opposite. You may start with the notion that you are only going to help people and not hurt people. You start by thinking that you are going to serve the heck out of them. Instead, you create chaos for yourself because eventually you are going to be exhausted. You will work your ass off, and resent the heck out of your customers.

When a person working from altruism reaches the end of their rope, finally they say, "I cannot do this crap anymore." When that happens, they start getting pissed off and then they overcharge their customers.

Every individual lives here in the balanced self—neither altruistic nor narcissistic—what I call the "love state"—gratitude for who you are.

If you get too prideful, you will create the opposite to bring you back. If you create too much shame and resentment, you will create the opposite to bring you back. Your feedback mechanisms of life are always trying to get you back to this middle state of gratitude and love, right here.

The universe is working in fair exchange; your awareness is not. If you are going to live in a state of creating money and income, then you will need to see the love and gratitude in your life. Your love and gratitude for yourself is what gives you the opportunity to have self-worth, which leads to self-love.

I will make a blanket statement that I normally do not like to do, but I will. Your income and your net worth are completely and directly related to your ability to love yourself. Your net worth and your self-worth are completely connected and proportionate.

If you have a low net worth, that means you have a low self-worth. If you have a low self-worth that's because you have pride in what you do and shame or resentment in yourself. If you hold onto these emotions, you cannot appreciate who you are from the inside out.

Spirituality vs. Materialism

Many people have the idea that spirituality is good and materialism is bad. We put money into the materialism category.

If we do good, that is by helping. Let me ask you a question. At any time in this book before this chapter did you glimpse the idea that if you hurt someone else you actually helped them?

It is interesting how one shift in consciousness changes our judgments about things because, until now, we have been taught that "doing good" is altruistic, and the more we help other people, the better we are.

What are the drawbacks of helping people? Take a moment to write two or three answers to this question.

When you come back to your reading, compare your short list with the following discussion. Disempowerment is one drawback—robbing them of the benefits of doing it for themselves. You get nothing in return. They do not learn for themselves. They do not get to see their reality. Dependency. You are putting them ahead of you. They become expectant of what you are going to continue to do for them.

Let me ask you a question. Is it better to help? Or is it better to allow the process just to be? Is it better to be altruistic and help them, or is it better to hurt them and be narcissistic?

In your altruistic self, you can really empower people. In fact, my work is based on this concept. Because when you really teach people to love themselves and to love their life, that is where empowerment happens. When you realize that the universe works in fair exchange and it is not better to hurt people or help people. In fact, every time I help people, I am hurting people. Every time I hurt people, I am helping people.

I might be severe with a student, but later, that student is going to have some epiphanies. She is going to wake up and start to see things differently.

But what if I had been nice to her—gentle and kind? Would she ever find the will to transform her life? No. In fact, she would remain stuck in her old way of doing things.

When a rocket is hurtling through the sky, if it gets off course from the wind, it will take a certain amount of force to nudge it back on course. Sweet words will not help at all, but a swift kick could be what that rocket needs to get back on track.

What I do is not attached to the idea of helping people or hurting them; it is more about serving people in the most effective way. I do not use strong language just to be a jerk. Serving people means that you know that whatever you do, you are going to hurt them and help them. And these are meant to get them moving in the direction that they want to go.

Change is uncomfortable, sometimes even painful.

If I sit in the world of compassion, trying to be nice—trying to be kind, I am never going to make any of my students transform. If I am addicted and attached to your opinion of me, I cannot ever transform you.

Some of you may finish my course, or this book, and go badmouth the heck out of me. I hope you do not, but if you do, it is okay. I already have contingencies set up. I will call in the rest of my students to counteract that. But some people do not like my intensity, and it is okay.

If you stay stuck in trying to do something good all the time, you are going to lose yourself in the process. You are going to beat yourself up. Because many of you believe it is better to give than it is to receive. It is better to do than to have. It is better to do better for others than it is for myself. This is altruistic programming that has been brought on by mothers, fathers, teachers, and preachers.

This idea that it is better to do for others creates guilt in the individual so that they avoid having. And guilt is the biggest powerful emotion, of all the emotions in your life which hold you back.

One of my students was on the verge of having surgery on his neck to handle a serious health issue. All I did was help him clear his guilt. Because we become trapped by our own guilt, our spirituality and our materiality become the constructs that guide not only our behavior but also the behavior within our physiology.

Most people suffer from an inner conflict. They see that materialism seems more powerful and they want to have money and material possessions. At the same time, most people believe in altruism, but believe it is better to do for everybody else rather than to have for yourself. With such an inner conflict those people are never going to win.

If it is only about doing for other people and never receiving, you never end up living in fair exchange.

If self-love is the answer, who is the person that gets paid first? Everyone else or yourself?

Naturally, it should be yourself. That is why the wealthy people of the world pay themselves first because they value themselves first. In your company, in your organization, in your world, who is the most important person? You are. Even your management of your finances is trying to wake you up to get you to value yourself.

Most people pay their bills, first—rent, utilities and other vital things, first, and then minor bills. After that, people pay their taxes. Whatever is left, some people put in savings.

Money tends to flow toward those systems which are more organized.

If you are not going to organize your own money, it is going to flow toward those systems which are more organized—the businesses to which you own money, the government, etc. If you are not going to organize your money, it is going to travel into those other, organized systems. It is going to go where it is protected the most.

Out of an emotion of fear, people tend to pay their bills first because they need to survive. But surviving for the moment creates future chaos! You will get a feedback mechanism which includes stress, anxiety and frustration. This mechanism tries to wake you up to the fact that you are not saving for yourself and not preparing for your future chaos. Your nervous system is trying to wake you up to this state of imbalance.

Even your health is trying to wake you up to this state of imbalance as if to say, "Hey look, you've got this future thing coming up. If you are not preparing for it and you are not saving for it, you are not serving yourself well. You are going to lose out."

The feedback mechanisms are there to help you return to a state of balance.

Student Feedback, Problems and Solutions

One of my students is a consultant, part-time, helping other businesses. He said, "Not really a question, but an observation of something that I am going through right now. I am working with a gentleman in merchant services. Without going through the whole story, I went back to sales—microscopes—and I was in merchant services previous to this, but I am still doing some consulting on the side. Part of the chaos that's going on in my mind—and you just spoke to it—is having conversations with this gentleman that I am doing some consulting with. He's a point-of-sale technology reseller in that space, and I am helping him get set up with payments.

"Part of the chaos in my mind is how do I manage all of this? It is becoming more real to me—I am becoming clearer about this—in terms of the value that I am putting on myself and what I bring to the table. That value includes not only how I can help him but also serve his clients. Having the knowledge, understanding and the awareness of those thoughts that are going through my mind—what fair exchange really looks like—and being able to have those conversations with this guy that I am consulting with to get paid. I am getting paid for the value that I bring and, at the same time, for how I serve him and his clients. If I didn't have this knowledge and some of this experience of what you are teaching, it would be even more chaotic."

Quite often, an individual ends up giving away their talent and their work. Guilt does that. And when the guilt involves a fixed, but wrong belief about being "good," the individual cannot easily see the solution to their problem.

Another student talked about how "help" can sometimes be destructive. "You were talking about how whenever we help someone, we're not really helping them. Well, I do that with our girls. Whenever one of our girls will come and say, 'Hey Mom, how do you spell this?' And I'll say, 'Honey, go get a dictionary. If I tell you how to spell something, I am not helping you. You know how to go through the process of figuring that out. You need to do it for yourself.' But what I need to do is to take what I am doing with them and apply it to my own life. How I perceive my own past experiences and how I have done, or not done that with other people, is becoming clearer to me. Changing that delusion of how I caused all this pain and how other people have never recovered from it—or whatever—but how I really did help them in the long run. Just like I am trying to teach our girls to learn on their own because that is going to help them, if I do not help them."

Most of us have been taught the myth of helping others, but not how to think about the consequences of our supposed help. Entire government bureaucracies have been built on this kind of insanity.

I still live there sometimes. I still fall back into that horrible habit. The more you do for somebody else, the more important you are going to be to them—or so it seems. But that is not true. If I wanted to, I could take every one of my students on a personal, one-on-one call and break through all of their barriers, but such "help" would not teach them how to think. And that is why I do not do it that way.

The purpose of my work is to teach each student how to think—not what to think without them understanding what they have learned. It does no good to learn something by rote which you cannot use in the real world. My aim is to have them master their own lives.

There is an old saying that you can give a man a fish and he will eat for a day, but if you teach him how to fish, he can eat for a lifetime.

As your love of self increases, you will receive the reward of financial increases.

Remember, a poor person will not be able to help others very much, but a rich person who loves himself and others will be able to hire hundreds or thousands, giving them the opportunity to add their value to the company and to the community, all in fair exchange.

Bottled-Up Anger

One woman had held her anger toward me for two weeks. "Yeah, I was angry," she said. "On your Q&A call, you talked about the benefits of anger, and I thought I went through it already and somehow it hit me that the way I have been, there's benefit to it. I felt this whole likeness lift off of me, but in the last two weeks I have seen far less cash flow than normal. I feel like the resentment has forced me to push it all away. I am just hoping that I am on the right track because I feel like I found the benefit of it. Now, I should be able to attract it back into my world, if that makes sense. I am doing the work, but then I am constantly second guessing myself to make sure I am on the right track."

I asked her, "Can I tell you why you are doing that?"

"Yeah. Why?"

"Because you are looking for an outcome from the work. Remember, when you look to something external to validate what you are doing, you create chaos."

"So, I should just focus on the process? That's the whole gist of it?"

"Yes, that's the whole thing. You might be thinking, 'If you do the work—Oh, I'll do this, and get more money coming in the door.' No. Don't do that. You just put an expectation on the work. It doesn't work that way. You've got to do the work to get to gratitude. The expectation needs to be internal: 'I feel grateful for this whole thing that happened.' The rest takes care of itself."

"Okay. Good. There are constantly things around me that are super negative, and I feel like I am not having correct expectations or realistic expectations, so that's why there's such—I don't know. That's why I feel like it is out of balance. Is that ... like, am I too positive?... like, am I too loving and giving and..."

I interrupted her. "Is it possible that anyone can be angry at me? How does that work?"

"I know. I was too positive two weeks ago, and now I am just angry." She hesitated. "No, I'm not. I'm back to feeling—I feel such a sense of peace, but then it goes and I am questioning. I keep going back to questioning and I think maybe it is because it is just different. I don't know."

"Well, let me ask you this. What is it that pissed you off? I am curious."

"Because I let other people walk all over me. I have to question—"

"And that's my fault?"

"Yeah," she replied. "It's your fault that you made me see how bad it is. Seriously, I was carrying other people's issues and thinking I could fix them. Like, I am giving everybody all their stuff. Not only was I trying to do too much, but I was like carrying it for them. I don't know. It was screwed up. But I'm letting all that go. I'm in the process of letting it go. I'm still—like, it just feels different for me, okay? What do I do now? I have to focus more on myself, but it's just different."

"Okay. Please listen to the language that you used. You are angry at me because I showed you that you are holding other people's stuff and they're stomping all over you."

"Yeah," she replied. "It is really about me."

"Oh, good. I'm glad we're on the same page with this."

"No. Like, it wasn't you originally. Now, it's back to—like I allowed this to happen."

"You can't be angry at anyone other than yourself. You can blame other people, but you can only be angry at yourself."

"Right. It's like you create a mess, and then you let it go. That's what's been going on for the last six weeks. It feels like it's a conflict and then it gets solved, and then it is something else that comes up and then it gets solved. Actually, it's been a lot of fun."

"Cool," I said. "Please let me explain something. There is no end destination. You are going to continue the journey of continuing through the journey. There is no end destination. It is just a journey. Okay?"

My final step to your journey of money is this: There has been nothing more powerful, nothing more true to understand than your own self-love.

Every aspect of your life comes along to wake you up to this because it is waiting for you to honor and acknowledge your greatness and your self-love. Emotions, money, relationships, family, business relationships, romantic relationships—all of it—everything that is there is to get you to wake up to the balance and the equanimity of loving yourself.

Your life is a reflection of you back to you.

If you can wake up to that, then you do not become a positive feedback system. Instead, you realize that the universe is trying to get you into a state of balance. When you get high and when you get low, it is wise to govern yourself. Because if you can govern yourself, then you do not need others from the outside to govern you. Keep your pride in check. Just because you make more money does not mean that you are better than anybody else. And likewise, just because you make less money does not mean you are better than anybody else. If you say that you did such-and-such for them, that is instantaneously pride. If they did this for you, then that becomes shame or guilt.

It is wise to balance these two out so you can stay in true balance with your relationships. When you understand what your values are and who you are from the inside out, then you can achieve a healthy balance. You get to move down the path of being authentic to yourself. Ultimately, you must govern yourself against these two emotions. There is pride to others and pride to yourself—each one thinking that the recipient of that pride deserves to have what they have.

Love from a state of positivity does not work. The only thing I know of which heals is this: love from a state of equanimity, meaning a synchronicity of both positive and negative—a balance of homeostasis—gratitude. Learn to be grateful for your life—for all of it, both the positive and the negative.

I have given you tools, strategies, ideas, details on how to use them and how to make it all work. Use them. The more you use them, the better your skill with them will become. The faster you get with them, the easier it will get. But get yourself centered as quickly as you can. The more you stay centered, the greater and greater gift you are going to have.

Working into the Future

Some of my students have voiced concerns about the future, after they have finished their current course work. One student asked, "The tools that you said that you gave us, is that the assignment prompts, or the assignment questions? Would you suggest a daily practice of something—like, using either one of those, or just starting from the beginning and continuing to work through those? Like, finding and being grateful for the things that maybe I have struggled with in the past?"

These are certainly possibilities. As I said earlier, this is all about improving the journey. No one is perfect. Even I will do some of the same work, over and over again to expand my field of influence and to correct my own balance. I will not do this every day or even every week, but I come back to this work all the time. Governing your mind is the greatest gift you can give yourself. Mastering yourself. Loving yourself.

I have been rich, and I have been poor. Both had their benefits. Both have served me. Both have done what they needed to do.

If you focus on what is your mission in life, you won't be so addicted to money. The reason you get addicted to money is because you focus on the outcome rather than what you are looking to do with your life.

What I have learned is that people who have money, do not worry about money. And the interesting thing is, this is not because they have money. The attitude comes first and the money follows. They manage it effectively, strategically, but they take away the emotion and they learn to love who they are. All of us have that gift—that capability.

I know I am being a little bit philosophical in this chapter, but that is okay because it is intentional. I don't know what path you are going to cross. I don't know if there is something that you are going to do with this afterwards, but I remain grateful to all of my students that they are working on their own self-love because it is the only thing I know that heals, that governs, that creates life—creates everything that you are.

If you can master that for yourself, then you can live the life you want. But if you get caught thinking of an unrealistic expectation of your life, then you will create challenges for yourself. Not that the challenges are bad. The challenges are needed. We need to evolve and grow. Life is a game of evolution. Where you are today financially does not mean that this is where you will end up. Love where you are today financially. Love your debt. Love your pitfalls. Love the challenges that you have financially. It does not matter where you are.

If you use money logically and you set up an independent financial plan, strategically, there is not a single person in the next five to seven years that could not become wealthy and financially independent. But if you are thinking that you are going to speculate and make tons of money, invest it, spend it on popping bottles of champagne and stuff like that, then you do not value money. What you value is the thing that money is about—the things that money buys. Value the money and hold onto it. Keep it close to you. See what it gives you.

See what opportunities having a million dollars in your pocket gives you. What is the benefit to you of having a million dollars in your bank account? I didn't say spending your money. I said just having it. You cannot get rid of it. It has to stay in your pockets. You cannot get rid of that million dollars because I know some of you will think, "I can buy this, I can pay off my mortgage; I can go on vacation." That is not what I am saying. I did not say what you can do with spending your million. Just having it. What would be the benefits?

Self Healing

I continue to be amazed by the things these lessons will trigger in my students. One student became critically aware of his own romantic life. He said, "Hey. I can't remember who was talking, but you were talking to somebody about if you were a disempowered woman, you're going to attract narcissistic men into your life and abuse into your life. That was last week, but I had this question come up. Because I am attracted, I believe, to disempowered women, and I didn't realize it until this video. What the hell do I need to do about it? How do I humble myself and bring myself back to the gratitude state from that?"

"You are already doing it," I told him. "You are in the process of doing it. You are waking up. I know where you are at. You are waking up to who you are right now with what you are doing. The reason you become narcissistic is that you have this hero's mentality. This is the viewpoint which says, 'I am going to heal and save everyone.' And a hero needs lots of money. Heroes need to be Superman: 'I am going to save the world.' But at the same time, you attract women who are disempowered.

"You've got to be careful," I continued. "I'm just trying to say, look, realize that you are being arrogant. When you sense that feeling return—yourself being in pride—humble yourself. Ask yourself, 'What's the drawback of where I'm at?' Govern yourself so that you are not narcissistic and you can actually be loving to the person with whom you are talking.

"My narcissistic side says, 'I want you to tell everybody you freaking know so that they can save their own life financially.' My altruistic side says, 'I want you to do it to help people.' My narcissistic side says, 'Look, if they come into my world, like one student is saying, her world has changed, her life has changed. Great. I can help them, but I am okay with making money in the process of doing it.' Both are there. I have built a business to be able to serve and help people. If I do not have a business, I cannot serve and help people. That's how you create fair exchange. That's a fair exchange offer."

Adding Value

In my world, my highest value task is teaching because my teaching brings people to the table. It also brings clients to the table. And both of these bring revenue to my business. The highest value task I can do—economically, in business—is to teach. Even for me as a father, the highest value task I do is teach. The more I learn and teach, the more I learn and teach, and the more valuable I am in the marketplace.

Assignment: Having Money

1. What are 100 benefits to HAVING a million dollars in your bank account? (Not spending it)

CHAPTER 19

Fear, Crisis and Money

Fear, crisis, and money. I think this is a fitting title for this chapter, for right now, at this point in the history of the world. Please remember that money is a resource. Please stop calling it a "tool" because it is not a tool. It is a resource. It is dependent. It is equal to the amount of value expressed. That's it. It is a resource which equals the amount of value that is expressed. If you do not express value to people, you do not have money. It just works that way. It does not go in the other direction.

I want you to conceptualize with me. Let us say you have this electromagnetic ring around you, which we do; we just don't know it. This energy around you, I call "resonance." Money has a resonance as well. It is a resource.

The electromagnetic energy around you is now looking at your resource, and your body goes into sympathetic mode. If you go into sympathetic mode, this electromagnetic ring gets challenged and contracts. Accordingly, money goes inward, and you go into hoarding and saving. You go into savings mode. "Oh, my God! I'm going to run out of resources." With the threat of no more resources, stress kicks in because you fear the loss of that to which you are addicted. No more resources means you need to save no matter what because you perceive that there will never be any more money. No more resources suggest that you need to contract and stop.

What that means is that as you stop and you go into contraction mode, you're in self-preservation. Self-preservation mode does not lead to being of value to other people because you think about the self—the id, not the ego. When you get to Get RYL (Rewire Your Life), you will understand what I mean by that. It is the id. You are protecting yourself. It is a survival mechanism—survival consciousness.

Compare this to the state of abundance. This is the "abundance mentality," as people like to call it, which I find funny. In this condition, there is always more than enough. This is when people have lots of resources because they provide value to the world. They feel good, and they are green (the color of money in America) and flush. When the person is green and flush, they call it abundance. When they do not have any resources, they call it "contracted" and "fear mode."

Neither of these modes are really true. But supposedly, in the abundant state, you give openly; in the contracted state, you take from other people.

The truth is that you have both actually going on. I just want you to realize this. You have the sympathetic mode going on with its intent of self-preservation, and you also have the abundant mode going on with its intent of the giver. On one side, you have the receiver or taker; on the other side, you have the giver or sharer. This is the person in between.

You need both of these to be in balance. You need to give and receive equally to be in fair exchange. You need to be in equal exchange to achieve that balance.

If you contract, in fear, you put yourself in sympathetic mode, and you contract and you contract and you contract. This fear represents the contraction of the ability for you to serve more people. As your electromagnetic ring contracts, you are going to serve fewer and fewer people. As you serve fewer people, you think more about yourself. You get trapped more in yourself and in your consciousness. Then, fear now comes in even more and you get more sympathetic. Your blood pressure goes up. You start getting more resentful, and you start getting angrier. You start creating fights and challenges. You go to Walmart and fight with people over toilet paper. You get frustrated with the world. That is all sympathetic living, survival consciousness.

Now, I am not saying be blind. Please understand this. I did not say, just give openly. This is the land where people get to when they sit and say, "Okay. It's always going to be good. There is never going to be a down-cycle." That is not true. There is no such thing as, "It's going to be good and never bad." The truth is that this delusion is not true. Even in the good lives the bad; and even the bad lives the good. It is always going to be in balance. The world of awareness has to match that. When the world of awareness matches the balance that exists in the universe, then you actually are able to provide more value to more people. From there you stay in fair exchange, and you actually raise your self-worth and your net worth.

Right now, when people are constricting and saying, "I don't know what to do. I don't know where I'm going to go. I'm lost," this is the time when they have got to expand their consciousness more than ever before. They are going to expand their thinking more than ever before to provide more resources. When they provide more resources, what is going to happen is that this bubble will expand. It will provide more value. That is why, right now, you have a choice with your consciousness to do either this and expand into it, or do this, and contract into it. The most important thing that lies in between is your thinking. It is the way you think about things. It is your consciousness, your awareness, the tools you use and the wiring in your brain.

If you think that saving a little bit of money is going to save you from changing the way you think, you have just gone into this contraction mode and caused yourself a hell of a lot more pain than you know what to do with.

My friends are calling me every day, right now. This is not for me; it's for them because they cannot control their reactions to fear. They are playing the contraction game.

You have the opportunity to expand. Crisis is bred in the market. As we experience more crisis in the world, everywhere around us, you have the ability now to expand and serve more people within this crisis.

So, how do you expand when your gut reaction is to contract? What do you need to do? How and what? Not "why." The "why" is already there. The world may appear to be collapsing, but someone creates a charity to help people in need. They turn it into an online nonprofit. Manufacturers get involved and suddenly there is a whole new generation of things being built and birthed. In reality, there is no crisis. That is the point I am making. If you change your wisdom and your awareness, you realize that your #1 asset is your wealth. Your #1 asset right now is your brain because the brain realizes that there is no crisis. That is where the wealth sits. That is where the money sits right there, for everybody.

It is not the time to play small with it. It is time to leverage other people's problems and to solve more problems. The more problems you are going to solve today, the more people who are going to follow you. This means that you are going to be more valuable—more of a resource to other people. More value equals more cash. It is just that simple.

As you expand out of the sympathetic, you are changing your way of thinking. Your entire being works on maintaining balance between the two intentions. You will always get new challenges in a new business. Along with them, you will also get a new awareness to help you out.

And as you expand your current sphere to give more, you get new challenges automatically. Your original electromagnetic sphere will morph into one leaning in the direction of giving, but then that in itself will create a different opportunity for you. This will happen every single time. The giving and receiving exist simultaneously at all times.

Those people who have home-based businesses or work with multi-level marketing with a major corporation need to change their consciousness during a supposed crisis. Those who do not change their consciousness will not evolve with the external changes; they will become stuck and will not see the growth that is possible. Those who do evolve are the ones who are going to skyrocket.

During COVID, classrooms shifted from physical buildings to online virtual. Teachers who could not make that transition were going to miss the boat. Home schooling is already a thing. Universities are already going online. Now, this has been standardized. Eventually, schools will hire more teacher's aides and not pay teachers as much. Teachers are going to be in dire straits. They have not seen it yet.

Everything is going to change. The economy has completely been thrown upside down. Now, the economy is going to run without the need of many things that have been complacent. It is time to trim the fat. That is all it is; it is trimming the fat. If you are not being of value, it is important you make sure you put more value in.

The people who get it are the people who are really going to live in abundance—in that place from protection to security to abundance. Those who are playing even on the higher level of security and into abundance, are going to get super wealthy.

The Depression of the 1930s was the greatest time for millionaires. Most millionaires made it during the Depression. Additionally, so many people became wealthy in 2008. You just don't hear about it because they are circling in different places than in the mass media.

If it is accessible to everybody, then it is not the truth.

Assignment: Fear, Crisis and Money

1. How are you expanding your value with respect to your business or occupation? If you do not have either, how are you being of service to others?
2. How are you going to serve more during this time?

CHAPTER 20

Breaking Down Money Myths

The Myth of 'Free'

The myth of free. If money is the measurement of the value you have placed into the universe, and if you expect it for free, that means you have put nothing out into the universe.

The notion of "free" money creates the consciousness of dissociation. If this is you and you are getting something for free, then that means you are going to be giving away things for free. From that disconnected reality, the electromagnetic sphere of consciousness we discussed will stay the same— static or unchanging, rather than evolving up the ladder of income.

If you're always looking for free things, then you're resonating, and giving of yourself for free because free isn't about guilt. When you have guilt and shame about money, you look for shit for free. When you value money, you do not look for things for free. You look to pay a fair exchange. You look to pay fair market value for what it is you are receiving.

I never once said I am giving this program for free. I am, however, now giving introductions for free, but that is merely a marketing cost from my perspective. From there, what people do is up to them. I want to make sure I provide enough value into the introduction to let people understand the value of the full course.

If you are ever in a situation where someone is giving you money, be careful about calling them "generous." Watch out! You will find that there is an equal demand to take money away from you. For example, government handouts; the government does not make money, so any handout it has to take from others. And if you think the government makes money by printing it, you are wrong there, too. Printing money devalues all of the currency in circulation. Only those who add value to our civilization are creating money—the resource we have been talking about.

Do not think for a minute that it is more blessed to give than to receive. Similarly, it is not more blessed to receive than it is to give. It is wise to stay in fair exchange with money.

If you are thinking that some person gave you money for free because of COVID and all of that nonsense, hang on to your seatbelt because someone else is going to come get it, and you are going to lose that supposedly "free" money. "Free" is a myth.

If you think you are getting something for free, you are going to lose your money somewhere else on another side, another bill, or something seemingly random, to keep you in balance. For example, Apple iTunes may randomly take your money, equal to the amount you thought you got for free.

There are many ways your finances can return to a balanced state. As another example, consider the effect of health insurance not covering the 80% you thought it would cover, but handled only 20%. This type of activity leaves you in the state of survival because, if you do not actually value what you are getting, then what you do is you disintegrate on the topic of having money.

Please understand that you are never getting things for free. You are getting things of value and you have to ask yourself, "What am I doing to receive that value? What have I done to earn that value?"

For anything you have received, what did you do to get it? If you cannot see what you did to get it, then you will be out of fair exchange with money. When that happens, you will lose it on the other side because money works in a paradigm of pride and shame. That is the emotional context of money. If you have shame around money, then you will say free is good. If you have pride around money, then you will say free is bad. If you are balanced on money, you are going to see that there is no "free" money. It is all balanced.

People who have the perception that they get things for free start taking advantage of people. People who give things for free start getting pissed off and eventually get resentful. It is wise to say, "You know what? I've got to stay in a fair exchange with what I'm doing." That is why I said before that I am not giving anybody this program for free. I have gifted some people the first month, and then they are going to pay for it because I am going to provide them with so much value inside this work, and then they will see how their lives change. But that is not free. The way it is set up, I make sure that I remain in fair exchange because you have the narcissistic side of your money and you have the altruistic side of your money. If you cannot balance these, you will never be able to build a business. The universe will humble you to bring you back to a state of balance and to help you stay in fair exchange financially. Money is the measurement to see how much you actually balance and love yourself.

Money is very simple. The more people love themselves, the more they make money. That is why people come to my programs and automatically make more money.

I do not teach you how to invest in anything. I do not tell you how much to put in index funds. I do not teach those kinds of things, but people make more money. I do not teach people how to go out prospecting for leads and how to create new sales strategies, but people make more money. Why is that? It is because, when you realize your emotions around money, then they balance themselves out. You can stay in fair exchange, and you can climb the ladder of evolution through fair exchange and balance. But if you stay out of balance with it, you will create more chaos for yourself.

The Upcoming Assignment

Go through all aspects of your life from birth, and recall every item you think you have gotten for free. For each item, as you recall it, find out what you did to earn it.

This exercise will change your life. You will stop the guilt and the shame. You will make more money. It will show up in your life seemingly out of thin air.

Student Questions

Unexpected Expenses, 'Extra' Income and Proper Management

One female student works in sales. She said, "So, I work 100% on commission, and sometimes I make more than others. It seems like when I have a significantly higher income amount, then there's additional unexpected expenses. If I spent more time valuing the work that I did or thinking about it or being in balance with it, is that what I'm missing?"

I answered, "You just aren't managing the money wisely. The only reason you have unexpected bills is because you have money you haven't managed wisely. That's the only reason for unexpected bills."

"To a certain extent," she replied. "But my dog ate glue and it was $2,500. My furnace went out, like stuff like that. Okay. I should have an emergency fund to pay for those things, but literally I made extra money. The emergency fund is not growing because I spent the money to use it, so what is wrong with me?"

"What you just said, 'I made extra money.' Listen to yourself and say, instead, 'I don't make extra money; I make money.' See? There is no extra. 'I make money.' There is no such thing as 'extra money.' If you think in your head it's 'extra,' then—bam! —it's gone because you don't need it. Your brain works on survival, not abundance. If you say that I have this 'extra money' lying around, that will be gone in a heartbeat because you have to account for every dollar that you make. If it's not set on a percentage or a principle or something like that, and you're not managing effectively, strategically every aspect, every dollar that you're making, and don't know what you're going to do with it, you will go into devolution and you'll create more unexpected expenses and say, 'That's not my fault. That's not my fault. That's not my fault.' Take the unexpected expenses, start putting it in savings, and start seeing what happens."

She paused thoughtfully and replied, "That percentage thing you just said, that's a big deal. I don't do that for everything, like to manage it on a percentage versus a dollar amount. That's a really good point. Thanks."

"You're an entrepreneur. If you're an entrepreneur and commission based, you get paid on percentage. You've got to now manage on percentage."

Paying it Forward

"Okay," said another student. "I'm curious about the process of paying it forward. You always hear this process of you receive and then you give, and then you encourage others to give. Is that a balanced system? Talk to me a little bit about how that fits into this."

"Did you see this weekend at the 'Cut the Bullshit' event that everything served, no matter what you thought? I said this weekend that service is the currency of the universe. Paying it forward doesn't mean you're doing something nice for someone. Because you pay it forward, you're also disabling and enabling someone's ineptitude for them to master their own life."

"I love that."

"So, paying it forward," I said. "They're being nice to us. I would be sitting there saying, all right, this person is paying us. I'd better put this into some sort of savings because what's going to happen is that eventually they're going to come around and hold that over your head.

"They paid you when things weren't there. They're going to want more from you later on, and, at that time, this other person is going to turn into an asshole. Because they give and you think you've got it for free, when they take it away, you now call them an asshole."

"True."

"Then you eventually resent them. At first, they're great. Later on, they're a prick. Versus the reality that they're both. And so, any person that's expecting something, to get something for free, and says, 'Oh, I got this for free. This is great.' But I'm not against getting things at a discount. Please don't get me wrong. I don't mind someone getting things at a discount, but there is value in it. You're using that value because you're valuing money. You're getting things at the best rate that you can. If someone is just giving you money, be careful. It's not for free. It will come back to haunt you."

Assignment Clarification

"I guess mine is the final one," said one of my female students, "which is a good one because it was just clarification on the assignment."

"Take everything that you perceive you got for free and go and see what you did to earn it."

"Back in the day, like elementary school?"

"Every single thing you think you got for free. My kids and I were playing Monopoly last night, and my daughter told me about a rule I don't remember being part of the game. I don't know if this is a real rule or one they made up. I don't know, but I just kind of went along with it. If you don't want to buy a property, then it goes to auction and then you have to bid for it. And my daughter and I are going back and forth on a $2 million property in the Monopoly game. I was like, all right, we've got five minutes left in the game, and we're going back and forth, back and forth, and I literally made the offer, and she let me have it for $300,000. I said, why did you do that? She was like, 'Now, you paid for it.' But I picked up an asset for $1.7 million less than what it was worth. She said, 'I know, but it's kind of like for free.' I said, 'No, this is discounted. This is smart negotiating because I'm going to use that money to help build other assets.' If you don't know what you're going to do with your money, why would the universe give you any more?

"Consider the topic of grants and scholarships. Same thing. You're not getting a grant for free. You are going to end up paying back for it. You're going to be paying the university. You'll end up using something. You're going to be indebted to them. Look at what you did to earn it. You worked your ass off to get it. It's still a fair exchange."

Assignment: The Myth of 'Free'

1. Take everything you have perceived you got for free, and find what you did to earn it.

CHAPTER 21

Credit and Debt

Do you have debt issues? In this chapter we will be looking at both credit and debt. The objective is to understand the psychology of these things. There is nothing wrong with credit. There is nothing wrong with debt. What is wrong with these is your perception of both.

If you have a credit issue, it is because you thought that you valued something more than you did, and you wanted more of it. You were willing to hedge your current state, and your future, on this, to put yourself into debt.

This is the narcissistic side—the side which says, "I deserve this." What happens is that you will take on credit at the moment because you are going to hedge your future on it. This condition sits outside the realm of fair exchange.

Let me give you an example of this. When people buy a car, they use credit to take on debt, unless they buy it with cash. Let us say it is a $30,000 car. You take on the debt for this car because in the future you are going to see more pleasure than pain. That is why you get the car, because you have a fantasy about the future. The economy and the society build up this fantasy of future pleasure—a house, a family, these cars and all the riches that come along with it, and you use credit to take on debt for it all.

What happens when you take on credit is that now you take on this debt inside of it. The credit becomes the side of your pride and the debt becomes the side of your shame.

If I were to ask a group of people, "How many of you have debt?" A great many of them, if not all of them, would lower their hands real quick because they are afraid to say that they have debt. This is because the common perception is that debt is bad.

My real estate people will say debt is good because they understand that there is such a thing as positive debt and negative debt. Both are important inside the realm of making money.

However, if you say that credit is good only and never bad, then what you will do is that you will take on large credit card debt, buy things on credit, and not be able to manage your finances and pay for the things you purchased. Just because they can give you credit does not mean you have earned the credit. Credit is earned, not given.

As an individual continues to take on more credit, they automatically put themselves into debt. And they will continue to do this until they can understand the drawbacks of credit. One side effect of taking on such debt is that now they get owned in their own mind. Their finances are now "owned" because they took something in a fantasy of the future, and they get caught in the trauma of the past.

Now, I am not saying credit is bad. Please understand that. Credit has a downside. Debt has an upside. But you only look at it as credit is good and debt is bad. That one-sided view is not correct at all. That is imbalanced.

Right now, small businesses are going to get this "free money" that is out there. Again, let us be clear: There is no "free" money. It is going to be paid somehow, some way. You are going to have to pay it back. Maybe not to the government. You will pay it back somewhere else. It is not free money because credit and debt stay universal in the grand scheme of the universe. Someone else will take that amount of money from you.

Let me give you another example. I had an issue one time where someone was supposed to pay someone else some money, and it did not come through. I was having some challenges with it at the time. This was some 10 years ago. At the same time, someone else who was supposed to give me money, did not give me the exact same amount of money. It is always collectively equal.

It is better to pay your debts, even if it is a little bit right now, and move toward full payment so you stay universally in fair exchange. But if you take on more credit than you can handle, you will create more debt than you can handle because the credit side is pride, and the debt side is shame. Pride and shame will stay hand-in-hand. They will always stay congruent, balanced. They are part of the four primary emotions.

If you take on credit, thinking, "Oh, my God! I just got a new credit card and I've got all these loans. I got approved with this line of credit." That sounds great, but what is the downside? You had better take a hard look at your situation and get your debt balance down.

About Your Assignment

Besides describing your beliefs about credit and debt, your assignment is to find the downsides of your credit and the upsides of your debt. And there is a clever reason why you need to do this assignment. When you got the credit card, you were super excited, and now, after you have spent the money on it, you are now pissed off because you have a debt and they are calling for their money back. These people are like, "Man, I've got all this debt, and I hate those debt collectors." They resent their debt.

If you resent debt—which is merely an interest in someone (the one who loaned you the money) receiving money—then you are not going to be receiving any money because whatever you resent you resist. Debt, credit, your paycheck—they are all attached to money.

Your assignment is to list the things for which you have credit and to find the drawbacks to those things for which you used credit.

If you bought a car, what was the drawback of that credit? The interest, the interest rate, managing it, having to pay a bill every month. Whatever the drawback might be, of the credit—not the debt. Merely getting approved for the credit made you think that you were better than you were. It made you think that you could have more. These things took you out of fair exchange and made you more emotionally chaotic.

Also, your assignment is to explore the benefits of debt. It gave you a car. It allowed you to get to work. It allowed you to produce for the family. It allowed you to take care of your responsibilities. It allowed you to give value to the marketplace.

If you have 14 credit cards, then do this exercise on all of them. If you have a mortgage, you do this for your mortgage. If you have student loans, do it for your student loans. If you have taken credit on 300 things, then do the drawbacks for all 300 lines of credit, plus the benefits of each debt. I promise you; you will become far more financially balanced after you have done this one exercise.

What will happen is that you will not get so chaotic around debt. You won't get so chaotic around business. You won't get so chaotic around your finances. You will balance your emotions on it.

Chaos and Positivity

During the COVID lockdowns, liquor sales were up because people would sit around and drink. And when people received stimulus checks from the government, they thought they suddenly had received "free money." More liquor sales. More chaos.

If you are doing this financial mastery program with a friend or associate, make certain you do the assignments separately. Every individual is unique and your own transformation may require something entirely different from that required by someone else.

If you think you have been stuck in a negative consciousness, as one student did, do not think for a minute that your goal is a positive consciousness on money. Your goal is a balanced consciousness where you have both the positive and the negative.

You are not going to make it positive because if you get positive, then you will get a positive trauma. I'm telling you, you do not want to be positive around money. You want to be governed around money—not positive.

Some people think that you have to be positive around money, but that throws you out of balance. Compare this to the tragic relationship. This is where someone has a relationship that was so amazing, that was so positively addictive in the beginning, and then all of a sudden, the other person just left? I am trying to tell you that the more positively addicted you become to money, the more you are going to lose it.

The more balanced and governed you are, the more you are going to keep it.

Assignment: Credit and Debt

    1-a. What is your belief about credit?

    1-b. Make a list of all your current sources of credit.

    1-c. Then, list 25 drawbacks to your credit.

    2-a. What is your belief about debt?

    2-b. Make a list of all your current debts.

    2-c. Then, list 25 benefits to your debt.

CHAPTER 22

Mission of Money

Universal mission of money. Most people in their life will go after money, not knowing what they are going to do with it. They want this thing called money without an understanding of what they are going to do with it. When you ask them what they are going to do with it, they do not really have an answer. They will say, "Oh, I'll go on vacation, and I'll do self-deprecating lower value tasks, and money will go to debauchery."

In other words, it will go into debauchery and low value tasks where it gets wasted and sent off to someone else.

Money circulates in society energetically toward those who value it the most. Those who value it the most take other people's debauchery money, and they organize it and put it into value. They will make sure that they organize it—every penny and every dollar, and maybe not to that extreme all the time. But their money will become organized because they value it.

Whatever you value, you organize. If you value your kids and their diets, you are going to make sure that what they eat is going to be organized. If you value their education, you are organizing their education. All of the things in their life are going to become valued inside of this urge to organize.

If I gave you $10 million, what would you do with it? You would not even know. And if you do not know, why would the universe give you money?

When you are financially organized, you have negentropy with money. Being financially disorganized means you have entropy with money, and entropy means "chaos." Another term for negentropy is syntropy, meaning "order." Most people's money is here in chaos. What they do is they look at money from this place of entropy or chaos because their debts are higher than their assets. They judge themselves on the emotions of the debt and minimize their assets.

The truth is that when you have chaos in your money, it is because you do not value it. The bridge to financial syntropy is understanding the value of money and increasing the value of it. Whenever you increase the value of something, you add more order to it.

This program is designed specifically to help you transform the chaos of money into the order of money. How do you do that? You rewire the freaking brain. You rewire your consciousness around it. You rewire the way you think about money.

Most people will tell you that they value money. But then I ask, "Do you have any?" to which they reply, "Well, no. I do not." That lack is because of this.

People rationalize their lack of money—their disorganized state. They make statements to make themselves feel better.

An individual is going to put themselves into chaos with money and we know this because they do not have any money. Their credit score is crap. Their money is zilch. They do not have savings, but they want all the riches that exist. They do not value this thing called money because they make no effort to organize it. Instead of organizing money, they dismiss it. And this dismissive attitude is because of the emotions surrounding money. What that does is create a loop back to chaos.

When I make the statement that money comes into your life and out of your life based on your emotions, it is a complete statement. The feeling in money is important; I talk more about this in my Inner Wealth program. If your emotions are taking you back into chaos, you need to realize that it is important to equal your debt/asset ratio because your net worth and your self-worth have to come together.

But if you do not organize your money, why would you get more of it? Think about that. If you have not organized what has been given to you, what could make the universe say, "Let me give you more so you can muck it up?" Think about it. If you were the universe, why would you give you more money?

If you are a parent and you give your kids food and they say, "I do not want to eat Brussels sprouts, to heck with this, to hell with you, Dad. I do not want to eat Brussels sprouts. I deserve better than Brussels sprouts." What is Dad going to say? "You are going to eat the food I made for you, and you are going to appreciate it, God damn it. I am not making anything else. If you want something else, you go make it." That is what you would say to your kid.

If you do not appreciate that—what has already been given—how do you get more of it? You do not. If you do not organize what has been given to you, how do you get more of it? You do not.

But if you say, "Hey, look, I am going to eat these today. I am totally grateful for the nutrition and the value that I'm getting inside of this. Universe, thank you for this. But I also want to make sure you know that I am not the biggest fan of this experience. I am grateful for it, and I can see the gratitude and everything inside of it. I'd like to experience something different." And the universe replies, "Sure. What would you like?" It is a different conversation that is going on. I understand I am anthropomorphizing the universe, but this is the effect of reality. I am merely making it a figurehead inside this conversation.

Now, if you are going to create money and put it in the state of negentropy, you are going to reach a point called a FIN—the financial independence number. This financial independence number is going to be the place where you say, "I've got enough money. I do not have to work." Great. But now what? Well, then you do not need to make money. What do you think happens to your money when you start to say, "I have extra, and I do not need more?" Watch that stuff decline in a freaking heartbeat. Watch it go down and watch it disappear because you are going to look now and say, "Hang on. I do not need it. I'm good." Then what happens is you create health bills and other, unexpected expenses. These show up to start depreciating your wealth.

If you are not continuing to do what it is you love to do, and by doing so, increasing the value of money, you cannot remain in fair exchange. This is because fair exchange involves what you are giving to the universe—what the outer world is receiving from your inner world. Nothing ever stays the same. A system either grows or declines. We see this as a hot iron gradually cools down or as a plant grows old and withers away.

If you are giving service and they are receiving your service, you will get rewarded in the form of money. But if you forget this component of serving—boom! Gone! If you do not serve, there is no receiver to give you money back. Then you are going to go to your savings, and it will start dwindling because your self-worth depreciates when you are not serving humanity. Your self-worth equals your net worth.

In the narcissistic side of yourself, you value yourself. On the altruistic side, you value others. In self-worth, you value yourself and others. That creates net worth.

Creating a Strategy and a Plan

Your upcoming exercise involves you getting organized. If I were to give you a million dollars today, what would you do with that money? How would you manage it? Figure it out. Do you have a system or strategic plan of what you are going to do with all that money that comes in the door? If you do not have it, there is no reason for you to get it.

Look at the people who are saying they have a plan. They are the ones who have money. That is your homework—your assignment. Do not speculate. Objectively, what would you do with that money? Look at it for yourself.

Perhaps you are the type of person who would say, "I would pay off my house, pay off my parent's house, and my kids' houses." Okay. Then what? Are you growing your asset or are you decreasing your asset?

Now, perhaps you are the type of person who says, "I have a purpose." And that's great. But that does not answer the question. What are you going to do with the money that is given? Because a purpose is an emotional statement. What you are going to do with the money is a very logical, objective statement.

What am I going to do if I get a million dollars? I am going to put this much in savings, directly. Then what type of savings? Are you going to put it in index funds? Are you going to put it in a simple bank savings account? What are you going to do? If you are not negentropic, meaning life increasing, then wherever you put that money, it is going to decrease.

That is the homework. Spend the time and be very calculating. Do not just generalize it with large, rounded numbers—$200,000 to this, $300,000 to this, $500,000 to that— "Okay. I'm done." Does your life really show that? If I looked at your life right now, you would not have five general categories of bills. No, no, no. You have far more, and what are they? Calculate them. Analyze them. Then look at it. How are you going to keep everything growing inside of that? If you have a business and you put a million dollars in the business or you put $100,000 in it, are you going to put it into overhead or into marketing or investments?

One student told me that she is going to buy five income-producing homes. Do you see the specificity in that? "Income-producing homes." She is not just going to buy five homes. Because she is looking at it as growth for her business. Be very specific with what you are going to do. Are you going to pay off debt? Are you going to pay it all off? Are you going to pay the minimum? In what order are you going to pay that debt?

If you do not organize how you approach money—I'm just telling you— it is all a fantasy.

Another student asked if she needed to include taxes in the plan. A great question. What that tells me is that she values business—not money.

So, I asked her, "What do you do?"

"My husband and I own a catering company for the Mavs and the Nuggets and the NBA teams and stuff, and then I just jumped into Primerica with the downfall of everything going on."

"Cool. So you value business," I replied. "Valuing business is very different from valuing money. Alright? If you value money, just say cash. If you value business, that is where you are saying post tax or pre tax because that's business money."

"I was just asking because if you're giving me $1 million and I have to pay the IRS, then I only have a little bit to work with. So, I wanted to make sure I really understood. Would you give me $1 million in cash, or do I have $1 million I have to pay my IRS tax and that's what I have to work with?"

"Let's just say straight cash. Then if you really want to take it another level, you can say, if my business earned $2 million, then what would you do? I run these types of projections all the time. It's fun playing with this stuff. I say, 'Huh, what would I do with that? Is it my money?' It is a great question you are asking. 'Is it my money?' Bottom line: You have got to organize this stuff called money."

Those who organize money the most get the most money to organize. That is where the principle of the "Secret" comes in. Like attracts like. I just gave it to you. Like attracts like and this is all about what you can organize—not what you fantasize.

Yet another student voiced their confusion about work/life balance. They said, "What you've discussed in these lessons and what you've said in your book, *Chasing Success*—these two things seem to be contradictory. It is not clear where I do not understand. But it seems as though sometimes we are concentrating too much on our job to earn more money. Your point is that we should have balance in both. We should work as well as have a balance in our life so that we do not compromise our health."

"No," I replied. "That is not what I'm saying. When you live in your highest values, then there is no compromise. You are just living in your highest values. The only reason you would ask me that question is when you feel out of balance with work and life. Right? In Get RYL *[Rewire Your Life]*, I go into two hours explaining the difference between work/life balance. But in your highest values—in what it is you love to do—you do not call that work. This is my life. I do not call it different. Do I work? Am I a Dad? It's just how I live. But if you say, 'I have to go to work,' is that separate from my life? No. It's part of my life. Is today Saturday? Is it Monday? I don't know. It's just another day of my life, and my life is doing the things that I love to do. It's not work. Does that make sense?"

Assignment: Universal Mission of Money

1. Given $1 million, what would you do with it? (Strategize/organize it; be specific)

CHAPTER 23

Tithing and Gifting

Tithing and gifting.

Let us start this discussion with the topic of muscle contraction. We are interested, here, in the conditions which trigger a contraction. Neurologically, we have two types of organisms out there. One is called an extremophile, and the other is a non-extremophile. An extremophile is configured to go all or none. Like a digital on-off switch, it is either contracting or it isn't. A non-extremophile goes basically midline, more meaning based.

With "all-or-none," your neuroreceptors in your body work in an "all-or-none" response. They sit at a threshold and they respond or act based on some conditional change or they don't. Now, what that means is this: An extremophile is also going to have a shorter lifespan and a highly emotional state for an individual—your neural action potential that sits within your nervous system. On a biochemical level, you have sodium and calcium channels that, in essence, are going to fire when certain conditions are met. All it needs is a certain response and—boom—it fires and causes a muscle to contract. Those action potentials are sitting there and as soon as it goes boom, they respond.

Now, it is sitting at a 90% action potential. That means 10% isn't there. All it needs is an additional 10% of more calcium and it goes into the muscle—bam! —we get a contraction. So, a muscle sits here at 90% awaiting an additional 10% of calcium. When that added 10% comes in, the calcium makes the muscle contraction occur.

You may be thinking, "What does this have to do with tithing?" It has everything to do with it. This is because 10% is the threshold to which your nervous system can respond. You will give 10% to make the muscle contract, but you will only be able to give 10% more, otherwise the muscle will shut off and it creates sufficient lactic acid to cause a spasm.

Why am I talking about 10%? This is because, neurologically, your brain can handle fluctuations of 10%. To illustrate this point, I asked one of my students to participate in a thought experiment.

"If you had $1,000, and asked for $1, would you give it to me?"

"Sure," she replied.

"If I asked for $10, would you give it to me?"

She asked, "Do we know each other?"

"Yeah. We're buddies. We're friends. We go way back."

"Sure."

"Okay. Would you give me $100?"

"I'd have to think about it."

"See my point? A 10% fluctuation causes some resistance to kick in." Then, I asked, "Would you give me $300, if you only had $1,000?"

"What do you need it for?"

"Buying groceries. $300. Would you feel comfortable giving me $300 if you had $1,000?"

"It would depend."

See what is happening? Now, she is going through a moral quandary. There is a moral challenge going on inside of her. Do I give him the money? Do I not give it? Now, she is asking me, "What's it for? Is it a good cause?" Now, she is justifying the act of giving by reasoning with herself. She is attempting to find the rationale to fit her emotional value structure.

The questions she asked, once beyond the 10% threshold, are now based on an emotional response. Does it fit her value structure or not? And so, that 10% fluctuation which someone holds is always going to act as the threshold for what they feel comfortable doing. This is what they can give without feeling a backlash of guilt, shame, or remorse. This is the science of it.

The Limits of Religious Giving

Now, I am going to discuss a topic which may offend some people, and I am okay with that. My intent is not to offend but merely to examine the facts from a different viewpoint.

Most, if not all, religious organizations have long known about this 10% threshold. They knew that their members could handle a 10% fluctuation in the mind without feeling guilt or shame. Churches, temples and other religious organizations have bills to pay. Like any business, they are concerned to grow their membership—their roster of customers. I have had the chance of meeting and working with pastors directly. I have done coaching and consulting with pastors, and they complain about the same damn things which concern any business.

How do we grow our business?

What do you think happened to the churches during COVID? They were all pissed off because, in many states, the government called them "non-essential" and forced them to shut down or pay a fine. Pastors were concerned: "How do I get people to give me money for my church so I can pay my bills when no one is coming in?"

If the state slaps them with a $5,000 penalty but they make $25,000 in tithing, then they would do it. Why not?

Tithing became a rule that religious organizations and spiritual institutions put into effect. They taught people to donate 10% of their money to a higher ordered system, and it makes them feel better. Because of that, the rule of 10% tithing came into play.

Depending on the group, tithing would protect you from going to Hell in the afterlife, or from coming back as an ant in the next life, or from not getting your 72 virgins, if that was what you were promised. Give 10% of what you have earned to the church, temple or whatever, and that will protect you in the afterlife.

Tithing, Savings and Taxes

One of my students brought up a number of concerns regarding this 10% figure.

"So, how would you handle the subject of tithing with your children if they said, 'I want to give 10%?' Would you give them the same example you just did? And what if they were like, 'So, it's just a decoy to make money, but I still want to give'?"

"Do it," I replied. "The altruistic side of you will do that because you believe it's going to give you more benefit than drawback to do it. Then do it. I'm not telling you not to do it. I'm not telling you it's wrong. I'm not saying any of that. I've donated thousands of dollars to similar organizations, and my parents still do. They feel good about it. And that's great. But understand, it is an emotional thing. You're doing it because you think it's going to make you feel good. It's still a fear-based mechanism to protect you from something else. I'm not saying it's wrong. I'm not saying it's a bad thing. I am saying, 'Okay. Do it because you want to do it,' and that's cool. But know where it's stemming from and know why it's 10%. Know what it stands for. Then if you choose to do it, then it's empowerment. I'm not telling anyone what to do with their money. I'm just telling you this is where the 10% stems from. It's written in the Papacy. I just put it away. It's written in the Papacy. If you go read the Papacy, it will unfold all the rulings. They know this 10% rule."

She asked, "Then how does that play with the 10% savings? We've been taught to give your first 10% as a tithe. A lot of people struggle with the 10% that goes to savings. It's like, I just did that."

"Now, watch this. It also says to take care of yourself first."

"Right."

"Isn't that an oxymoron?"

"Right," she replied. "That's why I jumped to the other side because when I'm teaching people about saving. They're like, wait, you want me to do 10% tithe, 10% savings, and then you talk about 10% investment, I'm left with 70% of my income. Are you serious?"

"And you haven't included taxes yet," I added.

"Yeah. I haven't gotten to that."

"And then if you have child support or alimony, then you've got to think of that, too."

"Right. And by the time I get through, my client has 30% of whatever we started with."

"So, what's your question?" I asked.

"I'm going back to the savings. Like, is there a rule or something around saving that we should know? Because I never knew this rule about tithing. I'm excited about it, but is there a rule around saving that we should know, that we don't know, or that you do?"

"First," I said, "save 10% for yourself. Pay 10% to yourself, first. I'm going to make a very large generalization, and I'll probably offend somebody. I'm just saying, if I do, that's not my intention. This has just been my observation. Okay? I have no problem with religion. I have great problems with people manipulating other people for the purpose of religion. I have a vast problem with that because that's not empowering people. That's blinding people in a state of fear to hold them captive so that you can buy another frigging jet plane. That's not empowering people. That's not educating people."

"That's why I struggle to have pastors as clients."

"If service is God's work, then why don't I let my money continue to serve my highest values. I would much rather do this than to give my money to some other guy so he can buy another plane or put up another fancy building. I don't see a value in it. I've seen people go to the pulpit and have nothing in their pockets and put everything in this. You guys don't know. I'm telling you. I've been backstage where the people in charge are just rolling in the cash, like nobody's business. We've worked with them. The kind of money that rolls through these churches, it's absolutely mind numbing. There is a guy right now—I swear—I was trying to videotape it. There's a guy putting water in a packet and calling it "miracle water" and people buy it because it's going to save them from COVID. He's capitalizing on people's fears and making people pay. People are going to do it. He's probably banking the hell out of it. He's not a dumb businessperson. That, to me, is robbery."

I have lots I can say on this subject. I avoid religion all day long until you come to my Delta program. Then, I rip it to shreds. I rip it to shreds because to empower yourself under the light does not diminish your light around other people. The true words of all religions, if you study comparative religions, are trying to tell you the same thing. It is trying to tell you that love exists. It is trying to tell you that love is an equanimity, a complementary, a balance. True love is not a one-sided polarization. It is not a happiness or a sadness. It is not rich or poor. It is an existence of gratitude. That is what I am trying to teach here.

I have a problem with people getting robbed by it. It is not objective; it is emotional. Money is not managed and kept, and the wealthy don't base it on emotions. You can make money with emotion, but you cannot sustain it for the long term.

Attitude and Management

A great many of my students struggle with this topic. With great effort, one woman attempted to ask her question: "So, I'm trying to think how to take out the—yes, I agree there is corruption in everything. But just to go back to the subject of tithing. We were lucky to throw $10 in at a time, here and there, when I went to a Bible study. This was covered, and I had to work up to it. There was no 10% in the budget. I guess, sort of like what you said, what we've been taught here is you need to invest in yourself and the money will show up. We experienced that when we started tithing as we moved up to that 10%. It just showed up in the budget. I guess what I'm thinking is, is it just the attitude behind it?"

"The management of it," I replied. "It's the management of it that's making more of it show up. When you put it into something that you value, you're only going to work up to 10% because you value it. I am not telling you to do it or not to do it. I'm not saying what is right for you or wrong for you. I'm not trying to say that. But if you value it, then do it. That means that you're going to create the budget—the room and the space—to make that happen. And in the same way, this happens when you value yourself.

"I've taken away the term 'spirituality' and I replaced it with 'self-worth.' I replaced it because service is the currency of the universe and everything that you do serves. Spirit and matter need to be at one with one another in order for you to express your values. So therefore, for you to be able to serve mankind, you have to value yourself. When you invest toward your highest values, toward your self-worth, it shows up."

My students, in their first two weeks doing this work, notice wealth coming at them from all different directions. That is why it makes sense that this increase is not based on any action. It is just because you valued it, it showed up. The more money you manage, the more money comes to you to manage. I can tell you how true that is. The better manager you become with money, the more money shows up for you to manage.

You may donate to a specific cause, and that is where you tithe. That can be your form of service to spirituality, so that is where you will take it. You have got to make your educated decision on what you want to do based on the information you have.

From 10% to Exponential Growth

One of my more creative students wanted to understand the limits with this idea of 10% growth. He asked, "So, that 10% fluctuation that the average brain works on, I'm sure there is, but is there a specific way that you can increase that?"

"Sure," I replied. "You can increase it. Are you talking about the vulnerability of it?"

He explained, "Like from what my understanding is, the average brain normally can handle 10% increments in numbers or in capacities. And then some people think really big. Like you've got the mom and pop shop down the street thinking at 10% and then you've got Steve Jobs and Bill Gates thinking at like 80% or something like that. Is there a way to extend the growth rate to this?"

"No," I replied. "It doesn't work that way. It's not a 'think big' type scenario. That has nothing to do with it. The way that it works, even Steve Jobs and Bill Gates, they took investments, they took on leverage, and they scaled. There's a whole different game that they had to play, too. And exponential growth can happen. I'm not saying it can't. But managing exponential growth is much more stressful and impactful.

"I'll give you an example. The stock market was sitting at 29, 30, 31, and then it dropped to 18 that day. Right? At 18 people were like, 'Oh, my God! It's never going to recover. What happened to those people? They flipped out. They lost their lid. If they couldn't manage that near 35% drop, they were out of the game. They left. They sold. Like, 'I can't lose anymore. The world is ending.' Then you had people who were sitting there with cash on hand and ready because they could manage and mitigate, manage the challenge, and would sit there—myself included—and we went that day and we bought and we bought. Because we can manage that much of a fluctuation because we've got the cash reserves, we can manage and mitigate the challenges that are in front of us. Whatever you can manage, you're going to prepare for.

"That is why I teach you guys the protection strategy. And if you are protected, you can manage against the greater fluctuations. But if you can't manage it, then you'll be afraid based on that."

He replied, "So, it's not necessarily a matter of comprehension. It's a matter of management. If you can teach yourself to manage more, then you can reach higher percentages."

"Right."

"I can manage 10% right now," he said, "but I could teach myself to be able to manage 25% to 35%."

"For sure," I replied. "Once you have more in it, right. Like one of the things I'll teach at Smart Money Live is how you can manage 50% and how you run your business on 50% of your assets. When you can get into that game, then it's like you're building a whole different life. But it starts by playing small—or better, by managing small—then moving to 3%, then 5%, then 7%, then 10%, then 20%. But if you don't manage that effectively, and I'm not preaching from an ivory tower, it took me forever and a day to figure this out. I was not born a smart money manager. Today I'm pretty good. Today I'm pretty damn efficient because I got my ass kicked so many times and I had to learn. That's what I'm trying to teach you guys because I've gone through it. I was really good at making money, but I couldn't manage it. So, you don't keep money. My emotions were involved and that creates more challenges. You've got to look at that for yourself. Yes, you can manage more if you can protect yourself from the loss."

Who Makes the Rules?

Another student pointed out the awkward difficulty he had found in church when they passed around the offerings basket several times during one service. He said, "I've been the type of person literally in church, they'll have three or four offerings in one service, and so I've got to give again. So I'm like okay, how am I going to take care of myself? Before I even give, I'm already knowing, I've got this and that to take care of. I've got all these things to take care of. But it's like, okay, I've got to give, I've got to give. And then they say, you've got to walk out on faith. You've got to have faith, right, and I'm like, well, I'm not going to be stupid either. I have to take care of myself. Through all of that process, it just helped me to really balance myself and be self-centered within. I'm not going to let the pastor or whoever that is dictate the amount of money I give, and on top of that because they have a way of making you feel ashamed if you don't give the amount that they're asking for. But my question is this: So, it really doesn't have to be toward a spiritual place of worship, or anything, just as long as you give? Because this principle about the 10% is just as long as you give to any good cause, that's the rule. Is that correct?"

I replied, "Look, someone's going to argue with me and say, who are you to make the rule? Right? So, I'm not going to sit and argue with that. At the same time, I used to sit there and say to my Mom that I would write the rules. Since you're talking about spirituality and religion, I used to be in the Hindu religion and the Hindu religious book is the Gita.

"I said to my Mom at a very young age, 'I'm going to write the Gita part two.' That's going to be my first book. She said, 'You can't do that.' I asked, 'Why not?' She's like, 'You can't write the Gita part two. You can't do that.' I said, 'It was written by a man. Why can't I be a man and write another book?' Someone put something down. They wrote it by hand. A person did it. If I sit and ask you, 'Who am I to make the rules?' I'll sit and say, at the same time, 'Who are they to make the rules?' You see my argument?"

"Correct."

"So, my rule is this: If you value yourself and put your resources toward the things you value most, you will create more money to give back to the universe. On the other hand, if you do something in a state of fear, you will lose more from all the resulting chaos. If you really want to be spiritual, live in your highest values, make as much money, create service, and help humanity."

Reciprocation Delusion

Let me add something here about a confusion that many people have on tithing and blessings. Some people tithe in church and expect God to give them blessings in return to help their business or to heal a loved one. One woman could not pay her rent, but decided to give 10% at church in order to receive this type of blessing. It does not work that way. You need to realize that God does not sit up there; God sits in your heart. Remember, when you work from the outside-in, you create chaos; when you work from the inside-out, you empower yourself.

When you tithe in church, or give to some charity you value, do it as an act of creation—not expectation. When you expect something in return, then you are no longer at cause, but at effect.

One of my students brought up this subject of expectations. She said, "Like you're tithing with the expectation that you're going to get something, but we've been taught not to do things in expectation. So, I'm like, okay, how are we dancing with this, Dr. T?"

"You've been taught not to. But people think that if you give to this, you'll get something else back."

"Right."

"Watch this. I'm going to really mess with your head. The most disempowered communities worldwide are the religious ones. This is because they anthropomorphically need something outside of you to give you 'faith' to ride through it. The most disempowered people will look to prayer to solve their problems when they don't understand. The mind—it goes to the temporal parietal lobe in the brain. We create God in the anthropomorphic nature of ourselves to help us navigate the fears of ourselves in society. That is the animal-based, human-based God. If you study the beginnings of where God comes from and where it stems from, this is what I'm saying. I'm not saying it is right or wrong, good or bad. This is human nature that we do this. Because of that, we portray this image.

"One winter, a few years ago, I was driving in Albany, New York. No phone signal, in the mountains, snowstorm, pitch black, at 3 miles an hour, and I had an hour to drive in it. I started talking to God. 'God save me. God help me. God if you get me through this, I'll do this.' Then, I laughed at myself. *You dumb idiot. You know better than to do this.* I was asking God to help me because I was so scared. In that extreme fear, we create a conversation with God to bifurcate our mind to help us manage the fear. That's what it's about. So, when you have an expectation on something— 'When I tithe, I am going to get something back'—that's a delusion. You're not going to get it back. Right? Now, you give your money away to something that has higher ordered organizational systems.

"To create an expectation on a tithe is kind of a false idea. The only reason people do it is because it is making them feel better. When they feel better, then they raise oxytocin and dopamine in their body, and then they go out and do something with their life. But when you are in your highest values and you do the things that you love to do, you create the same effect.

I'm not trying to teach you how to live in your lower values; I'm trying to teach you to live in your highest values."

When given a choice between "faith" and "worry," I will pick worry because worry gives me the feedback that I am not sufficiently prepared. Faith—the way most people do it—tells me I am blind and I have not prepared for things, so I have to trust something versus being prepared for myself. Worry creates empowerment; faith, the way most people do it, creates disempowerment.

Judgment Versus Love

One student told me how he had begun to realize how conversations he was having with other people were modified by fear in their own past—that the other person was reacting to the current situation based on some past trauma, perhaps in their childhood. He asked, "Any advice on how you manage the relationship?"

"We all have our own journey," I replied. "It's better to love them for where they're at versus judging them. Everyone is at a different level. You're not better or worse than any other person. You're just a human being going through your highs, lows and challenges. I wouldn't look at it from a place of judgment. That's what sometimes people do with my work. They say, I know a little bit more, so I get to judge you. That's not the purpose of the work. Right?"

"Right."

"The purpose of this work is to love them—not to judge them. But in the initial phases people put on the face of judgment because they can see things a little differently. Later, when this material is no longer so new, you will realize that there's nothing to judge."

Assignment: What are you tithing and gifting to?

1. What do you really want to donate/tithe your money to?
2. What is your afterlife cause that you wish to contribute to?

CHAPTER 24

Products Service Idea

Product or service or idea. All germination of business starts with a product, a service, or an idea—every single one of them. Now, they all need to get packaged and distributed. That is the business. That is, in general, every business. A product, service, or idea gets put into a package and then gets distributed to equal cash and value exchange. All business works this way— every single one.

One of my students and I had a fascinating discussion on this topic which should prove valuable toward your own financial mastery.

I started the conversation with a hypothetical: "Okay, I have this idea. I am a creative intuitive, and I don't know how to convert this into a business. I don't like business, and I don't like doing investment. Great. Fantastic. Can you package your product? Can you package your information? Can you package what you're doing and put it into a product?"

She replied, "I've already done it for years."

"Great. Let me go through the content first, and then we'll come back to your specific situation.

"You package it into a product and then what you do is you say, 'Okay, where is that product from? Is it intellectual property?' Most of my business is intellectual property, at this point. Is it a business? My business has something which is saleable. That has a value. Cash, money, social relationships, physical, what can you package? Can you package your body and sell it, or sell it as a model and whatnot? Health, can you package health in a bottle and sell a vitamin supplement? Can you package spirituality? Yeah. Every single area you look at is all packaging in all seven areas.

"Now, let us say that you don't like doing the business side. You can take your product because you packaged it, and then sell the IP of it. You can sell the rights to it. You don't have to run and operate a business. You have to find people who buy IP who can distribute it."

"What is IP?"

"Intellectual property. If you've created products or packages or programs, I would assume that most of them fall into IP for you."

"I'm a teacher, a Montessori teacher, and I developed three paradigms, working with parents, working with the children, for a higher level of training, a new breed of teachers, and also spirituality awareness that comes from consciousness down, not airy-fairy crap. In other words, beyond what all the Bibles have already told us and stripped them of their garbage and their bullshit."

"So, you want to ask, 'Who can I sell these three products to?' How can you sell the IP where every time they use it, you can make money off of it? That is one way to do it. There are multitudes of ways. The reason I'm saying this is because you don't have to run and operate the business if that's not what you love to do. At almost 70 years old, it's probably not what you're jiving to do. You're probably not saying, 'Hey, let me go deal with HR, or deal with management, or deal with people taking days off, and all that stuff. You've done all of that before, but you don't want to deal with that now."

"Right."

"So, you can partner with somebody or you can partner with a firm that does it for you. You can partner with an IP firm that goes out and sells it. You can partner and license it. You can create distribution streams that you just sell it directly and they go do it whatever the hell they want to with it. There are multitudes of ways, but the key that you have got to look at is how do you want to package it and where do you want to put it out? You have got to be able to market and sell it. If you can't market and sell it, you've got to look up firms that can market and sell it and then give them a percentage of it."

She replied, "Not really at the point or have the interest to sell it. I'm more interested in demonstrating and setting up a model school that can be replicated, and I would like to train the first group of a new breed of teachers. I do a lot of things where people say, 'You can't do that!' 'But oh, my God, she's doing it.' If they see the model, it stops a lot of the arguing and the 'you can't' responses. I just stop and say, 'I'm going parallel. I'm not going to fight with you. I'm not going to convince you of what you can't see.' So, I'm at the point where the greatest thing that I have is to be engaged with what I love to do, and that is working with the children in the school, training a group."

"Okay. When you take a product, a service, or an idea, you've got to find the distribution channels for it. Who wants it? You don't have to sell the product, but someone's got to sell the product. Nothing happens until something is sold. Period. Nothing happens until something is sold. If you're not selling something somewhere, your Montessori school will not exist. It doesn't matter. You can say, 'I want to set up a thing. I want to go leftwing instead of rightwing, but somebody has to sell that idea and has to have a value worthy of getting money. You need some kind of business profit for them to move forward with it. Without that, it's nonexistent. So, you don't have to do that yourself, but you have to have someone who does that. Right? You have to partner with someone at some level. Coming up, you'll see how you will have your traumas with money. You'll have to work through those and the past traumas you've had with relationships. But you'll also have to look at it and say, 'Okay. With all the products, services, and ideas that I'm putting in place, who can benefit from this information?' and then go sell it to them."

Assignment: Products Service Idea

1. Write out the products or services you provide that you can package.
2. What is the part you do not love to do?
3. Who and how can you partner with them?

CHAPTER 25

Transcending the Trauma

Amygdala—The Emotional Center

Inside the brain down in the middle, you have this thing called the amygdala. The amygdala functions as the emotional center of the body. What they have found is that the amygdala is where you hold onto the emotional or financial traumas that we speak of.

In past lessons, we have talked about the emotional management of money. People look at it and say, "I've got to learn how to manage money. I've got to do a better job of managing my money." This needs to include everything to do with financial consciousness.

In the older self-help paradigms, you learn about allowing yourself to have rewards for achieving specific goals. You hit a goal, and then you buy yourself something. That is an external, or outside-in, system. And remember, this type of arrangement leads to chaos. A better arrangement would be internal or inside-out.

In a moment, I want to tell you about a Japanese doctor who did a study around this. What he found is very interesting. But before we get to that and what he taught, I want you to understand some additional facts about the amygdala. It holds both the positive and the negative traumas of your life. It has been functioning in essence to keep you stuck in the cycles of positive or negative trauma. In order for you to be able to manage anything effectively, you have to be able to transcend the trauma. If you do not transcend trauma, you remain stuck.

What do I mean by transcend? You need to learn to love it. When you do that, it no longer has any leverage over you or your behavior. From this transcendent viewpoint, you can see it for what it is. You become objective regarding your trauma—no longer subjective.

If you have a subjective bias inside of your thoughts, what you think is now based on your emotions. So, anything that you have in your emotions is a subjective system.

You all know—some of you more than others—that something can start off being the worst experience on the planet, but can turn out to be the best thing that has ever happened to you. In other words, something that you can perceive as good.

If you transcend the trauma, you become objective and it will no longer be an emotional spot in your mind. You will have left the emotions behind.

Now, back to the Japanese doctor. He and his fellow researchers began with a question: "What in society helps people grow? What makes societies and people have a true level of growth?" They had been doing studies on depression and they found that this dark, emotional state is brought about through psychological processes. We know this. This is not new, but it is based on the amygdala.

The amygdala is the fight-or-flight system—hair-trigger, survival response system.

They did a study to find out which type of people would be the happiest. Now, watch this. If I were to give you a Rolex watch, you could sell it for $10,000. But what if I were to sell that same watch to you for $1,000? How many people would buy the watch and then go sell it for $9,000 profit?

What they found was this: The person who gets a bad deal and a person who gets a good deal have very similar amygdala responses. Their amygdalae are both equally active, creating emotional trauma on both sides. However, when someone gets a fair amount for a transaction, there is no amygdala activity.

What does this mean?

When you think you are getting a good deal, you become elated about it. You become excited and your amygdala starts firing. Dopamine levels go up. Same with your oxytocin and serotonin levels. You say, "This is a good frigging deal. I've got to act on this." You become addicted to the deal, and you cannot walk away from it. You have to act on it.

If you get a bad deal, you become resentful, frustrated, shameful, and guilty. That is what happens when you get a bad deal and this also activates the amygdala.

Both the good and the bad deal activate the amygdala and cause you not to transcend.

Fair exchange is the way you grow and transcend without having challenges. In business, if you are charging fair equity for what you do and you provide that value to somebody, and they get that value, then that is sustainable. There is no emotional charge to it.

Each of these—the insanely good deal and the rotten deal—creates the emotional charge that prevents you from growing. They hold you stuck, addicted, and trapped with money. Either of these can prevent you from managing money. The fact that you got a good deal on something prevents you from being able to manage it.

When either of these happen, it triggers the sympathetic nervous system.

Money has no meaning until you give it meaning. Money is not about setting higher rewards. It is not about making more. It is not about any of that. Money is merely a resource that is used to help you provide more and do more of what you want to do in life.

One of my students struggled to understand how all these topics fit together. She said, "So, if I understand this correctly, fair trade is really subjective, right? Because it's the value that I have for myself that determines what that fair trade is, right? Because if I think I don't deserve anything at all, well, then I'm not going to ask for much because that's fair trade, or I actually believe that I bring tons and tons of value to the world, then I can ask for a lot and that's fair trade. Is that right?"

"Yes, you're right. But that's just one side of it. If you don't believe you add value to yourself, then what's going to happen is that you're going to not want to go buy more and not want to do more for yourself. Then at the same time, if you get something for nothing, you're going to end up resenting that person."

In any exchange there is something being given. The currency of the universe is service. It is happening whether you see it or not. Your job is to become aware of it, and to see it.

Another student shared an interesting breakthrough. She said, "I was kind of having a really bad experience with my car mechanic fixing my car, and I was pissed off. I was so very frustrated and resentful toward them for holding my car. But suddenly, I caught myself building pride around that because I had wanted to be right. I was thinking, let me find an attorney. Let's see what we can do. And then I checked myself because, through my divorce, I was very successful using an attorney, and so I caught myself in this place of pride. I swear to God that the next day, the check engine light, which was the source of the concern, went off. Like, what the heck is that? Seriously. Anyway, I checked myself emotionally, and the next thing I know, the problem totally self-corrected. It was entirely weird."

"That's not weird at all," I replied. "That's a feedback mechanism, trying to get you back to your authentic self."

The work of financial mastery is focused on helping you transcend all these emotions and traumas that you have around money. If you are not making what it is you want to make, it is because you are not doing the work.

Fair Exchange and Reciprocity

Another student had a hiring example to share. She said, "So in business, if I hire a front desk person, and I pay them $7 an hour, I'm ecstatic because I'm getting this person so cheaply. However, they're accepting that job because they don't have high self-worth, and that really just brings the whole energy down in my office. It really has."

You have to pay in fair exchange so they can feel the value in the work. If you own them or you use money as a tool against them, and if they think they are getting a great deal or the short end of the deal, that is where you create long-term havoc financially. There is no good deal. There is no bad deal. There is just a deal.

"Okay," said one of my students. "So, I think you kind of just answered this, but you got me thinking. We felt like we got such a good deal on this boat. Like we were saying, 'Oh, we stole this thing,' but then what ended up happening is I had to rewire the whole boat, so it was double the cost. So, there really isn't any good deal. It's going to come out even."

It is always going to come up balanced. The other day, I had a few minutes waiting for my son, so I was online and decided to look at the marketplace and see what the hell is out there. Then, I saw a 2012 Porsche Cayenne for $3,000. My first thought was, "I bet you I could take this and turn it around and sell it. Just put it in the driveway—whatever—and someone will come buy it. I'll make some money on it. Then, I was like, "No! You know what? What are the real chances this car is really worth $3,000? In the ad, they claimed that it is in mint condition. "Mint condition, my ass!" There is more to this story than I want to know. It is too good a deal to be true. My student was right in her boat example.

"So, with your car idea," said one of my students, "I'm going to try to get a little bit more understanding. You're like, it's $3,000 and it's too good to be true, but maybe it would be a good deal for them because maybe they've got to offload the car quickly. Maybe they're in the middle of a move or whatever. So, really for them it's fair trade because they need to get rid of that car so they can move somewhere else. And they're going to make more money by moving, let's just say. So, wouldn't it be a fair exchange?"

"It can be," I replied. "I didn't want to pursue it. It could be good for someone else, if that's really what the situation is and the car is really worth that. I just looked at it and said to myself, *I don't really want to get involved with it.*

Both parties can feel as though they are getting a great deal. When that happens, it is a fair exchange. If one party feels as though they are cheating the other, then it is not a fair exchange. This is all about perception and the value you place on the things being exchanged. If you perceive that there is an imbalance, then you will end up creating more work for yourself to achieve balance.

One of my students was concerned about reciprocity. She asked, "How does the law of reciprocity fit into this? I never did a lot of trading with my business because I learned through just valuing and self-worth, but I understand the whole fair exchange. But how is that different from the law of reciprocity?"

I replied, "Reciprocity means that I'm going to put something out there and eventually it's going to come back to me. Right? That is the essence of it."

"Okay. And I don't normally do a lot of trades. Like if somebody comes to me and says, 'I'd really like to work with you,' like a massage therapist, for example, 'Would you be willing to trade your coaching for my massaging?' I don't normally do that."

"Because," I said, "you have a higher value and a higher essence of money, so you don't barter. Barter is a permanent state of fair exchange. That's where it started. I don't like barters because I value dollars and cents. I'm not against barter. Sometimes you have to barter."

"Yeah," she replied. "I've done them. I just don't do them all the time. It's very rare."

"So, again, what was the second part of your question?"

"How is this different from the law of reciprocity?"

"When someone feels that they're getting something for free, what they're doing is they're creating the emotions of guilt and shame in order to pay for that service. That's one side of it."

"Okay. Because they're getting it free?"

"They're getting value," I said, "and if it gets value to them, then they're going to say, 'There is value to this. I have to give back'."

"But giving back out of guilt and shame, right? Not out of an expansive way, but more of a constricting way?"

"It depends on the context. It's more of a constricted way if your reciprocity includes a perception of value inside of it. Let me give you an example. When I do my Inner Wealth program, I don't look at the numbers of how many people are going to attend. No matter how many attend, I give the best possible service to them. Whatever happens, happens."

She replied, "You don't have the emotional attachment to it for the outcome."

"I'm not putting that into the market or the energizing space. At the same time, there are people out there who say, this is lousy, so they turn it off. Great. There are other people who say this is the greatest thing since sliced bread. Great. They stay on. They perceive value. There is some reciprocity and what happens is that it makes itself back on the people who do want to stay on. It's called preeminence in that state. Preeminence—in essence providing value, being a resource to people."

"Right," she replied. "Because I believe that the service you provide is in direct proportion to the money that you make. That's kind of what you're saying, right, in a roundabout way?"

"Yeah."

She said, "The law of cause and effect."

"I'm transcending cause and effect."

"What?" she asked.

"I'm saying, every cause that needs an effect is an emotional charge."

"Hmm. But isn't there an effect with every cause?"

I replied, "What I'm saying is that you can live causeless and effectless when you transcend the actual challenge and the emotion of it. There is a causeless state. Like emotional states. What I'm trying to show you and say, in the balanced state, the essence state, it's a causeless state."

"Yeah," she said. "It's kind of like there's no emotional attachment to it and it's taking the ego out of it, right?"

"Ego is not a term I'm going to use. I'm going to say it's going to take the id out of it. And I'll show you what that is and why that is what it is."

"Okay. So then, I guess to re-verbalize it, you're not getting emotionally attached to the outcome of things. And not having expectations."

"Correct. I serve because I love to serve, not because of the impact and not because of the effect of it. I do what I love, not because I'm looking for an effect of that service on the backend."

Money and Your Personal Mission

Life is full of decisions and sometimes weighing our competing priorities is not so easy. One student shared his challenge between more money and his own personal mission.

"I am looking for—well, I operate a lot more from my mission now, thanks to you, and nearly every meaningful conversation that I have when I'm trying to create a future, I literally share it. And so I had a conversation with the national Vice President, who I reached out to, for Optum Behavioral Health because I believe that the work that you do has a place in healthcare. Optum and UnitedHealth Group are the largest insurers in the world, and so she took me up on an informational interview. I just chatted with her because I'm looking for my career path. I want to go where I can make the biggest impact. Through that conversation, literally within five minutes, I shared with her my mission. At the end of the conversation, she asked for more of my time. And at the same time, my boss knows that I'm looking for my next career move. He offered me another position. I looked at it. It's a position I would have jumped on because it is definitely more money, but it has nothing to do with my mission, so I'm just kind of like, 'Nah. Sounds great, thanks, you know. I'm not fueled by it at all.' This woman hasn't offered me anything, but I just feel more natural and at peace and kind of balanced when I'm pursuing that conversation. I take it that's what all this stuff is for me, right?"

"It is and it isn't," I replied. "I'm speaking on this in the context of money. You're in a greater state of your essence, so your essence has a greater conversation that is tied to your mission."

"Yes."

"That's the difference. Right? When you're living in your essence, then you're functioning from that state and you have greater value for what you do, for lack of better words."

"Yes. So, the conversation with her and being in that space is an investment in a new income. That's really part of what I'm pursuing. It's just a new context in which I can generate more money and also impact more people. Even though it's not turning into money right away, I still feel like it's a financial endeavor or pursuit."

"You don't value money, right? You don't value that money. You value meaning and impact a lot more than money."

"And I want more money."

"Maybe that's why you are more awake to doing that work."

"Yeah."

"And so, it's completely congruent to who you are. That's why. Now if someone had a higher value of money, they may say, 'You know what? Let me go see this and follow that money trail.' It just depends on the individual."

"Yeah. I follow the money, it's just not worth that for me right now. I do want to generate more, but like you said, my values are more about the impact."

Financial mastery is a skill you can take with you into any endeavor. And when you are internally aligned, you create far less chaos in your life.

Dopamine Addiction and the 'Good Deal'

"I wanted to get to something that you kind of covered a little bit on the Inner Wealth, but also on this call. Can we get addicted to the dopamine of getting a good deal? Like always on the hunt for good deals or always looking for these things?"

I asked, "Have you ever met an Indian person?"

He laughed. "Yes. Doing transactions. Yeah."

"God! They're addicted to that."

"Yeah," he said. "It's like you've already got a good deal. 'Oh no, but I want more!'"

"That's what I'm trying to share with you guys. Both of those—the 'good' deal or the 'bad' deal—create the same physiological response in the system—in the body."

"So now," he asked, "does that create more chaos monetarily, while the fair exchange keeps the balance, but it also opens the way for more money to come in?"

"That's correct!" I replied. "You're getting it. Now you're getting it."

"I'm working on it," he said. "It's a hard nut to crack, but yeah. Then also you said if you're not making the money that you want to make, then you're not in fair exchange. Is that imbalance with yourself or is it that you're just not in fair exchange with the universe?"

"There is probably more to it. I can't tell you exactly, but there's more to that. Potentially yourself, potentially others as well."

"Yeah. Because I've gotten a lot from your Inner Wealth program. I've gotten to love myself more and to take care of myself, my health and a whole lot more. So, I'm working on my gym right now, so I can do cardio and take better care of my body."

"Because I called you out on it. Just start doing it. Just start moving."

"More money showed up like right after Inner Wealth and also I was doing some more work at listening to some of your information about the 50 drawbacks of having money and 50 ways of showing gratitude for how you're making money, the 50 benefits of making money, and then there are the 100 drawbacks of keeping things where you are, or the pain. Like the other student said, he doesn't want it to be painful to stay where he is, so I'm working on that right now. But that also worked in harmony too with this Inner Wealth because I can no longer stay where I'm at, whether it's financially or whatever it is. But yeah, I'm going to get through that assignment; I appreciate what you said. It's got to be so painful to stay where you are that you move."

"It is super important," I replied, "because if it's not painful, you're not going to go do anything about it."

"Yeah. That's it. So with that, I also wrote out my goals and things like that too, but I also wrote out the 'why not' on those two, why don't you do this, or why don't you do that, so I can get that. Once I got the balance, more money just started showing up, and I was like, okay, this stuff actually works! Okay. Because it's the science of it and understanding this. I mean you really killed it this weekend on the science of it. It's like, that was good. And I wanted to ask this too because I was able to get a good deal on let's just say some knives that I've been looking at. Because I kicked butt, I said, okay, let me reward myself by getting the knives that I wanted, and it's like I got a killer, super killer deal on knives. Now it's like, okay, was that fair exchange? So understanding that, the chemical balance of it, is so important."

I replied, "When you get a good deal, automatically you perceive that the other person didn't get a good deal. Right? Unless they truly did. And they're not making that deal unless they're actually perceiving that transaction as valuable."

"They got a good deal on the other side because they got the money out of me and other things, so there was some fair exchange, but I was grateful."

I nodded with a smile of appreciation. "If you can be grateful for it, that's the key. That's the key behind it all. If you can be grateful for a deal, that's great and be in fair exchange with it. You're balanced. Balance does that to the whole thing. Good job, dude. You're getting it."

The great basketball player Michael Jordan played each game as if it were his last. My son looked at me and he goes, "Dad, that's what Kobe said."

I said, "I know. Do you see a trend here?"

He said, "Do you do that?"

I told my son, "I don't do each seminar like it's my last seminar. I do each seminar like it's my last shot to try to help someone wake up to who they are."

He replied, "That's interesting. Why do you do that?"

"Because there may be other paths on the journey for them, but I know that if I don't do whatever I can to help them, there's the potential they may not do anything."

We have something here that can help anybody who wants to be helped. So, I do look at my work with that same athlete's intensity. Sometimes it is too much for people. I respect that. And I take the downside of that as well.

End of the Roller Coaster

Sometimes students do not have questions but merely want to share their breakthroughs and successes. This one is worthy of mention:

"The promotion I was talking about, the first thing that pops into mind is 'more money.' Really, that's the first thing that pops into everybody's mind in a similar situation, but I looked at it—the responsibilities and the drawbacks. It was going to pull me from my family which is my highest value, and it just is what it is. I'm looking at both sides of it and whatever outcome comes, and there's no emotional attachment. I'm not pissed if it happens. I'm not happy if it doesn't. The back and forth, just to neutralize it like that, that goes with any type of deal that can come your way. If you can look at both sides of it because the first thing you know, like you were saying, emotionally it's horrible or it's great, but it's actually both. When you can do that, you're just not really on so much of a roller coaster. I mean, I was able to leave $200,000 a year in the oil field and I'm making a quarter of that, but I'm more fulfilled because I'm with my family. The money is still showing up as I do the work, and it's in a different form. Surprisingly, there's nothing missing. We're still in the same house. We're still in the same cars. There's nothing missing. There's so much to this work. Just the other day I got into the lesson's assignment and stuff came up. Then more stuff came up. I was like, whoa, I didn't even know that this trauma was there. Growing up, I had to live with my grandparents. I made money as a child when my Mom was in prison. We lived with my grandparents and I worked, but my grandmother took my checks and saved them. So, I had a resentment toward saving, and I didn't realize that until just the other day. I was like, holy crap. So yeah, I just truly appreciate it. Thank you."

Perspective on the Work You Are Doing Here

When you walk a mountain path from the valley floor, it is hard to understand the progress you have made unless you can see the entire path behind you, or at least your starting point. One student was quite surprised by his own progress when he gained some very helpful perspectives.

"First off, I totally forgot that we have new people on the program. It's amazing. But man! All you new people, just stick with this work because I didn't realize how much I was changing until you guys started asking the same questions I had asked like three months ago. And I was like, 'Oh, my God! I'm getting it. I'm getting it.' Now I'm all excited because I can see the progress I've made.

"Regarding my question, I don't remember who asked it, but it concerned the deals. If you feel like you're getting a great deal, and they feel like they're getting a great deal, that's equal. If I feel in my brain and know in my heart that I'm making a deal with someone in fair exchange, and then weeks later she comes back saying, 'Oh, my God, he ripped me off,' and she feels out of balance, but I'm still in balance. How does that relate? Because I know that everything's connected and so there's something here that I'm just not seeing."

"That's a great question," I said. "What she'll do is she'll create her own resentment and she'll see the downsides to the deal that she wasn't looking at before. So, she'll be forced to look at the downside. That's why in negotiation, you've got to be able to walk away. This is because you can see both sides of the coin, unless it's four sides of the coin—the pros and cons of having the deal and the pros and cons of not having the deal. Let me say it this way: Whatever you don't have an awareness about will be brought to your awareness to make sure that you actually learn to reach equitable exchange.

"I'll give you an example of this. I had a staff person against whom I was holding a massive resentment. She had worked for something like six weeks as an event coordinator. Even though it was during the time of COVID, firing her had nothing to do with COVID. After we let her go, she was like, 'I deserve severance. I deserve this. I deserve that.' I was like, 'Are you fucking kidding me? Six weeks, you don't deserve severance. You haven't done anything yet. Late all the time.' I had a list of complaints written up during her stay. It balanced out the times I had harbored positivity toward her—the benefits of that relationship. Until I could see what value she had brought, I was out of fair exchange in that."

"Okay."

"It's up to the individual to master their own fair exchange. Because it's happening regardless. We cover more of this in the Align Mastery program. But one other thought: You can't control someone else's awareness. You can only control your own. The universe is trying to wake you up to take off your blinders."

Extending Your Mission

This next student question ties in to the previous chapter, but this is how the breakthroughs typically happen. A future lesson or learning experience will help you align the data so that it suddenly makes sense.

"My question is kind of a follow-up to what we talked about last week about giving. Where it's like, why do I give to things? I've been thinking about it. Then the thing that you talked about today, which makes perfect sense to me, if I want to support a cause that helps promote things that I believe in or things that I find of value, is that a different kind of giving? Because I feel like I'm getting fair exchange. I give to different schools and I give to like NBIC and other organizations that I feel like even though it's a donation, my fair exchange from that is the work that they do."

I replied, "Not necessarily. You're giving value, so therefore you do it. Because it's still compensation for something that you're attached to."

"But if in my head it's a fair exchange, does it change? Because last week when we were talking, it seemed that if I give something to my kids or my grandma or something like that, that's not necessarily a fair exchange thing, but in this case because it's giving to a cause, and I feel like it doesn't give me an emotion one way or another, I'm like, okay, I'm giving these people money because they do work that I don't have the time or the desire to do, but I find it important."

"Then it's just extending your mission because it's connected to your mission in some way."

Assignment: Transcending the Trauma

1. When have you perceived you got a good deal? (30 drawbacks)
2. When have you perceived you got a bad deal? (30 benefits)

CHAPTER 26

Fear of Money

I would like to talk about a rather odd topic—the fear of money. When we are completely honest in our assessment of reality, we have to admit that money is such a weird thing as a construct. To be sure, everyone has their own story around money and quite often we hide part of that story even from ourselves.

Many people in our society perceive money as such a negative thing. We may have seen others do such horrible things in order to get ahead. Everyone has negative associations with money. At the same time, other people have perceived money to be very positive. The truth is that money is neither negative nor positive. Instead, money has a much more balanced game inside of it.

So often we get these polarized constructs of money from people who do not understand what money is all about. Then we subordinate our lives to their constructs regarding money. We become so certain of the construct we accept as valid that we miss the aspects of money which are not part of that construct.

There are so many hard-working people in the world—even outworking others under the table with their incredible work ethic—but without any understanding of money and how it works. Many others—especially those who stay at home and depend on the family provider—resort to hope and prayer as their guidance in life. Hope and prayer is not a strategy.

You have to go after your hopes and dreams, and do things in an effective manner. These negative associations work against you. So many negative traumas surrounding money, perpetuated by the people around you, distort your perception. Society and the people in it perpetuate those negative associations.

So many people have heard, while growing up, that money is a bad thing, or that you should not have too much money, or that money is a source of chaos or trouble. We have all been taught things like these by people who do not understand the context of money. Instead of wisdom, they impart their own chaos. This can include some religious people misquoting their own holy book, like, "Money is the root of all evil." The chaos is evil, but not money.

Please do not misunderstand me. Do not blame your parents for their shortcomings and misunderstandings. You need to remain grateful for all they have given you. When you view each challenge as a gift, you prepare yourself for financial mastery. Your parents, siblings, friends and associates have helped to give you your starting point. From here forward, what you want to do is be different. Everything from your past served a purpose which has prepared you for your future. But you do not need to remain there forever. You no longer have to remain in that financial place. You can move on to something else—something more empowering.

The challenge with which you are faced involves your current consciousness. And that mindset is based on a belief pattern that may include something like, "If I make money, I will become a bad person," or "If I make money, people in my community will judge me harshly."

When you are in a fear state with regard to money, you are stuck in the societal view which fears the attainment of money. This may not apply to you, specifically, but it is common enough throughout the world. Your problem with money may be nothing else than this. Maybe the problem is that, if you get wealthy and successful, your parents, your kids, or uncles and aunts—the ones with whom you grew up—are going to judge you on the subject of money. It may be that they are going to say, "You know what?

That's bad. You should be this other way." Maybe you are not subordinating yourself to your Mom and Dad, but maybe you are subordinating to the external family, or even bigger than that—maybe you are subordinating yourself to the society in which you live. Maybe the people in your community look at your new lifestyle and judge it as "expensive." But is that really true? Or is that merely one person's perspective? After all, the term "expensive" is a relative word.

Let me give you an example of this. I went shopping this past weekend. It was that special time of the year called "Black Friday" weekend. On Saturday, we went to the outlet mall and I said, "I'm going to go get some clothes. I need some clothes." We went to the store and I bought a bunch of sweaters and other things. While in the store, I looked over the selection and said, "Okay. Here's one sweater which is $50 and another one which is $100." Right? But if you have money, which sweater are you going to wear—the $50 or the $100 one? I want you to understand this. Think about this for a second. You value many things about a sweater—what the sweater does to your self-image, how it makes you feel, how it gives you the right look, and how long it will last. Would you pay more for these things? Of course you would. When the money does not matter, the sweater which does not have these things does not stand a chance.

Now, let us drill down into my example a bit more deeply.

The store where I bought the sweaters was Hugo Boss. I like Hugo Boss. In fact, I like wearing Hugo Boss stuff. At that store they had some crazy deals, like sweaters which were $180 marked down to $40 and $50. I was like, "Deal! Score! I'm in!" I could do that all day long. I bought a bunch of sweaters. Now, there was one sweater which was sort of nice, but it was not so different from the others I had already selected. Also, it was a bit more than I had wanted to spend on any one sweater, like $90. "Why not? I'll buy it anyway. That's fine because it will go with my suits." I rationalized it in my head to put it within my range of values.

"I can wear it at Delta," I told myself. "It can be a business expense." That is how I looked at it. Right?

But then I went to Banana Republic right next door to Hugo Boss. Of course, they also had sweaters there, but they were like $20 each.

Okay, here's the thing. I saw my consciousness shift between the two scenarios. I was like, "Oh, my God! I should return all of these sweaters, and instead of paying $40 or $50, get these sweaters for $20." I thought, "I could get double the sweaters."

Have you ever done that before? You tell yourself, "I could get more of what I want."

Standing there in Banana Republic, I looked at myself and said, "Why would I want more sweaters? Do I want more sweaters, or do I want quality sweaters?" I shook my head and said, "No, I want quality. I want the quality that is going to make me feel empowered—make me feel like I'm putting on a Hugo Boss sweater." There is something extra to it—a different cuff, a better-quality material, a better cut.

Some people might say that it does not matter. After all, a shirt is a shirt is a shirt. But that is not true by any capacity. There is a difference in material quality and workmanship. Buying something from Walmart is different than buying something from Banana Republic which, in turn, is different than buying something from Hugo Boss. It just is. The quality, the fabric, the material, the cut, the lining—there is a vast difference in the final product.

So, I told myself, "You know what? I'm not going to go and buy all these sweaters. I want to have quality over quantity. I like a couple of these sweaters. I'll buy a couple, but I didn't need to go return all the other ones and buy all of these."

While I was at the store, I was thinking about my students, saying to myself, "I need to make sure I share this lesson." I had found myself returning to an old mode of thinking. I had been taught this by people who did not know any better—by our parents, our family, our society, our friends. You can have more for cheaper, but then you look at it and say, "Well, okay, how long is that going to last?" A Banana Republic sweater may last a year whereas a Hugo Boss sweater may last three years. Which one do I get more value out of? You have got to think about that. It is about the value that you are getting.

It is not about the consumption of what you are getting. The Hugo Boss sweater is going to provide more value over several years. That will be the case, unless I destroy it, or gain lots of fat or, better, lots of muscle, and then have to upgrade my wardrobe.

On the same day, I needed to find some new bedroom furniture. A buddy of mine said that he had gone out a couple of months ago and, at one place, they wanted $400 for an end table! Incredible! I was like, "We can get something for $50. We'll just keep it at $50." Then he said the key word which told me a lot about his inner self; he said, "What's the point? Nobody's going to see it anyway." So, what did that tell me very clearly about this? They have money to show people they have money. His shopping is based on a search for significance and the importance of money.

I do not look at it like that at all, actually. The most important thing is the experience of having that end table. If you think about it, your end table is the thing that's next to you the most—for the longest single period in your day. Your desk and your end table are the two tables which you have next to you more than anything else. Think about this. Is it that you want to have the cheapest because it does not show to other people, or is it that you want to have nice things because you value yourself? It is a matter of focus; the former is outside-in; the latter is inside-out.

As I am posing these ideas to you, I hope I am stimulating your brain to think about these things. Because when you do things on the premise of trying to serve everybody else with a desired self-image and attempt to look good for people, you will always have a restriction of money. Your intent will negate your money. If you are looking for the rewards and the accolades of people for money, then you are going to negate money. You are going to push it away from you. Because money is not about trying to impress. I suspect that you have done it. I have done it. Very likely, we have all done it. We have all tried to impress people with our money, and then money disappears.

But when you provide value and meaning, and you value yourself, then you are going to take better care of yourself and you're going to surround yourself with greater quality of possessions. Some people may look at this effect and say, "I'm not as fortunate as you. I'm not lucky enough to do that." No, no, no! You are just as fortunate because you have the ability to think. Money only comes to those who have the ability to think. Those who think can create money.

There are rules inside the labors of consciousness. The labors of consciousness, if you look at it closely, are manual. This is just how money will flow in society. You have labor, then you have a manager, then you have a leader, and then you have visionary creators. These are stages through which money travels. CEOs of companies make the most money. Why is this? Because they are usually the visionary who created the idea. They are the visionary who started it, had the guts and the responsibility. My company—the team that is here—would not exist if I had not had the balls to step up and say, "You know what? I'm going to go do this thing." It would not exist otherwise. Everybody in my company has a job because of that vision, and therefore, it is my responsibility to provide value to the world so that my company has its revenue in place. But a CEO is not just the person who is sitting there saying, "I just make money and I just manage things." No, no, no. They are the one who had the entrepreneurial vision to set it all up to begin with. Then there is the visionary founder afterwards as well. But they are the ones who had the vision to create this thing. Because money travels to those who have ideas that serve the most to the least.

Money travels to the ones who have the ideas who have the most.

Whether you are in a network marketing business, an entrepreneurial business, a doctor, or whatever it is you are, you are the CEO of your life, and the more free energy you create, the more opportunities you create for your life.

So often people get stuck in this idea that they are going to manage their way to success. Please understand I am not against saving. I will say this. People think that they are going to save themselves into becoming millionaires—save themselves into becoming rich. It is not going to happen. First, you have got to provide a lot of value so that you can save lots of value.

Right? Trust me. I am a big proponent of saving, but you will never be able to save enough money.

The reality is this: The average American household makes $36,000 a year. You have to get insurance. That is costing families $1,000 a month. You have to feed yourself. And then there is rent. If you have kids, you have to have a two to three-bedroom apartment or something like that. If you live in Brooklyn, goodness! You are paying an arm and a leg in Brooklyn. If you are in the suburbs you are paying $1,600 to $1,700 a month for an apartment. How do you survive? How do you save? What are you going to save? $100 or $200 a month? I am saying this so that you can understand the full context of why this is the case. Some of you become so scared of the $100 to $200 a month that you forget the big picture. Some of you become so scared of the idea of $100, $200, or $300, but nobody went to their deathbed and said, thank God I saved that $100. Nobody does that.

Be wise with your money. I am not telling you to spend it frivolously. You have to provide value. And you need to provide value in the money areas you fear most.

I feared teaching. I was afraid that no one would want to listen to me. Why would people listen? Why are people going to be there to hear what I have to say? Am I going to say anything different or sufficiently valuable? Are people going to listen to what I have to say? Are people going to value what I have to say? Well, I think people are starting to, at least. I think there is some value that people are getting.

What if there are people who are not getting any value? Is that okay? Is it okay not to provide value to people? This is another subject I want to address in this same conversation. Who are you providing value to? Some of you are going to say, "Everybody." But you are not providing value to everybody in a business. You are providing value to specific people.

While discussing this topic in my Financial Mastery course, I asked my students, "How many of you are entrepreneurs?" All of them were. And this fact was by design. The marketing had been aimed directly at them.

Do not be so afraid of what people are going to say about you. Do not be so caught up in other people's stories because—you know what?—they are going to have stories about you regardless. Here is the thing that they are going to tell you. They are either going to tell you that you did an amazing job in changing their world, their business, and helping them grow; or they are going to tell you that you were their friend and at least you hung out together.

In this regard, two things are keeping you stuck, financially—the friends and the positive trauma of the association onto which you are holding. The negative traumas are not what are keeping you stuck; only the positive traumas!

Think about this for a moment. If you are making $1,000 a month, all your friends have $1,000 a month. If you make $10,000 a month, then you hang out with people who have $10,000 a month. The more money you have, the more opportunities open up for you.

I suspect that some of my readers are probably playing the game of micromanaging pennies instead of creating opportunities. Some of your micromanagement is preventing you from seeing the big picture.

Consider this example: Say, for example, that you make $3,000 a month, and then one month you make a whopping $10,000. Your friends and family think you are doing good. You feel the dopamine rush and you say to yourself, "I'm doing good." This continues until you get around other people who say, "$10,000? Okay, cool. That's good." You get comfortable with the idea, but comfort is the kiss of death.

Yes, comfort is the kiss of death. I want you to realize that. You may look at it and say, "Well, okay. I'm comfortable." But you never take a chance on yourself. While stuck in comfort, you never say, "Hey, look! I can do more; I can be more. I can push myself to another level." This is not because you want to make more money; this is because you want to make a bigger impact from the inside out. It is not about the money when you already have the money. You have to go get the money to make it not about the money.

How do you get the money? You provide value to more people. You go serve more people in the things that you love to do. It is not going to happen accidentally. This is why I am giving you the creation blueprint.

You have the ability and the opportunity to connect to more people, to provide so much more value, if you get out of your own fear and out of your own way. The key is to make sure that you serve more people. But it is your fear that is preventing you from doing these things because it is the fear that makes you significant. It is the fear that keeps you self-important.

Drop the need for self-importance and learn to connect with more people. Touch more people. The more people you touch, the more money you make, I promise.

You may think that you have to be important and recognized to be significant and important, but that is the wrong focus. This may seem counterintuitive to some. Just go give to people—not blindly, not frivolously. Go connect with more people so that you can give to more people.

Assignment: Fear of Money

1. Whose negative perception of money have you subordinated to in your life? (25 ways this has been a benefit to you)
2. What would be the benefit to you of having a quality item even if no one else will see it? (25 benefits)

CHAPTER 27

Cost of Money

Building Toward Financial Independence

The cost of money. In this chapter, I plan on shattering more of your false realities on money and making you wake up. I need to do this because there are a lot of people telling and selling a lot of bullshit, so it is time to wake up to all of that.

So, there is a cost of money.

If you have $2 million, and you are collecting 8% ROI, you are making about $100,000 a year. You may be thinking, "Oh, my God! I'm making $100,000 a year. That is a lot of money." Okay, I would have to agree. Most people do not make $100,000 a year. The average in America, at least, is about half that.

But there is something called a rule of 72 and the doubling of money. Some of you know this. For some of you, it is basic and simple. If you have $100,000 now, what is it going to be worth 15 years from now? Because you have inflation at 3% to 5%. So, in 15 years from now, what are you going to have?

Over 15 years it is going to be 50% of that. In 15 years, you are going to have $50,000 worth of buying power from the original $100,000. I want you to think about this for a second. If you think that $2 million today is going to give you $100,000 a year, that is only for today. If you do not have $2 million today, and you merely wait until 15 years from now, that $100,000 is going to be equal to $50,000 worth of value in today's market because inflation keeps growing and the costs keep growing. In other words, the dollar of today is worth less in the future in terms of real purchasing power.

Right now, I will say this at the same time: With the current economy and the way things are, inflation is going to grow much faster, so the value of the dollar is going to be less and less, so what people are going to have 15 years in the future may well be less than $50,000 of purchasing power for their original $100,000. But, for argument's sake, let us stick with the more recent inflation rate.

For example, let us say you are 40 years old. When you are 55, that $100,000 is worth $50,000. When you are 70, it is worth $25,000. When you are 85, it is basically worth $12,500.

Now, think about your $2 million. So far, I am not saying you are appreciating it. I am not saying it is growing. I am not saying it is doing any of that.

If you do not learn to value money, which I'm trying to get you guys to do through this whole program, that $2 million which you have in the bank will give you an ROI of $12,500 a year in buying power after 45 years, and you cannot go spend from that $2 million each year because—what happens when you spend it?

Simple answer: Your ROI goes down.

Then how much money do you really need in your bank? How much money do you need to make in order to live the lifestyle that you want? Do you need $5 million, $10 million, $20 million in the bank to make that you have a passive income of say $100,000 a year?

If you have $4 million, it is going to be worth $200,000 now, so it would be $100,000 in 15 years, then it would be $50,000, then it would be $25,000— at successive intervals of 15 years.

In this example, I am not including appreciation, and I am not making my assets grow. I am simply taking principal.

Do stock markets go up and down? Yes, of course they do. You know that things change all the time.

If you want to live on a passive stream of income to be financially independent, you want to make sure that you have passive money. Passive money means that you are completely free for the rest of your life to make what you want.

If you want $100,000 a year when you are 85 years old, and you are 40 years old, you need about $10 million in the bank today, without investing any, without putting in any more money, without growing it at all—just straight principal.

Of course, if you have that kind of money, you are going to be wiser with it. But I am simply saying this because I want you to comprehend what is the cost of financial independence. Some people will likely get depressed when they look at this number.

But this is a wake-up call. The only way you are going to get to those numbers is if you put service into the mix—adding significant value to your community.

The only way you are going to do that is by accomplishing three things:
- By learning to value what you do (the work that you are doing),
- By learning to value money (not possessions; get reality with your money),
- By learning to invest and grow your money.

You can work a job or a business. It makes no difference which way you go. But whatever it is you are going to do, you are going to have to grow that wealth. If you do not do this, you are living in a fantasy with regard to money.

Financial independence does not happen if you do not value money. You can also fail to make that happen if you do not learn to clear the traumas, if you do not learn to reevaluate and rebalance your money, and if you do not learn to increase your value structure and to make it more important in your life.

But everyone wants to teach you financial freedom. There is no such thing as "financial freedom." Virtually no one is completely free because you need to remain vigilant. Something can happen that can make you go bankrupt overnight. Perhaps Bill Gates and Mark Zuckerberg are two exceptions; they are sufficiently well protected that they are not likely to go bankrupt.

Targeting Financial Independence: Finding Your Number

You have to look at your numbers when considering your future and the possibility of financial independence. So, what is your financial independence number and what do you really want as a result of all your work? Now, many of you have conversations about legacies for your kids and what you want to leave behind for them. That is a valuable part of your planning. But consider the following.

If you have to make $10 million to live a $200,000 lifestyle when you are 85 years old, how do you get to that level?

How many people reading this have the aspiration of having a greater lifestyle as they grow older? How many people want to have a great lifestyle as they age?

But look at reality, ladies and gentlemen. Look at the reality of what is in the world. Does that happen to most people? Of course it does not. Most everyone in Western society has that fantasy, but nobody puts in the required strategic work. Nobody does the work to make sure that they are truly financially independent. This is the topic which interests me most. I am not interested in teaching you a bunch of hype on it. I am interested in making sure that you actually have the strategy to say, "Okay. Here's what I want my lifestyle to be." If you want a $50,000 lifestyle, God bless you. I am not here to judge you on your goals. I am not here to say that this is what is right for you and that is what is wrong for you. But I am pretty sure that you would want to go into your retirement with wealth, to be able to travel and do the things that you love to do, right? Most people do not get that opportunity. What they do is they end up with one doctor's visit after another because they do not value the finance which would give them the independence they desire.

If you want to have financial independence, become financially disciplined. Get very disciplined. Get organized with your money. Get disciplined with what you are doing. Learn to master your life and learn discipline with your money. Know where your money is going, organize it and make it grow. Do not keep it stuck in small situations. Do not play small with your money.

Some of you are so afraid of money that you will not spend it on yourself or spend it on something else because you are afraid that you cannot make more. That is why I am saying these things to you because I want you to get that realization: How much money do you really need to live the life you want?

I have no doubts that some of my readers think $1 million is a lot of money. But now, how many of my readers realize that $1 million is not jack shit right now for the long term? There is a reason 99.8% of the world never achieves financial wealth. There is a reason for it. Only 0.2% of the population will ever become financially independent. That's it. Only 0.2% will and the other 99.8% will not because they are living in a fantasy about money.

Here is what happens when you do not become financially independent. You have to look to other people because eventually your physical body is going to give way to age and infirmity. More than likely, you will not be able to work at the same level, doing whatever it is that you are doing. Or maybe you are blessed enough that you can continue until the very last day of your life and I hope you are so blessed. More likely, eventually—physically—you are going to change and have to do something different.

My employees are going to take my voice and record it onto an audio box and it is going to keep going on. I am going to create videos and audios when I am lying in bed at 92 years of age, teaching people how to be inspired. But if you do not have a strategy in place for when you stop working, then you are going to lean on things like Social Security.

Depending on Government Management of Your Money?

Where do you think Social Security is going? It is not going to last. You have got to think about that. It is not going to survive in our generation. Some of you are younger. Some of you are a little bit older. Whatever your age, Social Security is not going to be there throughout your senior years. Do you think it is going to be there when you are 65 or 70 years old? And brace yourself, for I am going to get a little harsh, here. Even if you do have Social Security, do you really want to live on the government's handout? I do not think you would be reading this book if you wanted to live on a government handout. You could say that you invested into it. "It's my work—my money!" But it is not your work. You put money into the Social Security system so that they can grow it tax free and then give it back to you. You simply do not realize how you are being manipulated in the system with your own money because no one is educating you on this topic. It is your money that you put in, they grow it tax free, and they say, "We'll give you 2%," all the while they made 20%. And maybe you thought you were getting a good deal.

Again, I am not a financial advisor, so please understand that I am not giving you financial advice. Instead, I am teaching you about how to relate to money. You can go to a financial advisor and they may have this conversation with you; they may not. You have got to empower yourself with money.

Seeking Financial Advice

When I was 27, I went to a financial advisor. He was an advisor connected with the Edward Jones group—an older guy, perhaps 55 or 60 years old. I told him, "Look, I'm making some decent money." At that time, I was making what I thought was a lot of money for my age, and the level I was at. To me, it was a big deal. I went in and I said, "Hey, I'm looking to invest money. I want to learn to invest. Can you help me?"

"Yeah, sure," he replied. "Absolutely. How much money do you have?"

I said, "I have a couple hundred thousand dollars. Let me invest it and start growing my money."

"Okay," he said. "How much do you want to do?"

"We'll probably start with $50,000 to $70,000. But before I invest with you, I need to see your portfolio."

He looked stunned. "Why would you want to see my portfolio?"

"Because I'm not going to give you my money if you really don't know how to manage it. I need to see what you're going to do with your own money and if you have it. If you don't have it, you're going to mismanage mine."

And he would not show me his portfolio.

"You're not getting my business unless you show me your portfolio."

"It's against policy," he told me, telling me this and that to make his excuse sound plausible.

"Well, good," I said. "It's against my policy to work with people who aren't going to show me what they do." So, I left.

Nearly every financial advisor is either broke or living paycheck to paycheck. I do not care who it is. This is unbelievable! Why would you take financial advice from someone who is not financially sound?

Please understand that I mean no disrespect. If you are in financial services, you have to master your own money before people are going to bring their money to invest with you. I hope this will be a wake-up call. A financial advisor needs to provide proof: "Here is my portfolio. It's worth $3.5 million." Great!

If you are investing in a hedge fund and they said, "We manage $1 billion in assets," and a competitor said, "We manage $1 million in assets," which one do you think is more stable? Naturally, it would be the $1 billion in assets. With whom are you going to feel more secure and safe? Again, the $1 billion in assets. The size of their fund shows not only their skill but also their longevity. And, of course, verify what they tell you.

If you do not have money mastered, please do not expect people to invest with you. Otherwise, you are merely living in a fantasy. Savvy people will not invest with what you are not. It is like, if you need surgery, you will not go to someone who dreams of being a doctor one day. People who value their money expect a professional with a proven track record.

My goal for you, in this book, is not whether you figure out how to do benefits or drawbacks. My goal for you in this program is for you to master and empower yourself with money so that you do not have to live financially disempowered later on in your life.

I do not trouble myself with whether or not a student makes $100 million or creates a passive income pulling in $100,000 a year. I do not care. I want each student to be fulfilled, living in his or her highest values, doing what they love to do. And I want each student to have the money to be able to do more of that and to be of service to the world. These are the things I care about.

I am not the guy who is going to tell you that, you have got to go make millions and millions of dollars. I am all about having you move beyond the "go chase it" mindset.

If you want to make millions of dollars because you want to provide service to the world, then you should be financially served because of that. But if you are sitting there saying, "I need $100,000, $200,000, $300,000, or $1 million a year for my desired lifestyle," then you are playing too frigging small with your life. This is what I am trying to show you with this program.

I am trying to get you to wake up to the fact that you have been playing too small with regard to the reality of what you could be in your life.

Which is wiser: Making lots of money and nothing else, or making money, saving, protecting and building a large investment for yourself? If you do not do these things, who is going to come save you if tragedy strikes?

If you pour everything you make into an expensive house, without thinking of the other aspects of financial mastery, you may find that you need a reverse mortgage just to get your money back out in an emergency—messy business with lots of lost momentum and added interest payments from your lost equity. Converting from one type of asset to another will always cost you.

You have got to read more and to think more about what happens if the unthinkable actually happens. How are you going to live? How are you going to be empowered with your money?

Student Feedback

Overcoming Past Trauma and Loving Your Customers

Quite often, the realities of financial mastery can be somewhat depressing to students who still feel the grip of money fantasies. It takes time for the body to become used to a new way of feeling about money and the new consciousness acquired through these lessons.

One student shared her horror stories of past trauma. She said, "Totally depressed. I'm laughing because I'm trying not to cry. First, yes, I feel sad, depressed, and everything. It's bringing back an old injury where I lost $1.5 million because I trusted somebody to take care of my money. I was young and I was busy doing other stuff. It's like now I'm the age that I am, and I don't know if I'll ever feel grown up around money."

"Keep doing the work," I replied, "and you will do that. You're a neophyte in the process. You're very early inside of this process. You will. But can I ask how old you are?"

"Yeah. I'm 58."

"So, 58. Fantastic. I want you to realize that people make millions and millions of dollars in their 60s, right? Don't ever limit yourself saying, 'I'm 58 and that's it. I'm screwed, over-the-hill, done!' No, no, no! Create an opportunity for yourself by doing the bioresonance of your current passion. How do you take what you currently do to many more people? How do you take what you do to serve people to hundreds, thousands or even millions of people? That's what you've got to figure out how to do. When you do that, then more people will give you money. I say this almost every single time I talk about business. Love your customer so much that they have no choice but to refer you to others."

Corporations these days tend to cut back on customer service. They give their customer service reps quotas, if they have representatives at all. Those quotas are based on quantity instead of quality. Any customer who has a thorny, oddball issue is going to be trampled in the rush to close the customer service ticket. This reality makes great service a rarity. And when you give even merely "good" service, customers feel downright pampered. If you give them 5-star, top-of-the-line service, you become unforgettable in the customer's mind. And the feeling lingers with them long after they have forgotten the details of what you did for them.

A massive percentage of my new students are from word-of-mouth referrals. I love every one of my clients who show up, even the ones who are sometimes quite annoying. I know what it is like to struggle with these concepts—the frustration, the confusion and the uncertainty. Helping my clients overcome those dark emotions with regard to money is a large part of my joy.

I push and I want you to win, but it is not going to happen if you do not value your customers, if you own a business. I am so glad when a student becomes pissed off by some of this material. The required transformation for financial mastery requires that you go through a great deal of emotional turmoil and resentment until you can value money.

Past Traumas and Future Ailments

On the subject of past traumas, another student wanted to understand more deeply the effects on her future. She said, "When you are talking about this, I had a thought. Do the traumas of the past catch up later in life—later in years? Is that why we all have physical ailments that prevail late in life? That's a thought I had when you were talking and that inspired me more to do the work—to cut out those traumas. But then I had another thought: Am I just making excuses of like, 'Oh, let me use that as my reason to do the work,' that I wasn't sufficiently butt-hurt over what you said about financial independence and needing the $1 million, $10 million or $20 million to fund the lifestyle I want."

"Let me tell you this, then. If this doesn't mess you up, then I don't know what will. Traumas which remain unhealed will stay in your physiology for the rest of your life. They are a festering sore which will lead to ailments because of that."

"Yeah, I get that," she replied. "I'm just wondering—my real question here is this: Am I still making excuses for why I need to do the work? I understand that this motivates me more than the money."

"The question is, do you want to be sick?"

"No. Of course not."

"Well, then do the fucking work."

"Yeah."

"Let me give you an example. One of my students had a rash, and I just told them to do the work. Last week, the rash went away. There's no question. This stuff is mind/body connected. I don't care if you want to make more money or not. You've got to look at it and realize that you have all the tools in front of you. However, you may not value yourself enough to do it. So, start doing the work. Put one foot in front of the other, making plodding, incremental progress. Be inspired! At Inner Wealth, I talked about the 'movement coefficient' which can help in figuring out why they are not doing it. But beyond any tricks to help you overcome your procrastination, I'm going to tell you quite bluntly, just start doing the fucking work. Just put it in your schedule and let it increase its value. Every step you take can help increase your own self-worth or bring you closer to realizing that self-worth."

"Thank you."

Gain, Loss and Transformation

Another student told me, "I wasn't really depressed by this lesson. The modules, and especially Delta, helped me realize something beyond the obvious. I think something you say a lot is, 'energy,' but money, also, never goes anywhere; it just changes form. Who was it that said that she lost a lot of money, like $1.5 million. I have harbored so much guilt over a bad business deal that I got conned out of, but after doing the work, I realized that nothing was truly lost. I realized that the connections I had made through that bad deal led to the solar deal which I put together for passive and residual income. So, I didn't actually lose that money. I spent it on the connections that got me to the next level."

"There you go," I said with a smile. "You saw where you transferred that money to a greater opportunity. Good job. That's a great realization. Let me just add to that, too. For those of you who are sitting there saying, "I lost money," you don't lose money; you transfer it. Money is never lost. It transfers from one form to another. You've probably heard me say this, but if you haven't, let me repeat it here: The masses play at gain or loss; the masters play at transformation."

"Perfect."

"In this work," I said, "it's designed to help you value money because you'll change the forms of the things in your life that you value the most. You'll always change what you have in order to create the form of the value that you want. But if you want it in the form of money, then you're going to find it in the form of money. If you don't value money, you'll put your wealth in other forms. But this can backfire. If you are not fully aware of what is going on, you'll judge yourself and beat yourself up, thinking that you should have had the money. You know how many people get into their 60s and 70s and 80s and thought retirement was supposed to be different? It's truly insane. I don't care how old you are, just take care of the money. Once you do that, you won't have to worry about the money. Like I said last week, it's not about the money until it's about the money. Just so we are aware and cognizant of that."

"Thanks, Dr. T. I'd like to add something about the transformation that relates to the inflation module you just did. I had a lot of guilt and shame because I was brought up thinking one way about things. My parents were always trying to get out of debt, get out of debt, get out of debt. And then finally, they got their credit cards paid off, and it was like, 'Whoa! We're out of debt!' And so, my mentality growing up was that debt is bad, but when you transfer money from debt, this creates a whole new dynamic. Like, I have a couple of loans that are 2% and 3% and that's below the inflation rate. I look at that like it's free money because the amortized interest is less than normal inflation, so I'm like, hey, I'm actually making money on holding this debt longer. That was a huge mind shift that I had to go through because all the way to my 30s it was debt's bad, debt's bad."

"Right. A lot of people believe that," I replied. "Once you understand and take away the emotion of money, then you can start looking at debt as a better use of money. If you have a 1% loan or mortgage your money is going further by not paying off the loan and putting it somewhere more productive."

He said, "That's lower than inflation."

"I've got money. Having debt that costs 2% and taking that money and appreciating it at 5%, I'm making 3.5% on my money, if it's appreciating. When you start taking the emotions away from money, you just look at money as a resource to gain a larger ROI. Entrepreneurs think of ROI; employees think of debt."

A Final Word on Trauma

One female student had a great deal of difficulty early on with this material, but the problem she experienced can apply to anyone at any stage. She had long known of her own trauma with regard to money, but kept expecting something to change even though the trauma she already knew about did not need to be uncovered. And this should tell you something. If you think you have found the source of your problem, but the problem persists, then you have not found the true source of that problem. Uncovering past trauma can be quite cathartic. Simple awareness of such trauma can render powerful healing within your mind and the mind's effect on the body. And awareness is part of responsibility. When you accept responsibility—and remember, this is not "blame"—you take charge of your life. That is the meaning of responsibility.

My advice to the young woman was to continue to do the work. She needed to dig more deeply to find the true, root cause of the difficulty. You might remember the primary, secondary, tertiary and quaternary levels of drawbacks. Peeling away each layer gets you closer to the pay dirt you need with regard to trauma. Awareness and then responsibility gives you the transformation you require.

Even as you finish this book, you may well need to continue to do the work, perhaps going through the exercises another time, cycling through, digging more and more deeply until you have thoroughly excavated the resources of your mind. I, too, continue to do these exercises, discovering new levels of freedom.

Discovery, learning and more profound levels of responsibility should become a perpetual lifestyle for anyone serious about financial mastery.

As always, I love to hear from my students, whether they are from a classroom setting, an internet seminar or from reading a book. I want to hear of your successes because they might inspire others to take up for themselves the work which you have started.

Assignment: Cost of Money

1. What is the "cost" of your current Financial Independence number?
2. How will you create more services to invest and grow your money?

Dr. Alok "Rewire" Trivedi

The Lifestyle Performance Expert

Dr. Trivedi is a media personality, human performance Doctor, founder of the Trivedi Performance Institute, and the author of *Chasing Success: Lessons in Aligned Performance.* Dr. Rewire has been featured on CBS, NBC, Fox News, Global News, *Entrepreneur Magazine,* and Amazon Prime. People worldwide have sought him out—CEOs, celebrities, professional athletes and entrepreneurs—to rewire their thinking with his science-backed approach, helping them to transform their health, wealth and relationships.

The Trivedi Process is a scientifically proven method for helping people heal from chronic ailments and to rewire the fear, beliefs and habits that hold them back so they can achieve the life they've always dreamed of having. Dr. Trivedi created this process while founding and building one of the largest healthcare clinics in the country, seeing over 1,250 patients a week.

Using his health background, coupled with 27 years of study, he is an expert in the mind/body connection, the science of success and fulfillment, and human behavior. He developed his own approach, which now includes 92 techniques and tools to rewire the brain, and has helped over 500,000 people and businesses worldwide.

Clients have included the FDIC, Berkshire Hathaway, WNBA stars, professional golfers, Olympic tennis players and corporate executives.

In 2021, Dr. Trivedi's team was named #672 on the *Inc.* 5,000 list of the fastest growing companies.

Other Books by Dr. Trivedi

Chasing Success: Lessons in Aligned Performance, DASH Enterprises (2017).

Connect with Dr. Trivedi

Facebook—https://www.facebook.com/DrAlokTrivedi/

Instagram—https://www.instagram.com/dr.rewire/

Tiktok—https://www.tiktok.com/@dr.rewire

Twitter—https://twitter.com/DrRewire

YouTube—
https://www.youtube.com/channel/UCf6D1A8xbgNoWp3ofGO23sA

Website—https://DrRewire.com

ACCESS YOUR FREE GIFTS

Just to say thanks for buying and reading this book, I would like to give you a few free bonus gifts, no strings attached!

To Download Your Free Gifts Now, Scan the QR Code Below:

I appreciate your interest in my book, and value your feedback as it helps me improve future versions of this book. I would appreciate it if you could leave your invaluable review on Amazon.com with your feedback. Thank you!